Kenya's Foreign Policy and Diplomacy

Evolution, Challenges and Opportunities

Kenya's Foreign Policy and Diplomacy

Evolution, Challenges and Opportunities

Boaz K. Mbaya

Published by
East African Educational Publishers Ltd.
Elgeyo Marakwet Close, off Elgeyo Marakwet Road, Kilimani, Nairobi
P.O. Box 45314, Nairobi - 00100, KENYA
Tel: +254 20 2324760
Mobile: +254 722 205661 / 722 207216 / 733 677716 / 734 652012
Email: eaep@eastafricanpublishers.com
Website: www.eastafricanpublishers.com

East African Educational Publishers also has offices or is represented in the following
countries: Uganda, Tanzania, Rwanda, Malawi, Zambia, Botswana and South Sudan.

First published 2019

ISBN 978-9966-56-433-7

Printed in Kenya by
Printing Services Ltd

CONTENTS

Dedication xiii

Foreword...xiv

Preface..xvi

Acknowledgements xx

Acronyms and Abbreviations xxii

Introduction xxvii

    Orientation towards the East xxxi

    Kenya Foreign Policy, 2014 xxxii

    Emerging issues in international relations.................xxxiii

    Environmental diplomacy............................... xxxiv

    Kenya's Foreign Policy in perspective xxxiv

PART I: CONCEPTUAL BASIS OF FOREIGN POLICY 1

CHAPTER 1: The National Interest in Foreign Policy 2

    Establishment and recognition of a state............................ 2

    The national interest... 3

    Recognition of a government..................................... 5

    The national interest as a driver of state activities.............. 6

    US Foreign Policy under President Trump........................ 7

CHAPTER 2: The Making of Foreign Policy 11

    The process of formulating Foreign Policy 13

    Policy framework... 14

    Articulation of Foreign Policy 14

    Projection of power... 15

    Collective action 17

CHAPTER 3: Diplomacy and the Implementation

of Foreign Policy.. **19**

Sanctions as an instrument of Foreign Policy................... 21

UN sanctions and international focus on North Korea ... 25

Role of the Ministry of Foreign Affairs in implementation

of Foreign Policy... 26

Coordination and strategy 27

Communication between Ministry Headquarters and

diplomatic missions.. 29

Intelligence gathering.. 30

Other tools of diplomacy.. 33

Strategy in Foreign Policy.. 33

Security of diplomats 34

Appointment of ambassadors and other

diplomatic staff... 35

PART II: KENYA'S FOREIGN POLICY FRAMEWORK, SOURCES,

PRINCIPLES AND ITS EVOLUTION **37**

CHAPTER 4: Establishment and recognition of Kenya as a State **38**

Kenya's Foreign Policy framework 38

International dynamics at independence 39

Principles guiding Kenya's Foreign Policy......................... 40

Sources of Kenya's Foreign Policy...................................... 40

Evolution of Kenya's Foreign Policy 42

Democracy and good governance in Kenya 43

Public participation in governance 46

Corruption: A threat to national security 48

Poverty and food security.. 48

Coastal problem: Threat of insurgence.............................. 50

CHAPTER 5: Jomo Kenyatta Presidency, 1963-1978 51

Early years of Kenya's Foreign Policy.................................. 51

Concentration of power in the presidency......................... 54

Policy differences between Kenyatta and Odinga 54

Sessional Paper No. 10 of 1965 57

Kenya's response to the wave of socialist rhetoric

in Africa in the 1960s.. 58

Look West policy 59

Early years of Kenya's role in conflict resolution 59

Jomo Kenyatta's Foreign Policy legacy............................... 60

CHAPTER 6: Daniel arap Moi Presidency, 1978-2002......................... 63

Politics of Moi 65

1982 Coup and Moi's transformation 66

Kenya's Foreign Policy after the end of the Cold War....... 67

Decades of lost opportunities 68

Rise to power of progressive leaders in Africa.................. 68

President Clinton's Visit to Africa exposed Kenya's

isolation.. 69

Clamour for a new Constitution 71

Moi's Foreign Policy legacy 71

CHAPTER 7: Mwai Kibaki Presidency, 2002–2013............................ **73**

    Initiative to publish Kenya's Foreign Policy 75

    2007/2008 post-election violence..................................... 77

    The Constitution of Kenya, 2010..................................... 78

    Kenya's Foreign Policy under the Grand Coalition
    Government 80

    Diplomatic miscalculation 81

    Kibaki's Foreign Policy legacy... 83

CHAPTER 8: Uhuru Kenyatta Presidency, from 2013 .... **84**

    Uhuru's Kenyatta's first term 86

    Challenges ahead 89

    Uhuru's Kenyatta's Foreign Policy legacy 90

PART III: REGIONAL RELATIONS, SECURITY CHALLENGES,

MEDIATION AND CONFLICT RESOLUTION.............................. **91**

CHAPTER 9: Regional relations and security challenges

    for Kenya.. **92**

    Threats to Kenya's territorial integrity 92

    Al-Shabaab attacks 94

    Territorial threats from Uganda 96

    Threats from political instability in South Sudan............. 98

    Threats to strategic economic interests............................ 98

    Trans-boundary security management 99

    Joint Border Security Committees 100

    Kenya/Ethiopia defence pact.. 100

Management of security along the Kenya/Ethiopia
border.. 101

Refugee problem... 102

Proliferation of Small Arms and Light Weapons 103

CHAPTER 10: Mediation, Peace Efforts and

Conflict Resolution 105

Kenya's role in conflict resolution................................... 106

Mediation as an instrument of Kenya's Foreign Policy. 106

International focus on the Horn of Africa 108

Sudan peace process... 109

Negotiations for a new agreement................................. 111

Declaration of Principles 112

Death of Dr. John Garang.. 113

South Sudan's power struggle strains relations with

its neighbours... 114

Impact of South Sudan power struggle on

regional economies.. 115

Uganda peace process 117

Ethiopia peace process 121

Somalia reconciliation process 122

Kenya's Foreign Policy on Tanzania 126

Tanzania's role in the 2007 election crisis in Kenya 127

Mozambique peace process.. 128

Instability in the Great Lakes Region........................... 134

Conflict in Eastern Democratic Republic of Congo 135

PART IV: REGIONAL AND MULTILATERAL DIPLOMACY **136**

CHAPTER 11: Regional Diplomacy **137**

Origins of regional cooperation in East Africa 137

The East African Community 139

Political marriage in the East African Community 141

New East African Community 141

Kenya's Foreign Policy and the objectives of the
community 144

EAC milestones and national policies 144

Inter-Governmental Authority on Development 144

Common Market for Eastern and Southern Africa 145

African Union 146

CHAPTER 12: Multilateral Diplomacy **148**

The Non-Aligned Movement 150

The Middle East conflict 150

International terrorism 153

Rise of militant Islamic groups in the Middle East 154

Islamic State of Iraq and al-Sham 156

Foreign Policy dilemma over the
International Criminal Court 158

Background to ICC's involvement with Kenya 158

Assembly of State Parties' Conference at The Hague 159

United Nations Organisation 160

UN Security Council Reforms 160

Chapter 13: Environmental Diplomacy 163

Fourth UN Headquarters 164

Deforestation.. 166

Convention on prohibition of international trade in endangered species.. 167

Developments thereafter 168

PART V: LOOK EAST POLICY, EVALUATION, CONCLUSION 170

CHAPTER 14: Look East Policy 171

New thinking 172

China's emergence from a peasant society to a global

power.. 174

New economic realities.. 174

Chinese interests in Africa 175

Assertive China.. 176

Strategic decision.. 177

CHAPTER 15: Kenya's Diplomacy on the World Stage.................... 178

Track record 178

Quality of Kenya's diplomacy.. 178

Internal political dynamics in Kenya's Foreign Service 179

Promotion, protection and defence of

Kenya's interests abroad 180

Tours of duty for envoys 181

Setting SMART objectives.. 183

Leadership in the region.. 185

Pro-action.. 185

Clear policy position.. 186

Kenya's diplomatic infrastructure......................................187

Suitable deployment...189

Kenyans in the diaspora...189

Goodwill ambassadors..191

CHAPTER 16: Conclusion.. **192**

Conduct of Kenya's Foreign Policy...............................192

The Constitution of Kenya, 2010....................................193

Internal dynamics in Kenya's Foreign Policy.................195

ICT in diplomacy...196

The future 197

Bibliography...198

Index 199

About the Author 214

Dedication

To my dear wife, Florence, who sacrificed her career to support me and for bringing up our three children, Felix, Fidel, and Della. It would have been impossible to stay as a family without her sacrifice. Together, they encouraged me to write this book after I retired from Public Service.

Foreword

Today, as Kenya takes an even greater leadership role on the world stage, forging broader international alliances and reshaping closer cooperation with our regional neighbours, we face a decisive moment when we must lead by example and not allow politics to trump professionalism in the exercise of our Foreign Policy. Amid a worldwide resurgence in national identity politics and widening fractures among the nations of the world, Kenya's vibrant democracy can remind the international community that there is strength in diversity, and that power endures through merit and compromise.

It is natural that, in a country with as diverse a population and a geography as our own, complex forces guide our national interest and our relations with other regional and international powers. Ambassador Boaz K. Mbaya's book distils much of the detail of this complexity in a manner that will undoubtedly serve as a thoughtful reflection on our diplomatic history; both for those of us that have lived it, as well as for the next generation of Kenyan thinkers and leaders that must lead it going forward. In this book, Ambassador Mbaya has composed a constructive critique of Kenyan diplomacy and foreign relations since independence, focusing on the responsibility of our Foreign Policy to pursue national interest through projection of our national interest and founding values. He lays out a compelling history of diplomatic ideas and thought, tying together the development of Kenya's international relations with the practice of Foreign Policy in all modern democratic societies.

Kenya's international relations have been strongest when they reflect the ethnic diversity of our country. In these challenging times for international relations, Kenya's political and economic leadership role in Africa today – more than ever – must reflect the inclusiveness of our society. Chronicling the competing interests and various perspectives with which our leaders since independence have managed our relationship with the rest of the world, Ambassador Mbaya uncovers how the seeds of our national consciousness today can continue to bear fruit in new ways.

Kenya's Foreign Policy at independence was, unlike many of our neighbouring countries, born out of the need to turn from armed rebellion against the colonial power into peaceful co-existence in the community of nations. This book makes a strong argument that the true test of our independence came when our founding fathers successfully undertook this shift, and that the continuous practice of diplomacy was key to these efforts. Our non-aligned Foreign Policy, as informed by the Cold War realities, allowed our political and economic relations to mature over the early years after independence and laid the ground for a prosperous and promising future, which Kenya offers its citizens and neighbours today. Ambassador Mbaya is right to point out that this inspired realism can be credited for the increasingly important role, which Kenya today plays as a force for peace and prosperity in Africa, and in the world as a whole.

The professionalism of the Foreign Service Office is a valued public good serving all Kenyans, when it transcends domestic political divisions to defend collective national positions. The inclusiveness of our civil service at its founding under Jomo Kenyatta must continue to inform the further professionalization of our diplomatic corps today. The lesson one can draw from Ambassador Mbaya's volume, is that waning inclusivity in our political process would threaten Kenya's emerging leadership role on the world stage.

It is my distinct hope that today, as Kenya matures as a democratic society promoting peaceful trade and commerce at a global level, our next generation of leaders and great political minds can find inspiration in Ambassador Mbaya's book. Kenya has much to thank for the efforts of its diplomats and the technical skill of our Foreign Service professionals, and this book commends their efforts in an important and valuable way.

Dr. Mukhisa Kituyi
Secretary General, UNCTAD
Geneva, Switzerland
June 2018

Preface

Ambassador Boaz K. Mbaya has written an excellent text on Kenya's Foreign Policy and diplomacy. This excellence is attributed not just to the fact that this is the pioneering book on this subject, but because its coverage of themes is wide and encompassing.

Since Howell's seminal work on the Foreign Policy of Kenya half a century ago, there have been many outstanding journal articles and book chapters on the subject of Kenya's Foreign Policy. These have investigated various areas of Kenya's Foreign Policy. After fifty years of the examination of these various themes, it became increasingly evident that the time was ripe for a comprehensive text on the theme. Ambassador Mbaya's text fulfils that promise and does so in a very intellectually fulfilling approach to the subject.

One of the most important contributions of the book to the theme of Foreign Policy in Kenya is the inclusion in the discussions and analyses, sections on Kenya's diplomacy. Essentially, there is a school of thought that says that the foreign policy of any country cannot be analysed in the absence of an analysis of how the country's diplomacy is conducted. The relationship between Foreign Policy and diplomacy is captured by the fact that, while Foreign Policy is concerned with a philosophical statement about the themes that inform the country's approach to its international and regional relationships, diplomacy is concerned with the implementation of that Foreign Policy. Indeed, there exists the belief that while a country may have a good Foreign Policy, it will not make any headway in the absence of proper diplomatic strategies for its implementation. Ambassador Mbaya's pioneering book, *Kenya's Foreign Policy and Diplomacy: Evolution, Challenges and Opportunities,* takes this relationship into account. In doing so, he has produced an intellectually worthy text, and in the process, challenges practitioners to continue giving life to the Foreign Policy that has been articulated.

The structure of this book is at once revealing, exciting and challenging. Part I of the book analyses the generic conceptual basis of Foreign Policy. This Part is made more relevant by the inclusion of a short but penetrating chapter on the national interest of Kenya. It is often forgotten that the whole structure of Foreign Policy and its making is centred on the national interest and national values of the country. The making of Foreign Policy is then covered in a similarly short but insightful chapter on the process, policy framework, and articulation of Foreign Policy, and related issues like the projection of power and collective action. These early chapters lay the groundwork for one of the best chapters in the book on diplomacy and the implementation of Foreign Policy. This well-written chapter alone makes Ambassador Mbaya's book a worthwhile contribution to its subject.

Part II examines Kenya's Foreign Policy framework, sources and principles of its evolution. In this chapter, Ambassador Mbaya divides this discussion into two broad but related parts. He inspects the evolution of Kenya as a state, and the principles guiding its Foreign Policy and its sources, including very pertinently the constitution and the national anthem. The second theme of this Part successfully analyses Kenya's Foreign Policy under the four regimes since its independence: the Jomo Kenyatta years, the Daniel arap Moi years, the Mwai Kibaki years and the start of Uhuru Kenyatta years. This approach to the analyses of the Foreign Policy of Kenya is intellectually challenging. But it might have been better to examine Kenya's Foreign Policy in the first fifty years, running to the first four regimes. The reason for this is that it is intellectually difficult to reach any serious conclusions about a regime when still serving its term and whose Foreign Policy is still evolving. However, Ambassador Mbaya carries it off admirably.

Part III of the book analyses Kenya's Foreign Policy and diplomacy in the context of regional relations, security challenges, mediation and conflict resolution. This Part of the book is made better because it is the first time that these themes have been analysed by a practitioner, in contrast to the more academic writings that have been variously offered on the themes. This practitioner's analysis derives its intellectual power from its ability to match Foreign Policy decision making in Kenya – and its diplomacy – with the challenges that the very dynamic regional and international environment throws up to decision makers. In particular, the chapter on Mediation, Peace Efforts and Conflict Resolution provide the refreshing views of decision makers as they attempted – and managed for a time – to create a regional niche for Kenya's Foreign Policy and diplomacy.

Part IV of the book inspects Kenya's Foreign Policy and diplomacy from the perspective of regional and international diplomacy. This part specifically examines Regional Diplomacy, Multilateral Diplomacy, and Environmental Diplomacy. These chapters cover a whole range of issues that challenged policy and decision makers. It does so from the perspective of a practitioner engaged in problem solving for the multiple challenges that were confronted by Kenya's Foreign Policy and diplomacy.

Part V of the book examines the Look East Policy in Kenya's Foreign Policy and diplomacy, and evaluates Kenya's Diplomacy on the World Stage in Chapter 15. The intellectual importance of this chapter is that, it engages important issues in the management of Kenya's Foreign Policy and diplomacy. These issues of management have only been analysed in a couple of academic articles before this. In essence, this part and particularly Chapter 15, tease out issues of Foreign Policy that while important, are generally ignored in the existing literature. It is a valuable and inspiring chapter because, while written by a practitioner, it does not shy away from the often-ignored analyses of the Foreign Policy and diplomacy of Kenya.

In the past decade or so, the study of international relations and diplomacy has become one of the fastest growth areas in various universities in Kenya. The study of international relations and diplomacy has also developed to a stage where the subject is also offered in post-graduate courses in the academy. Inevitably, all these undergraduate and post-graduate programmes in Kenya have courses on the Foreign Policy of Kenya, and related aspects of diplomatic practice. Ambassador Mbaya's book clearly fulfils an urgent need, and fills admirably a lacuna in university level education in these areas.

But this is not the only dimension from which this admirable book will be welcomed. It is a book that aspiring diplomats of Kenya, and more seasoned professional diplomats will find useful: for some to learn about the evolution, development and challenges of Kenya's diplomacy and Foreign Policy, and for others to benefit from the core insights offered in the book as they endeavour to refresh and freshen up their perspectives, knowledge and analysis about the themes of this book.

Ambassador Mbaya is the most appropriate person to have written this book. He joined Kenya's Ministry of Foreign Affairs as a cadet (they were not known as such in those days), and rose through the ranks to become an ambassador and Permanent Secretary. As Permanent Secretary, he contributed to innovations in Kenya's diplomacy that still endure. He could easily have written a typical memoir of his time at the Ministry of Foreign Affairs. Instead, he chose the more challenging approach of producing a more wholesome text of the related themes of Kenya's Foreign Policy and diplomacy. He has succeeded in this endeavour, and is to be congratulated for having brought the many issues and perspectives on Kenya's Foreign Policy and diplomacy alive.

There already exist a fair number of post-graduate master's and doctoral theses on Kenya's Foreign Policy, and a fair collection of academic journal articles and book chapters. There will also be many future texts on Kenya's Foreign Policy and diplomacy. These books of the future will introduce new perspectives and analyses, and fresh insights on the subject. They will without doubt be important analyses on emerging aspects of Kenya's Foreign Policy and diplomacy. But Ambassador Mbaya's pioneering book, *Kenya's Foreign Policy and Diplomacy: Evolution, Challenges and Opportunities* will not wither or perish because of them. This welcome book will be one for the ages, and will always have a place whenever and wherever issues of Kenya's Foreign Policy and diplomacy are discussed.

Prof. Makumi Mwagiru

Adjunct Professor of Diplomacy

Strathmore University, & Former Director,

Institute of Diplomacy and International Studies (2003-2012)

University of Nairobi Karen, September, 2018

Acknowledgements

It is not possible to thank everyone who has contributed to this book. However, I wish to single out the following: my former colleagues in the Foreign Service of Kenya and in government for interest and encouragement to write this book and for cooperation and evaluation of the original manuscript.

I am indebted to Bernard Chahilu, a writer, who suggested extremely useful structural changes on the first draft. His recommendation that I include a chapter on evolution of Kenya's Foreign Policy singularly helped to focus on the theme of the book. Chiboli Shakaba-Induli, a Management Consultant, made suggestions which improved the structure of the first three sections of the book.

I thank Ambassador Ochieng Adala, for peer-reviewing the section on evolution of Kenya's Foreign Policy, mediation and peace efforts; Ambassador Franklin Esipila, a Consultant, for suggestions on content and presentation; Ambassador Nehemiah Rotich for comments on environmental diplomacy, and Ambassador Marx Kahende, a Consultant, Public Policy, and writer, for comments on approach, content, policy orientation and strategic expectations.

I am grateful to Prof. Macharia Munene, for his insights on: Sessional Paper No. 10, of 1965, on Kenya's economic policy, Kenya's ideological differences with Tanzania and Uganda, and their economic blueprints in 1967 (Arusha Declaration) and 1969 (the Common Man's Chatter), respectively. Prof. Munene is Professor of History and International Relations, United States International University-Africa (USIU-A), Nairobi.

My sincere gratitude goes to William Mayaka, a Development Consultant, who was Personal Assistant to Mwai Kibaki, then an Assistant Minister for Economic Planning in 1965, for his insight and experience on Sessional Paper No. 10. Mwai Kibaki later became President of the Republic of Kenya from December 2002 to March 2013.

I am highly indebted to Prof. Makumi Mwagiru for overall academic evaluation of this book. Prof. Mwagiru provided guidance on the theme of the book, the concept of national interest, Foreign Policy formulation and evaluation of Kenya's Foreign Policy articulation as well as the general structure of the book. His endorsement in the Preface succinctly captures the objective of the book. I sincerely thank him for his efforts.

I am also grateful to Andrew Mbaya, a Consultant (CPA), for cleaning up the original manuscript and for general evaluation from a reader's point of view; Beatrice Asienwa, a Development Consultant and Ambassador Albert A. Musalia for their comments on the initial draft; Mabel Tumwebaze for proofreading and, Benson Shiholo for excellent editorial work on the book to its final publication.

Overall, I thank my former colleagues in the Ministry of Foreign Affairs, and all friends who encouraged, and challenged me in discussions on different aspects of the book.

Ambassador Boaz K. Mbaya
Nairobi,
December 2018

Acronyms and Abbreviations

9/11	–	9th September 2001, the date terrorists attacked the World Trade Centre and the Pentagon, USA
AAEC	–	Afro-Asian Economic Cooperation
AGOA	–	African Growth and Opportunity Act
AMISOM	–	African Union Mission to Somalia
ANZUS	–	Australia, New Zealand, United States of America
APRM	–	African Peer Review Mechanism
ARC	–	Association for Regional Cooperation
ASP	–	Assembly of State Parties
AU	–	African Union
BRICS	–	Brazil, Russia, India, China and South Africa
CAP	–	Commonwealth Assistance Programme
CFCs	–	Chlorofluorocarbon emissions
CITES	–	Convention on International Trade in Endangered Species
COMESA	–	Common Market for Eastern and Southern African (States)
CoP	–	Conference of Parties
CPA	–	Comprehensive Peace Agreement
CRCK	–	Constitutional Review Commission of Kenya
DFI	–	Direct Foreign Investment
DoP	–	Declaration of Principles
DRC	–	Democratic Republic of Congo
EAA	–	East African Airways
EAC	–	East African Community
EACSO	–	East African Common Services Organisation

EAH	–	East African Harbours
EAHC	–	East African High Command
EAP&T	–	East African Posts and Telecommunications
ECOWAS	–	Economic Community of West African States
EPA	–	Economic Partnership Agreement
EPLF	–	Eritrean People's Liberation Front
EU	–	European Union
FRELIMO	–	Front for the Liberation of Mozambique
FSR	–	Free Syrian Army
G20	–	Group of 20
G7	–	Group of 7
G77	–	Group of 77
G8	–	Group of 8
GDP	–	Gross Domestic Product
HIPIC	–	Heavily Indebted Poor Countries
HIV and AIDS	–	Human Immuno-Deficiency Virus/Acquired Immune Deficiency Syndrome
ICC	–	International Criminal Court
ICT	–	Information, Communication and Technology
ICU	–	Islamic Courts Union
IGAD	–	Inter-Governmental Authority on Development
IGADD	–	Inter-Governmental Authority on Drought and Desertification
IMF	–	International Monetary Fund
IOR	–	Indian Ocean Rim
IPPG	–	Inter-Parties Parliamentary Group
ISIS	–	Islamic State of Iraq and al-Sham
ITU	–	International Telecommunications Union

JAP	–	Jubilee Alliance Party
JCPOA	–	Joint Comprehensive Plan of Action
KADU	–	Kenya African Democratic Union
KANU	–	Kenya African National Union
KDF	–	Kenya Defence Forces
KHA	–	Kenyatta Home Again
KPU	–	Kenya People's Union
LAPSSET	–	Lamu Port-South Sudan-Ethiopia-Transport (Corridor)
LEGCO	–	Legislative Council
MAGA	–	Making America Great Again
MDC	–	Movement for Democratic Change
MoU	–	Memorandum of Understanding
MRC	–	Mombasa Republican Council
NAFTA	–	North American Free Trade Agreement
NAK	–	National Alliance Party of Kenya
NARC	–	National Alliance Rainbow Coalition
NATO	–	North Atlantic Treaty Organisation
NCTS	–	Northern Corridor Transport System
NDC	–	National Defence College
NEPAD	–	New Partnership for Africa's Development
NFD	–	Northern Frontier District
OAU	–	Organisation of African Unity
ODM	–	Orange Democratic Movement
ODM-K	–	Orange Democratic Movement-Kenya
OECD	–	Organisation for Economic Cooperation and Development
P5	–	Permanent Five (Permanent Members of the UN Security Council)

PLF	–	Palestinian Liberation Front
PLO	–	Palestinian Liberation Organisation
PNU	–	Party of National Unity
RECs	–	Regional Economic Communities
RENAMO	–	Mozambique National Resistance Movement
SADC	–	Southern African Development Community
SAHRAWI	–	Western Sahara Democratic Republic
SALW	–	Small Arms and Light Weapons
SAPs	–	Structural Adjustment Programmes
SDGs	–	Sustainable Development Goals
SGR	–	Standard Gauge Railway
SHIFTA	–	Bandit or Rebel
SMART	–	Specific, Measurable, Achievable, Realistic Targets
SOEs	–	State-Owned Enterprises
SPLM/A	–	Sudan People's Liberation Movement/Army
SRRC	–	Somalia Reconstruction and Reconciliation Conference
TFG	–	Transitional Federal Government
TICAD	–	Tokyo International Conference on Africa's Development
TNA	–	The National Alliance
TPDF	–	Tanzanian People's Defence Forces
TPLF	–	Tigrinya People's Liberation Front
TPP	–	Trans-Pacific Partnership
UAE	–	United Arab Emirates
UDI	–	Unilateral Declaration of independence
UK	–	United Kingdom
UN-HABITAT	–	United Nations Human Settlements

UNCLOS	–	United Nations Conference on the Law of the Sea
UNCTAD	–	United Nations Conference on Trade and Development
UNEP	–	United Nations Environmental Programme
UNESCO	–	United Nations Educational Scientific and Cultural Organisation
UNIDO	–	United Nations Industrial Development Organisation
UNO	–	United Nations Organisation
UNON	–	United Nations Office at Nairobi
URP	–	United Republican Party
USA	–	United States of America
USSR	–	Union of Soviet Socialist Republics
WTC	–	World Trade Centre
WTO	–	World Trade Organisation

Introduction

Kenya's Foreign Policy and Diplomacy: Evolution, Challenges and Opportunities is a product of years of thought and reflection on the direction Kenya took in international relations after its establishment and recognition as a state. The decision to write this book was in part an attempt to study and appraise Kenya's Foreign Policy and diplomacy since independence. This required an objective analysis of the Foreign Policy, its basis, formulation and articulation in the face of the challenges Kenya had to overcome in pursuit of its Foreign Policy objectives. It examines how Kenya managed its Foreign Policy at different times since independence. It pays specific attention to the policy direction during the respective tenures of office by the four presidents Kenya has had since its independence. Towards that end, it brings out the actual Foreign Policy orientation, which characterised each presidency and how each contributed to its evolution over the years.

Kenya's Foreign Policy articulates the county's values, beliefs and aspirations. Like any other policy, it is concerned with institutions, and not individuals and, therefore, about the state itself. Individuals mentioned feature as its operatives and state actors because of their state positions or outstanding work performed on Kenya's behalf. Even though not all state actors, except the four successive presidents Kenya has had since independence, have been singled out. In Foreign Policy parlance, political leaders such as a president, monarch, prime minister, minister for foreign affairs, ambassador or appointed envoys symbolise the sovereign authority of the state.

It may be helpful to distinguish the terms *Foreign Policy* from *international relations*. Foreign Policy consists of the objectives a state sets out to achieve in its efforts to secure its national interest. International relations constitute interactions among states and other actors of international law in exercise of their rights, duties and obligations as defined in the Montevideo Convention. The Oxford English Dictionary defines diplomacy as the management of international relations through negotiations. It is the principle of negotiation which establishes diplomacy as the primary instrument for articulating Foreign Policy. The distinction between Foreign Policy, international relations and diplomacy is important in understanding the intentions and actions of a state upon its establishment and recognition by other states within the international system. It is from this premise that the reader will grasp the process of formulation and implementation of Foreign Policy.

Kenya's establishment as a state during the Cold War rivalry mainly between the United States of America (USA) and the Soviet Union, demanded a delicate balance in establishing relations between the West and the East. Kenya crafted its Foreign Policy to secure a role and place for itself among the community of nations and earn the respect of other states, after it emerged from the yoke of colonialism. It designed its diplomacy to articulate its Foreign Policy with flexibility so as to adapt to the changing international dynamics.

At the time of writing this book, no one from within or without Kenya had written a comprehensive book on the subject. The challenge on non-availability of reference material while compiling the book was overcome through consultations with key informants. These included retired ambassadors and other public servants, who recounted their experiences and participation in the management of public affairs of independent Kenya. *Reminisces on Kenya's Early Diplomacy* illustrated Kenya's early experience in diplomacy. The book is a compilation of reflections by retired Kenyan ambassadors during a Symposium on Kenya's Early Diplomacy 1963–1993, held on the 16th and 17th September, 2009, and published by the Foreign Service Institute, Ministry of Foreign Affairs.

Other information sources included government circulars, blueprints, manuals, print media and my own experience as a career foreign service officer. The information and insight I gained from the consultations helped me put together a coherent narrative on Kenya's Foreign Policy since independence.

Some of the people I consulted played a significant role in the formulation of the country's Foreign Policy after independence. Their views provided valuable insight on the Foreign Policy intentions Kenya adopted at independence. The contents of this book have thus been gathered, in part, from these interviews, works on Foreign Policy, international relations and diplomacy and from my over thirty years' experience as an officer in the Kenya Foreign Service (KFS).

* * *

Foreign Policy is not an everyday conversation for ordinary citizens. Many citizens perceive Foreign Policy simply as "activities which take place outside the country and have no direct bearing on their daily lives". Yet, Foreign Policy plays an important role in defining a country's international image which impacts on their own perception as citizens. Foreign Policy articulates a state's national values, beliefs and aspirations in a strategy to influence other states and other actors to support its cause.

A state which articulates a sound Foreign Policy successfully persuades other states to view international issues from its point of view. A state's ability to articulate these attributes in relations with other states and actors of international law, enables it to promote, protect and defend its national interest. Kenya's Foreign Policy follows this general rule. Kenya's founding fathers settled on a pragmatic Foreign Policy which took into account the delicate balance between the US and the Soviet Union superpower rivalry and competition for global dominance. Kenya's adoption of a mixed economic development model turned it into an economic success story in comparison with its neighbours in East Africa.

In his book, *African Socialism in Two Countries,* Ahmed Mohiuddin provides an interesting comparative analysis of the interpretation and application of economic paths which Kenya and Tanzania adopted respectively. He discusses how their respective strategies defined the ideological differences which have characterised bilateral relations between the two countries to this day. Ahmed concludes that the capitalist path Kenya took enabled it to develop a strong economic base that has made Kenya become the biggest economy in East Africa. The different approaches were, to a large extent, responsible for the political challenges which faced the defunct East African Community (EAC) and contributed to its eventual collapse.

Kenya emerged from colonialism perceived as a revolutionary state on the basis of the bitter war of independence the Mau Mau waged against the United Kingdom (UK), which resonated well with many independent African countries such as Tanzania, Ghana, Algeria, Mali, Guinea, among others. Mzee Jomo Kenyatta focused on consolidation of Kenya's independence. He demonstrated leadership when he adopted a non-aligned Foreign Policy for Kenya, which made it possible to pragmatically relate to the West and the East. This pragmatic approach in Foreign Policy, in particular, enabled Kenya to foster friendly relations with the West, which proved critical to its ambition to secure the right to host the headquarters of the United Nations Environmental Programme (UNEP) and the UN Human Settlements (UN–HABITAT) in 1972 and 1974, respectively.

Kenya's role in peace efforts transcends the sub-region. It has participated in UN peacekeeping missions in Namibia, Sierra Leone, and Liberia in Africa, and in Lebanon, former Yugoslavia and East Timor. President Moi's two-year tenure (1981-1983) as Chairman of the Organisation of African Unity (OAU) solidified his interest in the peaceful resolution of political conflicts and intensified Kenya's role in mediation. These underline the principles guiding Kenya's Foreign Policy, namely; peaceful co-existence with neighbours and non-interference in the internal affairs of other states.

The non-aligned Foreign Policy made it easier for Kenya to play a leading role in mediation and conflict resolution in the Horn of Africa and the Great Lakes Region during the 1980s, despite Cold War rivalries, and the support different protagonists received, from either side of the ideological divide. Peace diplomacy, in Kenya's Foreign Policy in these two regions, took centre stage during Moi's presidency through to the early years of Kibaki's presidency. Two factors underlined the principles that guided its Foreign Policy: the quest for peace in the sub-region and the need to secure markets for Kenya's goods and services.

Kenya's geographical location in the midst of countries enduring insecurity and political instability informs its Foreign Policy on regional peace and security, which inevitably affects its own security. Kenya faces challenges due to an influx of refugees and proliferation of Small Arms and Light Weapons (SALW) from neighbouring countries. Its role in the Sudan, Uganda, Somalia, Mozambique and South Sudan peace processes stems directly from its concern on the political situation in the countries surrounding it. This approach was challenged by the post-election violence of 2007/08 which threatened the attainment of Kenya's Foreign Policy objectives, and hastened the need to address issues of good governance, democracy, corruption and ethnicity, which have bedevilled it since independence. Historical focus on personalities, property and greed in the country's politics, have not permitted articulation of a coherent and effective Foreign Policy. The Constitution of Kenya, 2010, has addressed some of the issues. Its full implementation is likely to create an environment conducive for articulation of a successful Foreign Policy abroad.

The fragile political situation in the Horn of Africa and the Great Lakes Region calls for decisive action to secure peace, security and political stability to guarantee sustainable economic development. Issues of governance, lack of democratic culture, weak state institutions and personalised rule have compromised the ability of the countries to grow faster and expand their economies.

Ineffectiveness of state institutions, bad governance, ideological and personality conflicts and greed, have exacerbated both natural and human-made disasters, such as drought and deforestation, which complicate the fragile eco-system leading to food insecurity and famine. Peace and security issues have, thus, taken centre stage in Kenya's Foreign Policy. The objective is to manage and mitigate the situation in order to improve the economic well-being of the people in neighbouring countries as well as secure markets for Kenya's goods.

Orientation towards the East
In the period from independence in 1963 to 1989 when the Cold War ended, Kenya took advantage of the dynamics of the Cold War to enjoy warm relations with its western development partners. However, the post-1989 period presented a challenge, which caught the country unprepared for the new dynamics in international relations that emerged. President Moi displayed unwillingness to embrace the new dynamics in international relations which were thrust upon the world. His reluctance proved costly to the country. The changed circumstances needed an innovative Foreign Policy to meet the challenge. Most of its western partners introduced tough conditions to guide their economic relations with Kenya. The new hard-line approach almost brought Kenya to its knees. Only France and Japan continued to support Kenya. Kenya was forced to adapt its Foreign Policy, as a direct consequence of demands by its traditional development partners, by turning to countries in the East, notably China and India, for alternative economic partnerships to sustain its economic development.

Kenya's Foreign Policy and diplomacy faced serious challenges after the 2007/2008 post-election violence, which threatened the security, unity and stability of the country. Intervention by the international community saved Kenya from degenerating into chaos when pressure was put on its leaders to negotiate a power-sharing arrangement. The negotiations led to a National Accord which created the post of Prime Minister. The accord further provided for the establishment of a local judicial mechanism to deal with the perpetrators of the violence. Two commissions of inquiry were formed to determine the causes of the violence and the credibility of the elections, respectively. The Commission of Inquiry into Post-Election Violence was chaired by Justice Philip Waki. It examined the causes of the post-election violence and recommended further investigations and possible prosecution of ten Kenyans whose names were sealed in an envelope and addressed to the International Criminal Court (ICC) at The Hague.

In the absence of a local judicial mechanism, the ICC was mandated to try the cases. Kenya's inability or unwillingness to establish the local mechanism led to the indictment of Uhuru Kenyatta, Francis Muthaura, Major General Hussein Ali Mohamed from the Party of National Unity (PNU); and William Ruto, Henry Kosgey and Joshua arap Sang from the Orange Democratic Movement (ODM). The names of the remaining four persons were not made public by the court.

The Constitution of Kenya, 2010, has contextualised the Foreign Policy and its relation to issues of governance, accountability and integrity. The provisions of Chapter 1, Articles (5) and (6) of the Constitution of Kenya, 2010, compel Kenya to respect its international obligations as defined by the treaties which it negotiated or acceded to. The constitution further compels Kenya to observe basic human rights, good governance and the values, beliefs, aspirations, as well as rights and duties, which the Foreign Policy articulates. Kenya promotes peace, security and stability in Africa, and recognises the importance of international cooperation and collaboration on issues which pose threats to international peace and security, such as terrorism, development and possession of ballistic missiles and nuclear weapons.

Kenya Foreign Policy, 2014

Publication of the *Kenya Foreign Policy, 2014,* has helped address some of the questions on Kenya's Foreign Policy. The written Foreign Policy documents the evolution of Kenya's Foreign Policy from independence. It states that:

> Kenya's long struggle for national liberation from colonialism set a strong foundation for its Foreign Policy orientation. The architects of our Republic underscored the inextricable link between national independence and humanity's freedom, equity and inalienable right to a shared heritage.

> Kenya assumed its place as a sovereign state and actor in international relations upon independence in December, 1963. Since then Foreign Policy has been guided by a strong belief that our own future is inseparable from the stability of our environment as the basic source of national survival and prosperity.[1]

The *Kenya Foreign Policy, 2014,* offers insights on issues which Kenya considers critical to peace and security both within and without its borders.

---

1   *Kenya Foreign Policy* 2014, pp. 14-15.

Its development of domestic and foreign policies has been influenced by the need to maintain a peaceful and secure country. Decolonisation, independence, the political tensions, which characterised East/West ideological competition and economic relations between the developed and developing countries played a key role in determining its early Foreign Policy orientation.

Kenya aligned its Foreign Policy in response to the constantly changing dynamics of international relations. It was influenced by consolidation of the state and a vigorous defence of its sovereignty and territorial integrity, and the high expectations of its people. National security is a priority as a pre-requisite for economic development and a pillar in the country's involvement in conflict resolution in the Horn of Africa and the Great Lakes region.

The principle of good neighbourliness underpins Kenya's investment in its strategic position as the hub of transport in eastern Africa. The railway and road networks forming the Northern Corridor Transport System (NCTS) are serviced by the port of Mombasa, the busiest and most efficient sea port in East Africa. The expected development of the Lamu Port-South Sudan-Ethiopia-Transport Corridor (LAPSSET) will expand trade with South Sudan and Ethiopia. Kenya offers convenient airline connections to West Africa, southern Africa, the Middle East, South East Asia and Europe. It has a well-established information, communications and financial services infrastructure in Nairobi and other major towns. The transportation corridors, the ports and other infrastructure make Kenya a strategic place for business and investment in eastern Africa.

The 2007/2008 violence paralysed the transport system, compromising Kenya's strong position as a vital external trade link for Uganda, Rwanda, Burundi, eastern Democratic Republic of Congo (DRC) and South Sudan and should never be allowed to happen again. Kenya should ensure efficient operations to maintain a competitive edge in East Africa. It should firmly deal with governance issues such as corruption and strengthen democracy to create a stable political environment, capable of sustaining the vantage position the country enjoys.

Emerging issues in international relations
Globalisation and advances in telecommunications have turned the world into a global village. Distances which took early explorers years to cover are done instantaneously. The new realities have opened up societies whereby issues which had, hitherto, been regarded as internal affairs of states have

become major Foreign Policy considerations. These include: democracy, accountability, transparency, respect for human rights and freedom of expression and association. Western countries adopted and advocated them as core values in their international diplomatic and economic cooperation arrangements.

Kenya is bound to seek international cooperation in combating international terrorism, drugs and human trafficking, illegal migrations, and illicit trade in endangered species. Its Foreign Policy should incorporate support for issues such as drought and other natural disasters, and out-break of diseases such as HIV and AIDS, Ebola and malaria.

Environmental diplomacy

Kenya's Foreign Policy includes environment, climate change, protection of endangered species and global warming. Kenya has actively participated in international environmental diplomacy since independence. Its pro-active engagement was evident and remarkable in the 1960s and 1970s. The decision was a result of recognition of Kenya's strong environmental and conservation credentials. The position drastically changed in the 1980s when the government failed to deal with poaching, the destruction of forest cover and corruption, which compromised many of the environmental policies. As a consequence, the level of poaching of elephants and rhinos rose dramatically. Due to high population and abuse of state institutions, huge acreage of forests were de-gazetted and allocated to political allies for their support. By 2002, the country's forest cover had shrunk to 1.7% of the land mass instead of the 10% recommended by the United Nations (UN).

Kenya's Foreign Policy in perspective

Kenya articulates its Foreign Policy through a non-confrontational diplomatic style. This approach enabled it to balance its relations with western and East bloc countries during the Cold War. The same style has been used in its approach to peace in Africa. Kenya does not threaten its neighbours, but has been able to assert itself against challenges to its sovereignty and territorial integrity. It applied the approach in the 1960s to thwart the expansionist threats from Somalia by firmly dealing with the Shifta insurrection from within; and, in 1971 when Amin made an outrageous territorial claim on Kenya. Kenya enhanced the capacity of its military including purchase of F5 bombers from the USA. Similarly, Kenya opted to deal with problem of Migingo Islands in Lake Victoria, and the boundary dispute with South Sudan along the common border at Nakodok through international legal mechanisms.

PART I

CONCEPTUAL BASIS OF FOREIGN POLICY

This part discusses the conceptual basis of Foreign Policy from the establishment and recognition of a state under the Montevideo Convention of 1933. It explains in detail the concept of the national interest and how its core elements determine Foreign Policy. No entity can have a Foreign Policy before it is established and recognised as a state. It examines the process of formulating a Foreign Policy guided by the national interest of a state, and identifies its priorities and objectives to attain its goals. It further examines the role by different organs of the state in the formulation of Foreign Policy. The process of formulation of Foreign Policy varies from state to state, depending on the structure and form of government and international dynamics at the time.

Finally, this part discusses diplomacy as the primary instrument of Foreign Policy and the tools and methods a state applies in articulating its Foreign Policy. The Vienna Convention on Diplomatic Relations of 1961 and the Vienna Convention on Consular Relations outline guidelines on the conduct of diplomacy and consular affairs which envoys must observe in carrying out their diplomatic duties. Envoys who violate these protocols face sanctions including being declared persona non-grata and expelled. A state could, in addition, face political, economic or military sanctions. Use of sanctions as a tool of diplomacy gained prominence after the end of the Cold War in 1989. They are used to coerce, influence or penalise an offending state to extract a change of behaviour. The diplomatic, economic and military capacities of a state or states, which impose sanctions, usually determine whether they succeed or not.

CHAPTER 1

The National Interest in Foreign Policy

A state's Foreign Policy is determined by its national interest. The policy draws its legitimacy from a Constitution, which establishes institutions of state including structures and functions of the government. It is the government which formulates and implements policies of the state from the time it is established and recognised by other states. The recognition of an entity as a state grants it legitimacy to determine, decide and take actions both local and international to secure its national interest.

Establishment and recognition of a state

Establishment and recognition of a state under the Montevideo Convention of 1933 affirms its full authority over its territory to decide on its role and place in the world, its relations with other states and other actors of international law without reference to any other authority. Recognition of a state is an acknowledgement that an entity so established meets the following conditions: a defined territory, a stable population and a government. The convention assigns rights, duties and responsibilities. These include its ability to enter into relations with other states, defence of its sovereignty and territorial integrity, form a government to drive its activities, and provide security for its citizens, which the state is obliged to exercise under international law.

Recognition pre-supposes acknowledgement by other states, of a state's absolute sovereign control of the territory, the population and the power the state may exercise over that territory. Recognition occurs when other states recognise the capacity of a state to enter into relations with them and other actors of international law.

B. Sen, a former Indian diplomat, explains the question of sovereignty as follows:

> It is clear beyond controversy that a new community, however, it may come into existence, must fulfil all the conditions of statehood.
>
> The more important of such conditions are;
>
> (a) that the new community must have a government which is actually independent of the control of any other state,

(b) that the community has acquired sufficient degree of internal stability, and that it has a defined territory under its control which can be treated as the state territory of the new state.[2]

The respect a state has towards the other, forms the foundation of cooperative relations between them. It re-assures absence of hostility from one to the other. The point of departure would normally be the instruments of its establishment and recognition, which grants it the legal capacity to enter into relations with other states. The instruments define its sovereignty and territorial integrity from which emerge core elements of the national interest.

Recognition of a state is an acknowledgement that an entity possesses legal authority to engage with other actors on equal basis. Although the convention came into force in 1933, establishment and recognition of a state precedes diplomacy, yet the conditions for such recognition progressively developed from the concept of Greek city states to the understanding of a modern state. Singapore is a good example of a successful city state. It may conceivably be argued that the Vatican falls in the definition of a city state, although it lacks the classical definition in the sense that it does not exclusively control its territory nor does it have a quantifiable population within its territory.

Many African countries were recognised as states at independence upon which, by resolutions of the OAU in 1963 and the UN, they adopted colonial boundaries to define their respective sovereignty and territorial integrity. Two states have since emerged through self-determination and negotiations in post-independent Africa. These are: Eritrea which seceded from Ethiopia in 1991, after the overthrow of Mengistu Haile Mariam and South Sudan which broke away from Sudan in 2011, on the implementation of the Comprehensive Peace Agreement (CPA). Away from Africa, the Soviet Union broke up into 15 independent republics in 1991, after which Russia assumed the rights and duties of the defunct Soviet Union, including the permanent seat on the UN Security Council. Similarly, the breakup of Yugoslavia in the 1990s resulted in the creation of Slovenia, Croatia, Bosnia-Herzegovina, Serbia and Montenegro. Kosovo later broke away from Serbia, although Serbia, Russia and a number of other countries have not recognised it as an independent state.

The national interest

The *national interest* of a state comprises core elements namely: sovereignty and territorial integrity, national security, economic advancement, national

---

2   B. Sen, *A Diplomat's Handbook of International Law and Practice.*

prestige, national power and military capacity. The national interest of a state is not transactional, but defines national power and drives all activities of the state. The national interest of a state is permanent and eternal; it drives all activities of the state and its core elements determine the state's domestic and foreign policies.

Kenya's Foreign Policy and diplomacy is determined by its national interest. Upon recognition, Kenya began to exercise sovereign power over its territory. It formed a government responsible for law and order and for formulation of both domestic and foreign policies to secure its national interest. Kenya's Foreign Policy was designed to deal with complex international issues of a bilateral and multilateral nature, with other actors in the international system. The economic blueprint it adopted in 1965 struck a balance between its national interest and competing interests of other states. This provided it with a platform for engagement with other states to support its cause and earn respect for its people. This balance is best explained by Gujiral, who, writing on the Foreign Policy of India, observes that:

> A coherent Foreign Policy can only flow from clearly defined objectives on the domestic front. It is to promote the inherent strengths of a country that a government follows a certain policy in the external sphere...The principal objective of the Foreign Policy of the United Front Government is to further strengthen India's democracy, and ensure all-round economic and social development with justice and equity.[3]

Gujiral's argument is both informative and instructional when analysing Foreign Policy. It helps in providing an understanding of the link between Foreign Policy and how it advances the domestic agenda of a nation (in this case India).

The Montevideo Convention grants equal status to all states under international law, but the influence each state exerts on others depends on its political and economic power and military capacity. These factors enable a state to exercise immense political and diplomatic power in international relations. For example, the US projects enormous power and influence over international institutions such as the UN, the World Bank, the International Monetary Fund (IMF), the North Atlantic Treaty Organisation (NATO) and many others where it is a member because of its political and economic power, and massive, sophisticated military capacity.

---

3   Inder Kumar Gujiral, *A Foreign Policy for India.*

Recognition of a government

The recognition of a government refers to acknowledgement and acceptance of the *government of the day* of a state as by law established. Unconstitutional assumption of power is unlikely to be recognised by majority of citizens in the respective country or by other states. It brings into question the quality of government in terms of its legitimacy and lawfulness. It means that the government which has assumed power is not legitimate and does not enjoy the approval of the citizens. There is a distinction between recognition of *a state* from recognition of *a government*. This distinction is important in understanding the concept of national interest of a state. The recognition of Kenya at independence falls under state recognition while the transformation of, for example, Spain from a military dictatorship to a constitutional monarchy in the 1970s, Iran from a monarchy to a theocracy in 1979, and Nepal from a monarchy to a republic in the first decade of the twenty first century, are examples of recognition of the *government of the day* for those countries, respectively.

Kenya's attainment of statehood on 12th December 1963, when it received the instruments of independence from the UK, thrust it in the community of nations as a full actor. However, Jomo Kenyatta's focus on consolidation of independence and the new state somewhat diminished his direct involvement in Foreign Policy issues, until Idi Amin laid claim to Kenya's territory soon after the overthrow of Milton Obote in 1971. Amin claimed the territory from the Kenya/Uganda border to Naivasha in the Rift Valley; only about one hundred kilometres west of Nairobi.

Kenya faced the dilemma in its Foreign Policy towards Uganda over Amin's overthrow of Obote in 1971. Although Kenya did not recognise the change of government in Uganda or the manner in which it came to power, Kenya found itself in an awkward position because of its economic relations with Uganda. Kenya maintains good relations with Uganda because Uganda is its number one trading partner in the world. Uganda is an important market for its manufactured goods, while Kenya is key to Uganda's external trade through the NCTS and Mombasa port. Uganda is an important investment destination for Kenya. These ties remain a major contributor to Kenya's economic development.

Kenya's geographical location is critical to the decisions it took in defining its strategic interests, in a region characterised by tough terrain, desert conditions, insecurity, political instability, agricultural potential and a fragile eco-system. Its role in conflict resolution in the Horn of Africa and the Great Lakes Region was borne out of these factors. All in all, Kenya's Foreign Policy is predicated on its capacity, actual and potential, in pursuit of its national interest. Other countries in the sub-region and beyond, similarly, take into account Kenya's geographical location in formulating their policies towards it.

Kenya's location influences its Foreign Policy on peace, security and stability in the Horn of Africa and the Great Lakes Region, which constitute an important economic area. Other examples where a country's location shapes its Foreign Policy include the USA, which explains its Foreign Policy, when its leaders regarded threats or an attack on its territory to be so remote in relation to events in Europe, until President Woodrow Wilson took the US to World War I. World War I and World War II against Nazi Germany made the USA realise that it was not immune to threats of war or actual attack. The USA and the Soviet Union immediately embarked on projecting their respective power in countries which they considered to be in their spheres. The USA sought to influence the world through economic partnerships and aid. The reconstruction of Europe through the Marshall plan consolidated US influence in western Europe and precipitated the Soviet Union's drive to export its communist ideology in eastern Europe. It also appealed to many developing countries, which had or were about to emerge from colonialism.

The national interest as a driver of state activities
The national interest of a state drives all its activities and determines both its domestic and foreign policies. The success of a state's policies depends on its size, capacity and the influence it may exercise in the international system. Powerful states such as the USA, China and Russia, take advantage of the comparatively huge capacities they possess, in different sectors of their respective statehood, to influence situations to their favour across the world. When, in their view, this approach fails, they often resort to coercion, arm twisting or outright use of force to secure or defend their interests. Less powerful states such as Kenya, Cuba, Cambodia and Ukraine, must be innovative in the deployment of the limited capacity they possess to face powerful states and other challenges in international politics.

Morgenthau argues that the realist theory of politics operates in a specific political national outline in which political acts and their foreseeable consequences must be considered. A realist theory of international politics imposes certain expectations from the Foreign Policy of a state. He observes that:

The concept of interest defined as power imposes intellectual discipline upon the observer, infuses rational order into the subject matter of politics, and thus makes the theoretical understanding of politics possible. On the side of the actor, it provides for rational discipline in action and creates that astounding continuity in Foreign Policy which makes American, British and Russian Foreign Policy appear as intelligible, rational continuum, by and large consistent within itself, regardless of the different motives, preferences, and intellectual and moral qualities of successive statesmen…the kind of interest determining political action in a particular period of history depends upon the political and cultural context within which Foreign Policy is formulated. The goals that might be pursued by nations in their Foreign Policy can run the whole gamut of objectives any nation has ever pursued or might possibly pursue…What is true of the general character of international relations is also true of the nation state as the ultimate point of reference of contemporary Foreign Policy.[4]

Morgenthau's observation explains how the national interest defines those specific interests which a state articulates as a sovereign entity independent of any other authority.

Kenya's Foreign Policy is no different and has been determined by the core elements of its national interest. Its regional focus addresses issues such as peace, security and political stability with the purpose of establishing dependable markets for the country's goods. At the international level, the policy focuses on two issues; the first relates to essential economic partnerships to advance Kenya's economic agenda. The second focuses on international collaboration on issues such as the fight against terrorism, human and drug trafficking, climate change and international peace and security. Overall, Kenya's Foreign Policy seeks to define the role and place for the country on the world stage.

US Foreign Policy under President Trump

Donald J. Trump campaigned on a nationalistic platform pledging to "Make America Great Again (MAGA)" with the slogan "America First". He was eventually elected on this Republican conservative platform, beating Hillary Rodham Clinton. Immediately after his inauguration, Trump initiated steps to withdraw the USA from some of the agreements entered into by his predecessors, arguing that they were not in the USA's national interest. This radical view of the USA's role in world politics illustrates how President Trump exploited the USA's national interest to support his view of USA influence in the world affairs.

---

4   Hans J. Morgenthau, *Politics Among Nations,* Fourth Edition.

In Trump's view, the USA must re-assert its economic and military power and influence in the world. US withdrawal from the international system it helped create after World War II may not serve Trump's intention of "America First", but could end up isolating America, which will encourage China and Russia to challenge the USA for global leadership.

The USA is apprehensive of China's militarisation of the South China Sea, while a resurgent Russia flexes its military power with incursions in Georgia, Ukraine (annexation of Crimea and its support for insurgence in the east of the country) and Syria. As a superpower and the most powerful country in the world, the USA's national interest has far reaching implications to other nations. These include its political influence, and, economic and military interests around the world. The USA plays a critical role in the maintenance of international peace and security within and without the UN framework. Its intentions and actions affect the interests of other nations in a fundamental way. The actions of a US president in directing US Foreign Policy are both keenly watched and carefully considered by other countries.

US policies on immigration, and other major international issues such as trade, environment, and international peace and security attract the attention of not only its rivals such as Russia and China but also smaller nations which look up to it as a role model. Trump's pronouncements and actions in his first year in office on the UN were alarming, and if implemented could have far reaching consequences. He signalled the US withdrawal from the United Nations Educational Scientific and Cultural Organisation (UNESCO), the United Nations Framework Convention on Climate Change (UNFCC) 2015, and regional trade arrangements such as the North American Free Trade Agreement (NAFTA) and the Trans-Pacific Partnership (TPP).

The USA's political influence, diplomatic outreach, economic power and military capacity far outstrip those of any other country on earth. President Trump withdrew the USA from the Paris Accord on environment, TPP and the Iran Nuclear Agreement known as the Joint Comprehensive Plan of Action (JCPOA), signed on 14th July, 2015. He also re-imposed economic sanctions on Iran on account that the nuclear deal was not in the interests of the USA. This decision caused considerable concern among other signatories namely, France, the UK and Germany, as well as Russia and China. Germany, France and the UK may take legal measures to cushion their companies doing business with Iran from USA sanctions.

In a departure from international consensus, President Trump reversed the USA policy on the Middle East conflict by recognising Jerusalem as the capital city of Israel. The move upset the balance in the search for peace between Israel and Palestine and threatened the two-state solution to the problem. Furthermore, the US reductions in contributions to the UN, adversely affected UN's capacity to meet its international obligations.

President Trump's view of NATO caused misgivings among its members. If the trend continues, US withdrawal from its international commitments could threaten the system which has maintained international peace and security since World War II. US national interests affect those of other countries because of its capacity to influence situations across the globe. Henry Kissinger observes that:

> John F Kennedy declared confidently in 1961 that America was strong enough to 'pay any price, bear any burden' to ensure the success of liberty. Three decades later, the United States is in less of a position to insist on the immediate realisation of all its desires. Other countries have grown into Great Power status. The United States now faces the challenge of reaching its goals in stages, each of which is an amalgam of American values and geopolitical necessities. One of the new necessities is that a world comprising several states of comparable strength must base its order on some concept of equilibrium – an idea with which the United States has never felt comfortable.[5]

The US is still the pre-eminent superpower, politically, economically and militarily, but it is unlikely to enjoy an unchallenged superpower status as it did immediately after the end of the Cold War. Russia, its traditional rival, lurks in its shadows, while an emerging and increasingly assertive China is competing for supremacy as an economic power. China has made inroads in many parts of the world, especially in Africa, where competition for influence is at its highest ever.

President Trump's imposition of 25% and 10% tariffs on steel and aluminium imports, respectively, from China, the European Union (EU), Canada and Mexico which petitioned the World Trade Organisation (WTO) threatened not just a trade war, but the essence of multilateral system anticipated at the end of World War II. Trump may target the US flagship agreement with African countries – the African Growth and Opportunity Act (AGOA) concluded on 18th May 2000, under President Bill Clinton, as a platform for trade between the USA and Africa. This platform has witnessed increased trade between Kenya and the USA which

---

5   Henry A Kissinger, *Diplomacy,* Third Edition.

has led the latter to gradually overtake the UK to become Kenya's third most important trading partner in the world after Uganda and Tanzania. This significant development could be jeopardised by President Trump's view and actions which seem to define the USA's international engagement from a narrow business perspective. Kenya should be alive to these new developments, plan its strategies together with other African countries to respond to them and safeguard AGOA.

CHAPTER 2

The Making of Foreign Policy

Formulation of Foreign Policy by a state begins immediately after the entity has been established and recognised under international law. The first government by the party which ascends to power creates institutions of the state responsible for both domestic and foreign policies as determined by its national interest. The core elements of the national interest determine its Foreign Policy. When a state begins the process of formulating its Foreign Policy, it defines the framework of the policy based on the national interest.

The framework includes identification of objectives, the strategies, the means to achieve them and the time frame. A state, therefore, uses all means at its disposal to formulate, articulate and implement a Foreign Policy to secure a place and role among the community of nations. It uses its Foreign Policy to articulate its values, beliefs and aspirations to secure its national interest. The attainment of its objectives may be limited by the state's capacity, obstacles in its path, resource constraints or by treaty limitation. Whereas a nation demonstrates its capacity to act in its own interest without reference to any other authority, its actions must be governed by internationally accepted norms and by international law.

A state's capacity, actual and potential, to articulate a successful Foreign Policy, depends on its strength as determined by the elements of the national interest. Its ability defines the extent of its diplomatic capacity, economic potential and military power influenced by its: geography (territory and location), natural resources (food, raw materials, flora and fauna), industrial capacity (wealth and economic status), and military preparedness (hardware and technology).

The process of formulating Foreign Policy is guided by a state's Constitution which gives it legitimacy, and the structure and system of government. It is the government which determines all the activities that the state will undertake such as the defence of its sovereignty, territorial integrity, national security and economic interests. A state, thereafter, proceeds to define the strategies by which its Foreign Policy will be articulated on the world stage. The Foreign Policy must provide a road map specifying the form, content and objectives as a basis for interaction with other actors in the international system.

The quality of political and military leadership, size of the armed forces, population distribution and trends, national character (feel good factor and prestige) and morale, powered by good governance, are critical factors for a sound Foreign Policy. These elements constitute the overall policy framework which a state uses as its tool to influence other states and other actors in its favour. If a state succeeds in achieving this objective, it can claim to be projecting its power on the international scene.

In the event of a state adopting new values through, for example, political transformation, it must adjust its Foreign Policy to articulate the new values, beliefs and aspirations. A leading example in this respect is South Africa which in 1994, experienced a shift of political power from minority whites to the majority blacks. A democratic South Africa adopted new values, beliefs and aspirations based on the rule of law anchored in a new Constitution and provided a new basis of its Foreign Policy. The shift did not, however, affect South Africa's recognition as a state. The new basis of its Foreign Policy was anchored on democracy, good governance, respect for human rights, tolerance and an all-inclusive national character and behaviour. Its new approach enhanced the country's prestige in the world. South Africa's strong economy and military capacity catapulted it into a major player in Southern Africa and the African Union (AU). South Africa's admission into the Group of 20 (G20) is international recognition of the country as a major player in world politics.

The UK spearheaded the establishment of the Commonwealth of States in a new Foreign Policy drive to maintain its influence in newly independent former colonies. Its objective was to create a mechanism through which the UK could continue to maintain some degree of influence in the former colonial territories. It negotiated for the Queen, its head of state, to assume the titular headship of the group.

In 2018, the Commonwealth Heads of State and Government summit in London, agreed to retain the Queen's successor as its head, even though the position is not hereditary. Further, the newly independent countries which emerged after the demise of the British empire, agreed, by consensus, to categorise the heads of their respective diplomatic missions accredited within the Commonwealth Countries as "High Commissioners" instead of the traditional title of "Ambassadors" to express the special relationship.

France, on its part, formed the Francophone which grouped its former colonies in Africa, through which it hoped to maintain considerable political and military influence.

China oriented its Foreign Policy to support a shift in its economic policy from a Marxist model to free market, after the death of its leader Mao Zedong. The shift did not alter the political structure. The economic transformation shifted China's focus in its Foreign Policy, turning it into the second largest economy in the world after the USA.

International law obliges a state to employ legitimate means in articulating its Foreign Policy. Powerful states tend to take unilateral action to project their power, sometimes outside existing international mechanisms such as the UN. The wealthier and more politically powerful the state is, the more influence it will exert on other states and generally force through its point of view. The USA, for example, imposed unilateral sanctions on Iran (1979) and North Korea (1949), in addition to those taken by the UN, because of its enormous political, economic and military capacity. The USA takes a lead on many international issues because it is able to flex its power well above the other nations.

The process of formulating Foreign Policy

Foreign Policy formulation varies from state to state. It is usually influenced by the powers granted to a state's institutions, size of its economy, its military capacity and geo-politics. In presidential systems, Foreign Policy is the prerogative of the head of state. For example, the US president enjoys enormous powers in the formulation and implementation of its Foreign Policy. The US Congress, however, exercises some power on what the president may do on fundamental issues such as declaration of war and imposition of certain types of sanctions.

In parliamentary democracies such as India, Great Britain and Germany, Parliament plays an important role in the determination of Foreign Policy. In feudal states and dictatorships such as absolute monarchies (Saudi Arabia, Swaziland), military dictatorships (North Korea, Gambia) and single party regimes (Cuba), where political participation is either non-existent or severely restricted, or in monolithic systems (Kazakhstan, Venezuela, Iran, Syria, North Korea), in which the president assumes absolute authority, Foreign Policy becomes the preserve of the Chief Executive of the country.

In Kenya, the president has considerable powers in Foreign Policy. The Cabinet Secretary for Foreign Affairs exercises his/her functions on delegation from the president. The Ministry of Foreign Affairs plays a central role in Foreign Policy formulation and its implementation. In this role, the Cabinet Secretary articulates the Foreign Policy with full powers in keeping with the principle of sovereign authority. He/she does not require specific accreditation to exercise this mandate abroad.

Lord Palmerstone, a nineteenth century onetime British Foreign Secretary said of the mandate of a Foreign Secretary: *"The only business of the Foreign Secretary is the pursuit of his country's national interest."*[6] Palmerstone's statement demonstrates that national interest drives Foreign Policy.

Pursuit of the national interest may be undertaken through negotiations (diplomacy) coercion (economic sanctions), or force (military action). The strategy a state chooses to use must define the issues, mode of engagement, and an exit strategy. To project its power, a state must have well-grounded diplomatic machinery and network, a sound economy and military preparedness. Nicholson observes that:

> Public interest is rightly focussed upon the early deliberative stages during which the "the policy" is being framed and decided; the subsequent "executive stage" during which it is being carried out, affects them less immediately... Diplomacy is neither the invention nor the pastime of some particular political system, but is an essential element in any reasonable relation between man and man and between nation and nation.[7]

Nicholson's observation demonstrates a state's capacity to enable it to choose from the options available when pursuing its Foreign Policy objectives. The choice a state makes depends on its economic power, which enables it to pursue the targets its economic resources allow it.

Policy framework

A *Foreign Policy framework* identifies targets to be pursued before embarking on the process of formulating policy as determined by principles, tenets, values, beliefs and aspirations by which the policy is guided. Such a determination is critical in creating a road map for articulating the policy. A state, therefore, develops a comprehensive set of criteria and objectives to secure its national interest. The activities of the state such as investment, tourism, education, commerce and culture are vital interests that fit in any of the core elements of the national interest.

Articulation of Foreign Policy

A state may employ different means to articulate its Foreign Policy, which is designed to influence events abroad to the state's advantage. The means which it may apply depends on the objective and must be informed by its capacity to act, either alone or in concert with allies, to achieve the objective.

---

6   Lord Palmerstone was a British Foreign Secretary in the 18th century.

7   Harold Nicholson, *Diplomacy*, Third Edition.

In principle, Foreign Policy seeks to build bridges between states, even when the states are in competition with one another. All states aim at securing their respective interests from opportunities in the international system.

Competition may be in areas such as investment, financial and technical cooperation, and cultural, scientific and technological exchanges. When a state reaches out to the outside world, its objective is to present a picture of itself in positive terms in order to seek the cooperation of other states on issues of mutual benefit. It has to demonstrate the capacity to provide an environment conducive to cooperative relationship in political and economic fields and promote itself as a reliable player on the world stage.

The establishment of the UN in 1945 after World War II created mechanisms which imposed obligations on all member-nations for the maintenance of the international peace, security and order. This placed a big burden on nations to build good diplomatic infrastructures and networks to undertake complex diplomatic negotiations and other engagements. This requires intensive mobilisation of domestic and international resources. Such infrastructure includes international, regional and sub-regional organisations with specific membership conditions, treaties and conventions on specific issues or a range of issues; diplomatic engagement through the establishment of diplomatic relations, establishment of diplomatic missions, and ad hoc missions including official visits.

Diplomacy is complex and delicate. As the primary tool in the implementation of Foreign Policy, it requires considerable capacity and networks. A state must make strategic decisions on where to establish its diplomatic missions to serve its interests. Establishment of diplomatic missions involves setting up the infrastructure (hardware) and personnel and facilitation (software) capacity. Hardware includes physical facilities, buildings, vehicles, communications equipment and computers; while software includes diplomatic networking, human resources, content of the Foreign Policy, strategies and financial capital to service the outfits. A state reviews the options available before determining the best means to deploy to achieve its objectives through diplomacy.

Projection of power

A state has a number of options at its disposal in determining what action to take to achieve its Foreign Policy objectives. The options range from diplomatic influence over other states, economic power and military preparedness. Any one of the options may be taken unilaterally when the state is convinced that it has capacity to attain its objectives in a reasonably short time.

Alternatively, the state may choose to involve other nations through collective action at regional or international levels, if in its view, chances of success are more assured. Collective action is most effective in situations where economic power is applied through sanctions, or when it is necessary to take military action to forestall a threat to international peace and security. Military action (the stick) should be considered only when diplomatic and economic pressure (the carrot) have failed to resolve the issue. Selected cases below show some of the circumstances in which countries have taken action to safeguard their national interest.

In 2011, Kenya took military action in Somalia – in consultation with the Transitional Federal Government (TFG) of Somalia – to deal with Al-Shabaab when the group abducted foreign tourists from their holiday resorts in Lamu at the coast. The action was taken to pursue the terrorists to safeguard its economic interests in the tourism and security sectors. The abduction followed a spate of bomb attacks by Al-Shabaab in Nairobi and the three north-eastern counties of Garissa, Wajir and Mandera. Al-Shabaab's actions threatened not just the economy, but security of the country.

In 2012, the Kenya Defence Forces (KDF) become part of the African Union Mission to Somalia (AMISOM). Although Kenya has preferred a non-confrontational diplomatic style in its Foreign Policy, the nature of attacks by Al-Shabaab demanded a different response. Al-Shabaab, like other terrorist groups, is an invisible enemy with whom traditional diplomacy is impossible.

Ethiopia, too, took its military to Somalia in 2006, to deal with the radical Islamic Courts Union (ICU) which nearly dislodged the TFG of President Ahmed Yusuf, threatening to derail stabilisation efforts in Somalia. Ever since, Ethiopian troops unilaterally remain in the country as a deterrent against Al-Shabaab threats as well as supporting AMISOM's stabilisation efforts in Somalia.

In 1953, the US successfully sought the UN Security Council authorisation to take military action against North Korea in the Korean War with full knowledge that the Permanent Representative of the Soviet Union was boycotting Council meetings. US President Eisenhower's action pre-empted the possibility of a Soviet veto which would have denied the UN permission to sanction military action against North Korea.

Unlike the Korean War, NATO took action against Yugoslavia in the early 1990s, to punish it for its role in the Balkan conflict which led to the breakup of Yugoslavia. Similarly, the USA mobilised its allies against President Saddam Hussein in 2003, and later sought post-facto UN Security

Council authorisation at a time when Russia displayed weakness in its early independence following the breakup of the Soviet Union. The US deployed ten thousand troops in Liberia, Sierra Leone and Guinea in 2014, to assist in dealing with the Ebola disease outbreak. It used the military as an instrument of Foreign Policy.

A state which takes unilateral action against another must calculate the political and economic risk and assess the advantages to determine whether, indeed, intended action will serve its interests. The USA has taken both diplomatic and unilateral military actions in many situations globally, when it has concluded that its global political, economic or strategic interests have been threatened.

In circumstances where the USA considers it necessary to seek the support of its allies, it has not hesitated to bring together a coalition of like-minded nations to its cause, such as imposition of sanctions against Russia for invasion of Ukraine (2014), and following claims of Russian interference its 2016, presidential elections. The US supported the UK, as did other western allies, on the expulsion of Russian diplomats after the poisoning of a former Russian spy agent and his daughter in Salisbury in the UK in March 2018. The USA's western allies which possess enormous economic power and influence more readily join coalitions of the willing with far greater ease than its rivals.

In 1979, Tanzania went to war with Uganda in response to Amin's invasion of northern Tanzania in violation of Tanzania's sovereignty and territorial integrity. Amin had carved for himself a barbaric image at home and abroad which greatly helped President Julius Nyerere to mobilise Tanzanians as well as seek international support for military action despite the severe economic difficulties facing Tanzania at the time. President Nyerere received overwhelming international support to get rid of Amin. The Tanzanian People's Defence Forces (TPDF), which Nyerere led, expelled Amin's forces from Tanzania and marched to Kampala from where Amin fled to Libya and later on to Saudi Arabia, where he died in exile. Milton Obote returned to power for a second time.

Collective action

A state may opt to take action under the umbrella of a regional organisation or organisations to which it belongs after concluding that unilateral action would be way beyond its means or may not attract international sympathy or support. The critical point in this approach is the realisation by the state that it requires support for the action, or that unilateral action would expose it to unnecessary harm, sanctions or ridicule. Usually, a state opts for collective action in cases where it seeks wider acceptance of its action or concludes that it does not have the capacity to go it alone.

Intervention through a regional organisation takes place after diplomatic efforts or sanctions have failed to find a solution. In such a case, the UN Security Council must sanction military action. The advantage with this approach is that whatever action that is taken will have the authority of the UN Charter under which the UN Security Council exercises the primary responsibility in maintenance of international peace and security.

CHAPTER 3

Diplomacy and the Implementation of Foreign Policy

Implementation of Foreign Policy is complex and expensive. A state uses a number of instruments to implement its Foreign Policy; diplomacy, economic sanctions or military power, to pursue its Foreign Policy objectives. Diplomacy is usually preferred as the primary instrument for the implementation of Foreign Policy. This may include persuasion, coercion or negotiations through an international organisation with which collective action may send a strong message to the offending party. If diplomacy fails, a state may deploy economic sanctions (soft power) to force compliance.

Military power maybe deployed as a last resort where belligerence cannot be contained by peaceful means. A state which pursues a successful Foreign Policy earns international respect of its people and secures a role and place on the world stage. Diplomacy is the means by which states conduct and regulate bilateral and multilateral issues of interest to them. States deploy a variety of diplomatic methods to influence events in their favour. Successful diplomatic engagement must be supported by economic power, military power or other sources of power at the disposal of the state in pursuit if its Foreign Policy objectives.

The minimum requirement for diplomacy is the establishment of diplomatic relations between two states on exchange of Diplomatic Notes after a general agreement between their heads of state or, at least, their respective Ministers for Foreign Affairs. This may be prompted by a verbal agreement between the respective heads of state or government. Each state declares its intentions and desire to enter into and develop relations to foster cooperation at the bilateral and international levels on issues of mutual interest. Diplomacy facilitates communication, consultations and cooperation between states and with other actors in keeping with the principle of respect of sovereignty and territorial integrity of states. In the interest of peace, security and economic interdependence, a state must court the friendship and cooperation of other states in pursuit of its Foreign Policy objectives.

No state, however powerful, can afford to ignore its neighbours or other international actors and realise its Foreign Policy objectives. Success abroad may most probably be a result of collective action and articulation of economic policies into a consistent set of policies which may be articulated to attract interest from other interlocutors. In a competitive international climate, such as exists today, this requires a clear Foreign Policy designed to secure the state's national interest through peaceful means. A state must decide on the level and strength of representation on the basis of the objectives and targets it has set for itself. When a state concludes that its interests should be pursued more effectively by posting resident staff, it establishes diplomatic missions in countries of strategic value through which it pursues its interests. It must determine the staff strength in each mission, based on the nature and scope of work and intricacy of issues.

A state then develops a comprehensive strategy to accomplish this task by targeting strategic areas which have been identified for resident missions. The state must ensure that its members of staff are properly trained and prepared for the task. This enables the diplomats to explain the state's policies to foreign audiences in a manner that makes it easy for them to develop interest in the country. Diplomacy, therefore, plays a critical role in engagement by a state with other states and actors in the international system. Morgenthau observes that:

> Of all the factors that make for national power of a nation, the most important, however unstable, is the quality of diplomacy. All the other factors that determine national power are, as it were, the raw material out of which the power of a nation is fashioned. The quality of a nation's diplomacy combines those different factors into an integrated whole, gives them direction and weight, and awakens their slumbering potentialities by giving them the breadth of actual power. The conduct of a nation's foreign affairs by its diplomats is for national power in peace, what military strategy and tactics by its military leaders are for national power in war. ... Diplomacy, one might say, is the brains of national power, as national morale is its soul. If its vision is blurred, its judgement defective, and its determination feeble, all the advantages of geographical location, of self-sufficiency in food, raw materials, and industrial production, of military preparedness, of size and quantity of population, will in the long run avail a nation little. A nation that can boast of all these advantages, but not of diplomacy commensurate with them, may achieve temporary successes through the sheer weight of its natural assets. [8]

---

8   Hans J. Morgenthau, *Politics Among Nations,* Fourth Edition.

Morgenthau's observation is a powerful message which emphasizes the importance of diplomacy as an instrument of Foreign Policy, its symbolism in state to state relations, and for its value in negotiations. What then is diplomacy? The _Oxford English Dictionary_ provides a further understanding of diplomacy. It defines diplomacy as:

> The management of international relations by negotiation.

Satow's Guide to Diplomatic Practice defines diplomacy as:

> The application of intelligence and tact to the conduct of official relations between the governments of independent states...[9]

These definitions make the connection between the intentions of a state and those of others and why both consider it important to create a level of understanding through diplomacy. As a tool by which a state conducts its business with other states, diplomacy enables the state to express its opinion and exert its leverage to influence decisions in its favour. For this reason, the state requires a quality diplomatic service to execute its Foreign Policy mandate. Morgenthau further observes that:

> Nations must rely upon the quality of their diplomacy to act as a catalyst for the different factors that constitute their power. In other words, these different factors, as they are brought to bear upon an international problem by diplomacy, are what is called a nation's power. Therefore, it is of the utmost importance that the good quality of the diplomatic service be constant. And constant quality is assured by dependence upon tradition and institutions rather than upon the sporadic appearance of outstanding individuals.[10]

Thus, a state must choose its diplomats based on qualification, training, competence and merit as they are essential to the success of its Foreign Policy.

Sanctions as an instrument of Foreign Policy

The use of sanctions in Foreign Policy is not new. Records show that as early as the fifth century, Greek city states applied sanctions against each other to contain unfair practise in inter-city trade. The first known such sanctions were imposed by Greek cities of Sparta, Corinth and Megara against Athens in 432 BC, during a Greek diplomatic conference in Sparta, which was convened to decide if Athens had violated its treaties and whether it should be punished by war. Quoting the records of Thucydides, Nicholson observes:

---

9   _See Satow's Guide to Diplomatic Practice_
10   _Ibid._

The delegations from Megara and Corinth made long speeches to the Lacedaemonian Assembly in which they outlined their case against Athens. A motion in favour of war was put to the vote and was carried, first by acclamation and then by a numerical count... Thucydides' record of the Sparta Conference indicates that by the fifth century the Greeks had elaborated some system of constant diplomatic relations; that members of diplomatic missions were accorded certain immunities and great consideration; and that it had come to be recognised that the relations between states could not be managed or adjusted merely by ruse and violence, and that there was some implicit "law" which was above immediate national interests or monetary expediency.[11]

The dominant position Athens enjoyed against other Greek city states was clearly in conflict with their interests. The point to the coastal town of Megara was one of the city states most vehemently opposed to Athens' domination. This was evident from its reaction to the Conference in Sparta. The trade disputes and the murder of an Athenian messenger sent to deliver a message from the city of Athens triggered the Mega-Athenian war shortly after the Sparta Conference.

Use of sanctions

Sanctions are an important tool of Foreign Policy and may be imposed unilaterally, by a coalition of countries with similar objectives or by the authority of the UN Security Council. Historically, sanctions have been applied to express displeasure with a member of a club or group, if such a member is deemed to have violated its membership rules. The Greek inter-city states' trade disputes are a classic example. Today, sanctions are routinely imposed by big powers to protect their interests.

The UN was established to manage international relations through multilateral diplomacy. The five victorious founding nations – the USA, the Soviet Union, the UK, France and China (at the time represented by Taiwan), arrogated themselves veto power in the UN Security Council comprising five permanent and ten non-permanent members. Often known as the Permanent Five (P5), the other ten are elected on rotation for two years on the basis of regional balance. The P5 often paralyse decision making due to their respective national interests. Ideally, a proper regime of sanctions should be authorised by the UN Security Council. The US and the EU sometimes impose sanctions against target countries outside the UN system where Russia and China cannot exercise their veto powers. The USA and its western allies imposed economic sanctions against Russia

---

11   Harold Nicholson, *Diplomacy,* Third Edition.

and have tried to isolate it diplomatically over the annexation of Crimea (2014) and its support for insurgence in eastern Ukraine (2014) and for its perceived role (unproven) in the poisoning of its former spy agent in Salisbury, southern England as already mentioned.

Unilateral application of sanctions is likely to lead to dilution of international architecture for the maintenance of international peace and security. The US often imposes unilateral sanctions to serve its national interest, irrespective of existing protocols and what other nations may think of its action. In 2018, a combination of UN sanctions with those unilaterally imposed by the US and the threat of use of force may have contributed to North Korea's decision to engage in dialogue with South Korea and the USA.

Sanctions have been an integral element of international relations since diplomacy itself was invented. They may range from political and diplomatic isolation, economic marginalization, to the use of force. It is generally understood that sanctions may be imposed on a state which has, in the opinion of those pushing for them, breached international law. Sanctions must be supported by international legal instruments to which all the actors have acceded. Sanctions as an instrument of Foreign Policy do not easily yield tangible results. Their effect often depends on the size and influence of the country targeted, as well as the size and influence of the country or counties imposing them.

Diplomacy is the preferred means of managing international relations. When diplomacy fails to resolve a dispute, a state or group of states may impose economic sanctions as a means to negotiations or compliance of a targeted country. Use of sanctions as an instrument of Foreign Policy has gained ground since World War II as a form of soft power before resorting to military action, if need be. In general, states apply sanctions unilaterally, to pursue national interests or in concert with others, to impose collective punishment in defence of common interests.

The UN Security Council has the power to impose mandatory diplomatic, economic or military sanctions as punishment for non-compliance in the maintenance of international peace and security. The UN imposed sanctions against South Africa for its apartheid policy before majority rule in 1994. It also imposed sanctions on Rhodesia (now Zimbabwe), for its Unilateral Declaration of Independence (UDI) in 1965, and on North Korea because of first, the superpower rivalry (1953) and second, its nuclear weapons programme (2018).

Individual states have applied sanctions against other states to protect their national interests. The US, for many years, blocked Russia and China's membership to the WTO because of their human rights record. However, the real reason was their respective political systems which the US considers to be restrictive, autocratic and uncompetitive. In reality, the US government, under pressure from the US Congress and its private sector, took the hard-line position which feared competition from subsidised products imported from China and Russia. The UN cannot impose sanctions on Russia due to its veto power in the UN Security Council.

The economic sanctions imposed by both the UN and the Commonwealth against Rhodesia (now Zimbabwe), after Ian Smith's UDI on 11th November 1965, led to a vicious and intensified armed struggle for independence by majority blacks. The struggle finally resulted in a negotiated handover of power from the UK in 1980.

In both South Africa and Rhodesia's cases, the West applied the sanctions half-heartedly because of their vast economic interests. Western companies continued to invest in South Africa in blatant violation of the sanctions by establishing motor vehicles' assembly plants and investing in the mining industry which supported their economies back home in Europe and America. The US justified its purchase of chrome from Rhodesia on the grounds that Rhodesia was the only source of the mineral in the "free world". Yet the US could have bought the mineral from the Soviet Union. Such an approach helped prolong the existence of the racist regimes in South Africa and Rhodesia.

The OAU lacked the requisite robust mechanism to deal with rogue states. Its successor, the AU established the Peace and Security Council with powers to apply sanctions against any member-state where power was secured through unconstitutional means. The AU was conceived as an organisation for integration with emphasis on certain behaviour by member states. Cote d'Ivoire (2010), Mali (2011) and Egypt (2013) were temporarily suspended from participating in policy organs of the organisation when they underwent change of government through unconstitutional means.

The UN, the AU and the Economic Community of West African States (ECOWAS) have used sanctions to address cases where incumbent heads of state or government have refused to leave office after being voted out in elections. For example, Laurent Gbagbo refused to leave office after Alassane Ouattara was declared the winner in the 2010 elections in Cote d'Ivoire; it took the effort of ECOWAS and French troops to install Alassane Ouattara to power. Laurent Gbagbo was subsequently indicted by the ICC for crimes against humanity committed during the post-election violence.

Similarly, ECOWAS forced former Gambian President Yahya Jammeh into exile in Equatorial Guinea in 2017, after he denounced the elections won by President Adama Barrow. ECOWAS applied diplomatic pressure and threatened use of force to make him step down. The AU and the UN Security Council backed the regional organisation in its action to uphold the will of the Gambian people.

UN sanctions and international focus on North Korea
North Korea has been under sanctions for decades. The country was founded by Kim Il Sung in 1948 with help from the Soviet Union and has been run as a family dynasty for three generations. Its leader, Kim Jong Un is the grandson of the founding father. North Korea's adoption of communism made it heavily dependent on the Soviet Union and China. North Korea's isolation forced it to begin developing nuclear weapons as a deterrent against a possible US attack in support of its allies – South Korea and Japan.

North Korea invaded South Korea on 25th June 1950, with the support of the Soviet Union and the Peoples' Republic of China. The invasion caused the Korean War, which lasted until 1953. South Korea was supported by the USA, UK, Germany, and Ethiopia, among fifteen other countries. The USA galvanised international support and took advantage of the absence of the Soviet Union in the UN Security Council, to secure the Council's authority. The Soviet Union had suspended its participation in the Council, in protest against the USA's reluctance to recognise and admit the People's Republic of China as the holder of the fifth permanent seat on the UN Security Council, at the time held by Taiwan.

The Korean Peninsula has been an area of potential conflict for big powers ever since the war. Significantly, North Korea's neighbours – Russia and China – would not like to see it develop nuclear capability. Both have approved sanctions against North Korea at the UN Security Council. China, the biggest trading partner with North Korea, has been cautious in applying sanctions to North Korea because of its own strategic security interests. It is worried about a possible US military strategic deployment of weapons and troops in the Korean Peninsula, particularly in South Korea because of their close range to its own territory. Thus, China is reluctant to cripple North Korea for fear of influx of refugees.

Kenya's Foreign Policy on North Korea

Kenya broke diplomatic relations with North Korea due to pressure from its western allies, and from South Korea on ideological grounds when it declared its ambassador persona non-grata and ordered him to leave the country in 1968. Kenya went on to develop close economic ties with South Korea. The differences between Jomo Kenyatta and Jaramogi Oginga Odinga played a role as the latter was apprehensive that Oginga Odinga would collude with North Korea to overthrow his government and introduce communism in Kenya. Under the Grand Coalition Government (2008-2013), some Kenyan ministers visited North Korea, a fact that was out of step with Kenya's Foreign Policy since the 1968 expulsion of its ambassador from Kenya. The visits did not bring about a shift in Kenya's Foreign Policy towards North Korea. Diplomatic relations between Kenya and North Korea remain frozen. Kenya upholds UN sanctions imposed on North Korea because of its nuclear programme.

Role of Ministry of Foreign Affairs in implementation of Foreign Policy

The Ministry of Foreign Affairs is the principal institution which implements Kenya's Foreign Policy. It therefore has the responsibility of coordinating activities of the state abroad, including advising on imposing sanctions, where necessary. The ministry has, at its disposal, diplomatic missions established abroad which monitor and evaluate developments in their countries of accreditation. Diplomatic missions have a duty to report to the ministry on their assessment of any development which may impact on relations in the countries to which they are accredited. If a receiving state faces sanctions from one or a group of allied countries, the sending state will be advised by its diplomatic mission on their impact on relations with other states. Such updates are important for any strategy that the sending state may consider in its relations with the receiving state.

Diplomacy requires a wide and reliable network to support the pursuit of Foreign Policy objectives. The Ministry of Foreign Affairs determines, subject to financial and human resource capacity, the size of diplomatic missions, number of staff, as well as the level and compositions of ad hoc delegations sent out to represent the state at bilateral and multilateral meetings. Such determination is based on the magnitude, intensity and complexity of the respective assignment for the diplomatic mission or delegation. It then coordinates preparations for country positions in all policy areas for articulation (including voting) during bilateral and multilateral meetings. Its role in coordinating and processing information from the host country's diplomatic and intelligence network on issues of interest to the state is critical to sound decision-making.

In this era of information technology, telephone, television, and other media (print, electronic such as video links, and social media), are major information gathering tools for governments. No country can ignore Julian Assange's Wiki Leaks' revelations even if its sources may not meet the standards expected in diplomacy. Barston observes that:

> Changes in communication technology have affected several aspects of decision making. Speed of communication between the overseas post and the centre has significantly altered, as has the 'time' relationship between the decision maker and the event. The visual dimension of an event – drought, demonstration, the construction progress of a development project, armed clashes, military engagements – can be graphically captured both formally and informally by a range of actors. The net effect is to raise the volume of traffic and alter decision-making procedures.[12]

Social media and developments in information technology in general, have revolutionised information flow in many fundamental ways. Before these developments, international broadcasting networks had already introduced fast flow of information to decision makers. These developments have made the work of a diplomat more demanding as governments instantly get information through breaking news from media houses. A diplomat is often left to play "catch up", although his/her input remains critical in putting the developments into context to support the Foreign Policy of the country.

Coordination and strategy

The implementation of a successful Foreign Policy depends on sound strategies and effective coordination by the Ministry of Foreign Affairs. This requires intensive coordination through inter-ministerial meetings to develop strategies on diplomatic work prior to major bilateral or international meetings. Preparations for bilateral meetings are usually more issue-specific as opposed to multilateral types which are generic in nature. States make greater compromises in multilateral negotiations because of the diverse interest by different actors.

A sending state takes into consideration many factors in its decision to establish a diplomatic mission in a foreign country. The reasons for such decision, may be political, economic and military or based on some

---

12   R. P. Barston, _Modern Diplomacy._

strategic interests such as trade, investment, education or opportunities in tourism. A diplomatic mission is established to pursue elements of the national interest of the sending state. The receiving state has its own areas in which it hopes to gain from hosting the diplomatic mission. The most common include: security, tourism, investment, economic partnership and cultural cooperation between the sending and receiving states.

The overriding objective by the sending state is for the mission to pursue policies that secure its national interest. Each mission requires targeted marketing strategies, whose success depends on the quality of staff serving at the mission. The sending state decides on the staff strength, on recommendation by the Ministry of Foreign Affairs, based on the general as well as specific set of objectives to be achieved in the receiving state. The Ministry of Foreign Affairs does not, on its own, have the capacity to adequately staff the Missions in all fields of state interests abroad. Usually, for specialised functions such as trade and tourism promotion and immigration services, the line ministries are called upon to second specialised attachés to undertake tasks that require their specialised input. R. P. Barston observes that:

> A string feature of diplomatic process is the continuing fusion of domestic and Foreign Policy, the reasons for this are primarily the internationalisation of previously domestic issues, the erosion of the concept of domestic jurisdiction, transnational boundary-crossing transactions and globalisation of economics. Further, special sets of factors are found in regions in which there is substantial population cross-movement or non-observance of borders in integrative organisations (such as the EU). The main effect of the increasing fusion of domestic and Foreign Policy is to alter the nature of diplomatic activity, bringing into some policy areas and issues considered as 'domestic'... in the political category, the diplomatic agenda would include issues of governance; corruption; 'foreign' economic policy; international banking oversight (standards); sovereignty and oral hazard decisions (e.g. whether to support a failed state; participate in a banking 'rescue'; or agree to a 'sunset' clause ending preferential assistance to Heavily Indebted Poor Countries (HIPIC). To these would be added traditional political concerns such as human rights and rule of law issues.[13]

---

13   R. P. Barston, *Modern Diplomacy.*

Barston's observation explains post-Cold War international dynamics and realities when development partners introduced tough conditions for economic partnerships. His observations indicate emerging issues such as democracy, good governance and respect for human rights in international relations. The issues which inform international cooperation had hitherto, been regarded as domestic concerns of states.

Communication between Ministry Headquarters and diplomatic missions

Communication between diplomatic missions and the Ministry of Foreign Affairs is central to a successful implementation of Foreign Policy. Diplomatic missions provide information and recommend certain actions in furtherance of the sending state's interests, in addition to representing the sending state at state and official functions by the head of Mission or his designated representative (where protocol permits). The head of Mission is usually an Ambassador, High Commissioner or Permanent Representative. A person appointed to such a position is a personal representative of the head of the sending state.

Diplomatic Missions conduct multiple functions ranging from political engagements, commercial activities and provision of consular services. The staff in diplomatic missions have various qualifications which enable them to carry out different tasks on behalf of the sending state. Military attachés play crucial roles in countries of their accreditation in fostering military cooperation with the sending state. Similarly, commercial attachés focus on economic and trade relations, while immigration attachés deal with visa and other migration issues of the sending state.

Diplomatic missions are important "listening" posts for sending states. They gather information (intelligence) on a range of activities in the receiving state which they consider relevant to their mandate. This makes diplomatic missions invaluable sources of information from abroad for the sending state. Revelations by Julian Assange's Wiki Leaks which published the US diplomatic electronic correspondence between its embassies and the US State Department and Edward Snowden, Central Intelligence Agency (CIA) fugitive who escaped to Russia, released intelligence information which showed the secretive nature of US intelligence and how it drives its Foreign Policy. Similarly, the widely-read Wiki Leaks reports on the internet have revealed startling information on the diplomatic work of the US in many countries.

Intelligence gathering

Diplomatic missions play a central role in the implementation of a country's Foreign Policy. In addition to their role as "listening" posts, diplomatic missions explain the policies of the sending state in receiving states or to international organisations. The heads of mission – Ambassadors, High Commissioners or Permanent Representatives – are critical to the successful articulation of the country's Foreign Policy in the receiving states or to international organisations. A state without a wide range of diplomatic posts abroad will, generally, be limited in scope on what it can or cannot do to influence events in its favour. Small countries which have limited resources to establish diplomatic representation in many countries face such limitations. Many of them multiple-accredit the few diplomatic missions they have established abroad for lack of adequate financial resources.

The Vienna Convention on Diplomatic and Consular Relations obligates countries to conduct diplomacy by overt means. Yet, covert means including eavesdropping, wiretapping, recruitment of secret agents and double agents, and other forms of espionage by foreign powers in other countries, including its allies, constitute an important element of a nation's Foreign Policy exploits. The fugitive former CIA agent Snowden's revelations indicate an apparent systemic tapping of Germany Chancellor, Angela Merkel's communication by the US Central Intelligence Agency (CIA). President Barack Obama was forced to make a public apology in an embarrassing diplomatic stand-off between the two close allies which pursue collective group interests through NATO, the Organisation for Economic Cooperation and Development (OECD), the Bretton Woods institutions (World Bank and IMF), and the UN. German media reported links between the German intelligence service with the CIA spying on the EU and on the French president at the Elyse Palace. Information received from such and other sources form parts of reports which sending states value and use strategically to shape attitudes of the sending state towards the receiving state or on important international issues. Such information is processed and evaluated by its intelligence and security agencies to inform relevant policy areas of the country, including Foreign Policy.

The US accused Russia of meddling in its 2016 presidential elections. Consequently, it was forced to declare thirty-five Russian diplomats persona non-grata in what it described as "engaging in activities that are inconsistent with diplomatic work", a code term for espionage.

The US further closed two Russian diplomatic compounds in the US which it believed were being used for espionage. In a departure from traditional diplomatic practice, Russia declined to retaliate, perhaps in anticipation of better relations with the USA under the Trump administration. This action by an outgoing Obama administration was taken three weeks before President-elect Donald Trump was sworn in. Trump as candidate, urged Russia to hack Hilary Clinton's campaign headquarters. Trump may have not been aware of the implications of such campaign rhetoric, but it later came to haunt him when an FBI investigation was established to find out if there was any collusion between his campaign and Russia, in his election as president of the United States.

A diplomatic mission has full mandate to represent the sending state in a receiving state. Its staff consists of a range of political officers who handle diverse functions such as diplomatic, ceremonial (participation in national functions), political and economic matters. Intelligence officers may formally be assigned tasks of a political nature as cover for their real work – intelligence gathering. Their security background and training make it easier for them to handle issues such as security, international terrorism, drug and human trafficking, piracy, governance, environment and proliferation of SALW which have taken centre stage over traditional diplomacy. In addition, countries which can afford it post specialised officers to deal with technical issues such as communications, space collaboration, nuclear science and technology, among many other areas of mutual interest.

Most developed countries have established development agencies to manage their official development assistance programmes to developing countries. These are quasi-governmental agencies which operate as non-governmental organisations (NGOs). This position allows them to deal with local NGOs or the people directly with a view to influencing public opinion in favour of the values or systems of government they represent.

Developed countries use quasi-governmental organisations commonly referred to as NGOs to pursue their Foreign Policy objectives. Often, the NGOs provide support to social programmes in recipient countries which provides them with the opportunity to have an indirect say in the local affairs. The United States Agency for International Development (USAID), the Norwegian Development Agency (NORAD), and the UK's Department for International Development (DFID), Oxfam-UK and the Swedish International Development Agency (SIDA), play a major role in sociopolitical development in developing countries. They played a role in the fight for multi-party democracy in Kenya. Soft power by such organisations explains their role in the implementation of their countries' respective foreign policies.

The US passed the African Growth and Opportunity Act (AGOA) to maintain special trade relations with African countries. The EU has concluded Economic Partnership Agreements (EPAs) with regional economic groups among developing countries to achieve specific trade terms with them. EPAs will offer the EU an opportunity to manage special economic preferences with individual member countries, without which it will impose punitive economic tariffs to their goods exported to the EU member countries.

Countries such as China and Japan use their economic institutions to exert their influence. China has established an export/import bank, Exim Bank, to finance its economic ventures in Africa and other parts of the developing world. The bank finances projects undertaken by Chinese companies. Similarly, Japan established the Tokyo International Conference on Africa's Development (TICAD), a forum through which negotiations on infrastructural development is agreed and financed in Africa.

After the 11th September 2001 (9/11) terrorist attacks, the US undertook a major re-organisation of its government security agencies to address any gaps that may have caused lapses in analyses of intelligence information. The re-organisation brought the CIA, the Federal Bureau of Investigations (FBI) and the Immigration Service under Homeland Security. It is now responsible for all immigration services in an effort to control visa applications for visitors to the USA. All security agencies were also brought under the umbrella of National Security Agency. The Department of Homeland Security deals with threats to national security in a more coordinated way. The USA was forced to take these measures when Al-Qaeda claimed responsibility for the terrorist attacks on the World Trade Centre (WTC) and the Pentagon. The USA vowed to pursue and eliminate Osama bin Laden, and other Al-Qaeda leaders. Perhaps the biggest prize was achieved when the navy seals killed Osama bin Laden who was traced to a hideout in Abbottabad, Pakistan, garrison town, seventy kilometres from Islamabad on the 30th April 2011.

International terrorism has captured the attention of the world. It knows no bounds. Terrorists have the ability to strike any target. Even a country as powerful as the USA needs the cooperation of other states to tackle the problem. Terrorists have struck targets in France, Belgium, Uganda, Kenya, Nigeria and Somalia. International terrorism has become a priority Foreign Policy issue due to the threats it poses worldwide. The war against terrorism, drug and human trafficking, illicit trade in endangered species and other emerging issues require a coordinated multilateral and comprehensive response on a global scale. The international community has, through binding resolutions of the UN and other international organisations, resolved to take strong measures in efforts to deal with them.

Diplomacy is the most viable tool for engagement in tackling such issues. No single country, no matter how powerful, has the capacity to fight human and drug trafficking, international terrorism and other illicit trades on its own. Drug barons maim, kill and virtually terrorise populations in the areas they control, wherever it pleases them, at will. Their activities cripple normal economic activities and generally impact negatively on the international image of the country in which they operate. International action is necessary to effectively tackle them if any headway is to be made. Terrorism, human and drug trafficking have emerged as sophisticated and troublesome issues in international relations, which require new strategies and collective action to combat. Foreign Policy formulation must take these issues on board.

Other tools of diplomacy
International politics is complex and difficult to manage. Unlike national politics which deals with internal factors through a political system, international politics requires careful navigation of competing national interests of many actors. A state applies diplomacy as an instrument of its Foreign Policy to exert itself using a combination of means such as direct bilateral contacts, as well as use of third parties (in cases where direct contact is not possible for one reason or another). The latter method has been used by a number of western countries. For example, the US and the UK have maintained interest sections in other countries' diplomatic missions in Havana, Cuba and Tehran, Iran.

Other tools of diplomacy include: international conferences, ad hoc meetings convened to deal with specific issues and international negotiations on treaties and agreements.

Strategy in Foreign Policy
A state develops a strategy by defining what it wants and the means to achieving it in the most cost-effective way, thus, enabling it to carry out the

mandate to achieve its Foreign Policy objectives. The strategy enables the state to avoid making wrong moves, which could be costly to its interest. An effective engagement requires a good strategy, carefully selected personnel to undertake assignments on behalf of the state and its ability to build consensus around its policy objectives.

A state must therefore ensure that both its ad hoc delegations and diplomatic missions are staffed with the very best the state can produce in terms of human resource. The staff strength of each Mission established abroad or each delegation a state intends to send abroad must be relevant to the respective mandate of each mission. The mandate of the mission determines the strength of the delegation and what skills may be required among the members of staff for an overseas post or ad hoc mission.

Security of diplomats

Diplomacy is inherently a risky profession due to the varied interests of states. Apart from the focus on specific sectors such as trade and investment, it is imperative to critically examine the general security picture arising from the location of the diplomatic mission. Diplomats are generally well aware of how unsettling it can be to park a car in an area where it is conspicuous. It is, therefore, important to be conscious of what places a diplomatic agent may reside or socialise. A state must, as far as possible, pay attention to the safety of its diplomatic mission's premises, its diplomats as well as delegations sent to represent it abroad.

The rise of radical groups such as Al-Qaeda in the Middle East and Afghanistan, the Taliban in Afghanistan and Pakistan, Islamic State of Iraq and the Levant (ISIL), Al-Shabaab in East Africa, Somalia in particular, and Boko Haram in Nigeria, have complicated the international security situation. It cannot be taken for granted anymore. The challenges these groups have created require careful planning of security detail with constant reviews.

In addition to the security challenges posed by these terrorist groups, a negative perception of a nation's security status erodes the confidence of potential visitors and investors to the country. Special attention must therefore be paid to marketing a sending state as an attractive destination for investment, trade and tourism, which should include assurances about the security of the country, its people and of the visitors themselves. A state must consider members of staff with training and experience in security intelligence and immigration matters over upstarts with little relevant expertise and training sufficiently developed to handle these tasks.

Appointment of ambassadors and other diplomatic staff

The effective articulation of Foreign Policy is founded on sound structures and fair play for members of staff deployed to implement it. For example, appointments of diplomats should respect qualifications, training, experience and merit. These qualities should not be compromised by the desire to reflect the face of the country alone. The quality of a nation's diplomacy determines the success of its Foreign Policy.

A state must therefore carefully scrutinise all persons it may consider for appointment as its envoys abroad. Where necessary, as it happens with all countries, countries appoint non-career diplomats to head selected Missions. In such cases, the sending state should ensure that the appointee is supported by properly trained staff in the fields in which the sending state regards as vital to its interests. The instances where heads of Missions have been appointed from a pool of politicians who have unsuccessfully contested elections should be minimal. A state should carefully nurture a strong career service for its diplomats to provide professional competence to its diplomacy.

The state should exercise moderation and strike a balance between internal political and sectarian interests of political parties and leaders, and a professional diplomatic service, so as not to undermine the Foreign Service. Career officers who have toiled through the system with the hope of rising to the highest diplomatic level should be given every opportunity to move up the ladder. Their hopes are dashed when politicians are appointed to plum diplomatic posts, usually to keep them out of the country.

Some countries have established systems which balance between career and political appointees in a mix that does not compromise the quality of their diplomacy. It should be possible to achieve the mix with carefully thought out deployment of staff with relevant experience to achieve specific goals. Such deployment must be carefully done so as not to compromise expertise and experience. Some countries like the UK, for example, have created quotas between professional and non-professional diplomats of approximately 70-30 per cent respectively, to address this problem.

The quality of a county's diplomacy is critical to its articulation of a successful Foreign Policy. Regional or ethnic balance should not be the primary criteria in selecting persons for appointment to diplomatic posts. It could be achieved at initial recruitment stages to enable the officers undertake appropriate training in preparation for a career in the Foreign Service. Although some non-career diplomat appointees have done a good job, effective diplomatic engagement abroad must be undertaken by officers who have what it takes to navigate through complex diplomatic networks. A state risks its diplomats being dismissed out of hand by their counterparts who may be accomplished diplomats. A reasonable workable balance ratio should be roughly 75% to 25% in favour of career officers.

Under the Vienna Convention on Diplomatic Relations (VCDR) and the Vienna Convention on Consular Relations (VCCR), representatives of sovereign states and diplomats are respected and held in high esteem. Diplomats are expected to be conversant with the provisions of the conventions and should comply with them. Violations of the conventions often lead to sanctions against offending diplomats which may include expulsion. A the state is free to appoint any person to represent them, but care should be exercised to determine the calibre of such a person. Where non-career officers are appointed, the state could suffer the consequence of lukewarm interest in their commitment to the job. Many of them retain their interest in domestic politics at the expense of diplomatic work. This leads to the Foreign Service being turned into a dumping ground for those whose interest lies in political offices back in the country. Such deployment weakens the pursuit of Foreign Policy objectives and destroys the morale of the professionally trained career diplomats.

The quality of a country's diplomacy can only be enhanced by the deployment of adequate material and human resources under a prudent management. This will facilitate planning, coordination and implementation of Foreign Policy strategies. An effective system generates crucial intelligence information, well-researched background position papers and briefs with practical recommendations for decision making. A political brief on a foreign country, requires input from the relevant security agency, while an economic brief, on the same country, requires input from an economic agency.

PART II:

KENYA'S FOREIGN POLICY FRAMEWORK, SOURCES, PRINCIPLES AND ITS EVOLUTION

This Part discusses Kenya's Foreign Policy framework, principles which guide it, sources, evolution and how Kenya deploys its diplomacy to articulate the Foreign Policy. It examines the four successive presidential tenures which Kenya has had since its independence. Successive presidents focused on specific issues. Jomo Kenyatta concentrated on consolidating independence and nation building, Daniel arap Moi focused on mediation and conflict resolution, Mwai Kibaki addressed the revitalisation of the economy and Uhuru Kenyatta on the rehabilitation of infrastructure. Uhuru announced the Big Four Agenda touching on housing, food security, manufacturing and health.

This Part surveys the evolution of Kenya's Foreign Policy under the four presidents, in the relatively short period since independence, and the changing dynamics that shaped international relations before and after the end of the Cold War, which saw significant re-alignment in Europe as well as reality checks for developing countries in respect to economic partnerships. Kenya was forced to embrace change after it became clear that its pre-1989 development strategy would not work. Its traditional economic partners tightened their purses by insisting on good governance, democracy and respect for human rights as conditions for development aid.

CHAPTER 4

Establishment and recognition of Kenya as a State

Kenya was established and recognised as a state on 1st June, 1963 when it attained internal self-rule. On 12th December, 1963, it received the instruments of independence from the UK. Kenya existed as a dominion within the Commonwealth until 12th December, 1964 when it became a republic, following constitutional amendments which established it as a republic within the Commonwealth. Full statehood gave Kenya the legal capacity to assume its rights, duties and responsibilities as a state. It began to exercise these rights as a sovereign state without reference to any other authority.

Kenya's path to independence mirrored that of the USA, which rebelled against the UK to form the current union. Similarly, Latin American countries broke away from Spain and Portugal (Brazil) to gain independence. Many African countries broke away from the UK, France or Spain to become independent states. After independence, Kenya adopted a liberal economic policy, which defined its Foreign Policy strategies and objectives as informed by its national interest.

Kenya's Foreign Policy framework

Kenya's Foreign Policy framework is informed, and, indeed, defined by the core elements of Kenya's national interest, internationally accepted principles, as well as obligations imposed upon it by international treaties and conventions to which it is party. The Foreign Policy is anchored in Kenya's Constitution and other national symbols, executive circulars, planning blueprints, pronouncements, and the ruling party manifestos, from which it draws its authority. The Foreign Policy is formulated, articulated and implemented by the government, which has established state institutions for that purpose.

Governance structures define the values, beliefs and aspirations which Kenya's Foreign Policy articulates to secure the national interest. This foundation is important in understanding the symbiotic relationship between domestic activities, which the government undertakes in nation building, or enables the citizens to engage in, as provided for in its laws, and Foreign Policy. The rights, duties and responsibilities which Kenya assumed upon its establishment and recognition as a state will remain permanent and eternal to its actions as an actor of international law.

Kenyan diplomats and envoys articulate the Foreign Policy within this framework. The Foreign Policy objectives and strategies derive their legitimacy from the intentions and goals set out in the documents mentioned above. The governance structures and institutions established at Kenya's independence, to manage Kenya's affairs, focused on issues such as promotion of economic development to meet the social and economic needs of its diverse population groups. These are the factors that informed Kenya's domestic and foreign policies after independence. This Foreign Policy framework guides the articulation of the Foreign Policy globally.

The objective of Kenya's Foreign Policy is to secure a place and a role for itself on the world stage. It is also designed to foster economic development and good relations with its neighbours and other states, so as to secure markets for its goods and services. To accelerate economic development, Kenya has not only adopted a pragmatic economic policy, but focused its Foreign Policy towards dealing with security issues and political instability in the neighbouring countries, with a view to fostering a peaceful environment conducive to economic development. The desire for peace has all along influenced the choice of mediation and conflict resolution in Foreign Policy, to address the problems of trans-boundary insecurity, refugees, proliferation of SALW, human and drug trafficking, terrorism and piracy.

International dynamics at independence

Kenya's independence at the height of the Cold War meant that it faced difficult choices on which path to take in its Foreign Policy. The rivalry between the US and the Union of Soviet Socialist Republics (USSR) created diplomatic hurdles Kenya needed to overcome so as to advance its economic agenda. The founding fathers opted for a non-aligned policy through which Kenya was to maintain friendship with and benefit from both the West and the East. Non-alignment helped Kenya achieve two goals; first, the country articulated a pragmatic Foreign Policy which steered it away from confrontation with its western economic development partners. Second, Kenya maintained good relations with the East and the developing countries allied to it. This equilibrium helped it negotiate the right to host UNEP and UN-HABITAT in 1972 and 1974, respectively.

Principles guiding Kenya's Foreign Policy

Kenya's Foreign Policy is guided by universally accepted principles. These include: sovereignty and territorial integrity, peaceful co-existence with its neighbours, promotion of regional cooperation, adherence to the UN Charter and the AU and its Constitutive Act. The Foreign Policy articulates Kenya's national values, beliefs and aspirations namely: promotion of national unity, promotion and protection of human rights, upholding democratic practices, equality of citizens, fair and just governance, maintaining diversity of Kenya, an enlightened Kenyan public and tolerance. These values represent the view which Kenya would like the international community to associate it with to secure their respect and support. The respect for sovereignty and territorial integrity of other states is founded on the commitment, which Kenya agreed to, upon its establishment as a state. Peaceful co-existence creates an environment conducive to the conduct of good neighbourliness and mutually beneficial relations with others. They define the context in which Kenya views other states, and establishes the basis of diplomatic relations, upon which cooperation for mutual benefit is founded.

Sources of Kenya's Foreign Policy

Kenya formulated its Foreign Policy at independence in 1963. Its basic tenets have remained largely unchanged, although it has undergone orientation in response to the prevailing dynamics in international relations. Kenya's founding fathers relied on the instruments of independence which Kenya obtained on 12th December, 1963. The process of formulating Kenya's Foreign Policy started when Jomo Kenyatta, the founding Prime Minister and later President, declared that Kenya was to pursue a non-aligned Foreign Policy. Kenyatta acted in response to the Cold War dynamics of superpower rivalry between the USA and the Soviet Union.

In formulating its Foreign Policy over time, Kenya relied on its independence Constitution, the National Anthem, executive circulars and pronouncements, and other policy documents such as Sessional Paper No. 10 of 1965, successive ruling parties' manifestos, and national development plans. The Vision 2030, developed during Mwai Kibaki's presidency and adopted in 2007, The Constitution of Kenya, 2010, the Kenya Foreign Policy 2014, which was finalised during Uhuru Kenyatta's presidency are further sources of Kenya's Foreign Policy.

The Constitution

The Constitution is the primary source of Kenya's Foreign Policy. The independence Constitution defined the framework for Kenya's Foreign Policy from the start, but was badly mutilated during the presidencies of Jomo Kenyatta and Daniel arap Moi, to transfer power from other state institutions to the presidency. The erosion of democracy and institutionalisation of bad governance and corruption which became a hallmark of their administrations, resulted in a negative impact on Kenya's international image. The Constitution of Kenya, 2010, has addressed most of the issues which underpinned bad governance in Kenya and has given a new life to its Foreign Policy.

The Constitution has rationalised and distributed state power, strengthening checks and balances between the executive, the legislature and the judiciary. It encourages collegial and more consultative processes in public policy-making. It has also specifically anchored Foreign Policy in its provisions as part of the laws of the country. The Constitution has removed immunity from prosecution of a sitting president for crimes against humanity and genocide, and obligates Kenya to respect its laws and to honour its international obligations agreed to, through treaties and conventions. Chapter 4 of the Constitution contains a comprehensive Bill of Rights for the citizens which give meaning to the values, beliefs and aspirations which Kenya's Foreign Policy articulates.

Kenya national anthem

The national anthem stands out as one of the few national symbols which remain original. The three stanzas of the national anthem encompass core elements of Kenya's national interest, with a powerful rallying call for national unity and identity. It urges citizens to work together to uplift their standards of living and speaks to the hopes, expectations and aspirations of Kenyans in reference to the sacrifice and loss of life the people of Kenya endured to gain independence. These are the values which Kenya's Foreign Policy articulates. The national anthem succinctly captures core elements of the national interest, values, beliefs and aspirations which Kenya's Foreign Policy articulates.

> Oh God of all creation
> Bless this our land and nation
> Justice be our shield and defender
> May we dwell in unity
> Peace and liberty
> Plenty be found within our borders.

Let one and all arise
With hearts both strong and true
Service be our earnest endeavour
And our homeland of Kenya
Heritage of splendour
Firm may we stand to defend.

Let all with one accord
In common bond united
Build this our nation together
And the glory of Kenya
The fruit of our labour

Fill every heart with thanksgiving.[14]

Evolution of Kenya's Foreign Policy

Kenya's Foreign Policy has evolved to respond to the challenges the country has faced at various times since its independence. The Constitution gives a mandate to the head of state, to direct it, on behalf of the country, and its people, influenced by internal dynamics as well as international developments, well beyond Kenya's control. Evaluation of Kenya's Foreign Policy under the presidencies of Jomo Kenyatta, Daniel arap Moi and Mwai Kibaki is conclusive, unlike that of Uhuru Kenyatta who was yet to complete his term at the time of writing this book.

Jomo Kenyatta focused on consolidating the newly independent state and began the process of nation building. President Kenyatta embraced the motto *Harambee* (pulling together), in his efforts to create unity for nation building, after the liberation struggle for independence. Daniel arap Moi coined the *Nyayo philosophy* by which he sought to assure Kenyans of continuity with the Kenyatta policies. Moi anchored Kenya's Foreign Policy on peace and conflict resolution in Uganda, Sudan, Somalia, Mozambique and Ethiopia. Kenya's engagement in mediation and peace efforts was a major contribution towards resolving the refugee problem, proliferation of SALW and political stability in the Horn of Africa and the Great Lakes Region.

Mwai Kibaki was elected president through a wave of popular dissent against the Kenya African National Union (KANU), the independence party. He embarked on the revival of the economy by what was described as creating a *working nation*. Mwai Kibaki began the rehabilitation of infrastructure, developed two important economic blueprints (discussed

---

14   The National Anthem of Kenya.

in Chapter 7) and encouraged Kenyans to embrace the spirit of hard work for the development of the country. This was a major boost to the national interest.

Uhuru Kenyatta continued the projects either conceived or started under the Grand Coalition Government, such as construction of the Standard Gauge Railway (SGR). He launched its construction at the port of Mombasa in 2013. It reached Nairobi in 2016 before the end of his first term. His main focus was on completing the infrastructure, modernisation of the port of Mombasa, and the construction of the LAPSSET. LAPSSET transport corridor was intended to open up northern Kenya and link South Sudan and Ethiopia to the port of Lamu. These projects are critical to exploiting Kenya's economic potential and improving economic prospects for free movements of goods and people in East Africa. President Uhuru spent the better part of his first term fighting his indictment and that of his deputy by the ICC. His handling of issues such as the refugee problem, international terrorism and the ICC will ultimately define his legacy.

Although there were occasional setbacks throughout the period since independence, implementation of Foreign Policy under each president helped consolidate Kenya's international standing and image abroad.

Democracy and good governance in Kenya

Kenya has made tremendous strides in democracy and governance issues which had become problematic after the systematic mutilation of the independence Constitution. The current Constitution of Kenya was promulgated on 27th August, 2010. It provides Kenya with a sound legal framework for its government to exercise its power through properly constituted state institutions. Its framers included provisions, which make it hard to amend it and water it down for short-term political expediency. Any such tempering with the Constitution will affect Kenya's ability to protect its values, beliefs and aspirations, and render the robust public participation in decision making.

The promulgation of a new Constitution in 2010 was intended to cure governance issues to enable Kenya move forward. A full implementation of the Constitution will enable Kenya avoid relapsing into the old bad behaviour of personalising power at the expense of good governance, which had a negative impact on national cohesion, national security and economic development. Some communities have suffered historical injustices on issues of land, democracy, and inequitable distribution of resources across the country. The constitution is intended to consolidate the rule of law and improve the quality of government, which should allow the state to deal with issues of national security, food security, economic crimes and sabotage, and corruption.

Kenya's drive to develop good strategies, objectives and methods of articulating its Foreign Policy depends on a democratic and transparent political system. Its national government is the most important structure representing national power with a constitutional obligation to engage governments of other states and other actors in international relations. Kenya's Foreign Policy articulates its national beliefs, values and aspirations through specific, measurable, achievable, realistic and time bound (SMART) objectives to secure its national interest. This requires Kenya to balance between its available resources and a clear policy direction in order to achieve its Foreign Policy objectives.

Kenya's national security determines its people's self-perception, the feel-good factor about the country and its international image. These attributes are relevant to Kenya's ability to articulate a sound Foreign Policy. Issues such as human rights, fair administration of justice, public participation in policy formulation, equitable distribution of resources, level of preparedness of the security forces and collaboration with international partners are critical to the Foreign Policy of Kenya. The Constitution clearly provides for a balance between security of the state and enjoyment of human rights by the citizens.

The constitutional provisions that restrain exercise of power by the executive, emphasize people's rights and economic development, will consolidate peace, harmony and cohesion which will make it possible to articulate a coherent Foreign Policy.

Chapter 1 of the Constitution provides that international treaties and conventions to which Kenya is party, are part of the laws and constitutional provisions. Kenya is therefore compelled to uphold its international obligations as part of the implementation of the Constitution. Chapter 4 of the Constitution of Kenya, 2010, provides for a Bill of Rights for fundamental human rights for the citizens. It clearly indicates that human rights and fundamental freedoms are not given by the state and, therefore, cannot be taken away from citizens under any circumstances, except in the manner contemplated by the Constitution itself.

Checks and balances provided for in the Constitution played out when the Court of Appeal rendered as unconstitutional eight sections of the Security Laws (Amendment) Act which, in its opinion, violated fundamental human rights guaranteed by the Constitution. The judgement arose from a petition filed by the Coalition for Reforms and Democracy (CORD), and the Kenya National Commission for Human Rights (KNCHR), seeking constitutional interpretation of the contentious sections of the Security Laws (Amendment) Act. The High Court of Kenya had earlier, in a judgement by Justice David Maraga, struck off eight sections of the Act, touching on fundamental freedom of expression and the media, the right to bail or bond under reasonable conditions, and heavy fines on journalists for doing their professional work.

The non-refoulement[15] principle established by the 1951 United Nations Convention on the Status of Refugees is part of the Laws of Kenya by dint of Article 2(5) and (6) of the Constitution. In their judgement read by Justice Isaac Lenaola, a five-judge bench ruling observed that:

> "The ruling established the role of different institutions of the state in the maintenance of the rule of law and its ability to guarantee security for the citizens. This balance is important in affirming the rule of law in a democratic society as the basis of good governance."

The judges further observed that:

> "Section 12 of the security laws is unjustifiable in any democratic society to the extent that it purports to limit media freedom. We find it unconstitutional for violating the freedom of expression and media as guaranteed in the Constitution."[16]

The judges concluded that the law did not specify who would determine what undermined police investigations or what image would cause fear among the public and help the terrorists. The judgement provided relief to persons arrested on suspicion of engaging in criminal activities arguing that Section 20, which had amended the Criminal Procedure Code, was unconstitutional for being in conflict with the right of the accused to be released on bond or bail on reasonable conditions. The judges went on to observe that:

> "The provision was totally unjustifiable as it would lead to trial by ambush. Disclosure of evidence is very important to enable the accused prepare his defence."[17]

---

15 The practice of not forcing refugees or asylum seekers to return to a country in which they are liable to be subjected to persecution.

16 *See* Kenya, The Security Laws Amendment Act 2014, ruling.

17 *Ibid.*

The judgement emphasised the balance between protecting the rights of citizens and the need to have laws to counter terrorist threats. It entrenched the principles of democracy and good governance, which are important elements of the national interest. Significantly, the judges asserted Kenya's obligation to uphold international treaties as provided for in the Constitution. The High Court and the Court of Appeal upheld the principle of the rule of law in Kenya. The courts emphasised the basis of law in policy formulation and implementation. Law and order is critical to the survival of the state.

Public participation in governance

Public participation in policy formulation and management of public affairs is mandatory under the Constitution of Kenya, 2010. In Foreign Policy, this is critical to the elevation of democracy and good governance as benchmarks for international engagement. Under President Daniel arap Moi, Kenya struggled to respond to the changing international dynamism due to its poor governance. The political playing field improved a great deal after 2002, when he left power.

Kenya faces the challenge of national cohesion which leads to reclusive ethnic chauvinism and rivalry. When these factors combine with other historical injustices such as land grabbing, corruption, and the perceived tendency to rig elections, they compromise state institutions.

President Uhuru Kenyatta accepted the decision of the courts which provoked strong sentiments against it by party supporters while it was hailed by the opposition. The judgement generated debate on the independence of institutions of the state – notably the relationship between the judiciary, the Independent Electoral and Boundaries Commission (IEBC), the Executive, the National Police Service (NPS) and, indeed, the democratic structure itself which makes it difficult to articulate a successful Foreign Policy.

The nullification of the August 2017 presidential election by the Supreme Court was a major development in Kenya and Africa. Kenya became the fourth country in the world to overturn results of a presidential election. Other countries where presidential election results have been overturned are: Ukraine, Austria and the Maldives Islands. It was a landmark decision in electoral jurisprudence.

Kenya's appearance not to respect a transparent democratic system, the high levels of corruption and its failure to address historical injustices may be its Achilles heel in its quest for international respect and support.

Morgenthau observes that good governance is necessary for an effective Foreign Policy:

"The best conceived and the most expertly executed Foreign Policy, drawing upon the abundance of material and human resources must come to naught if it cannot draw also upon good government. Good government, viewed as an independent of national power means three things: balance between, on the one hand, the material and human resources that go into the making of national power and, on the other, the Foreign Policy to be pursued; balance among those resources; and popular support for the foreign policies to be pursued hitherto."[18]

Morgenthau's observation means that a country such as Kenya needs to demonstrate its willingness to accept and implement change through a transparent and fair democratic practice to sustain its international image and respect.

State institutions created by the Constitution of Kenya, 2010, have established a structure for good governance necessary for attracting beneficial economic partnerships, investment and trade. The rule of law is essential for Kenya to take full advantage of its strategic position to avoid being overtaken by its competitors in the region.

The Grand Coalition government (2007-2013) may be credited with improving Kenya's international image, particularly, its work in winning the referendum on the new Constitution in 2010. Kenya should ensure that it will avoid degenerating into similar circumstances in future. Kenya should invest in the transport, service sector, and communications to support its strategic position as a diplomatic hub or first port of call in East Africa. Internal political instability weakens its ability to act as a responsible and respected member of the international community.

Morgenthau observes that:

"It is not enough, however, for a government to marshal national public opinion behind its foreign policies. It must also gain the support of the public opinion of other nations for its foreign and domestic policies...Foreign Policy is being pursued in our time not only with the traditional weapons of diplomacy and military might, but also with the novel weapon of propaganda. For the struggle of power on the international scene is today not only a struggle for military supremacy and political domination, but in a specific struggle for the minds of men. The power of a nation, then, depends not only upon the skill of

18   Hans J. Morgenthau, *Politics Among Nations*, Fourth Edition, p 139.

its diplomacy and the strengths of its armed forces but also upon the attractiveness for other nations of its political philosophy, political institutions, and political policies."[19]

Morgenthau's observations are relevant in today's world as a classic example of democratic behaviour and good governance. Kenya should stand out by upholding its Constitution. Any attempt to dilute the provisions of its Constitution would be retrogressive. Instability from internal conflict weakens state institutions and compromises Kenya's ability to articulate its Foreign Policy.

Corruption: A threat to national security

President Uhuru Kenyatta declared on the 23rd November, 2015, that corruption was a threat to national security. As a core element of the national interest, national security as one of the determinants of Kenya's Foreign Policy compromises its ability to promote the values, beliefs and aspirations which its Foreign Policy articulates. Corruption promotes, feeds and props up criminal activities such as pillage of public resources away from intended use. Corrupt practices obstruct justice, increase poverty, weaken state institutions and damage the international image of the country. Kenya needs to strengthen governance institutions to firmly deal with the problem and other vices which obstruct justice and are major obstacles to the development of the country.

An effective legal system will fight graft and enable Kenya deal with vices such as human and drug trafficking, trade in endangered species, illegal migrants from Somalia and Ethiopia, many of who use Kenya in transit to South Africa from where they hope to move on to greener pastures in Europe and the USA which portray the country in negative terms and considerably damage its international image.

Kenya must address the claims to eliminate being viewed negatively by its development and trading partners. It requires political will and pro-active action to deal with these problems expeditiously, failure to which it will cast doubts on investment, tourism, trade, employment and attainment of Vision 2030. Security agencies need to act with resolve to tackle drug trafficking and save the country from being labelled a major human and drug transit hub from South America into Europe.

Poverty and food security

At independence, Kenya set out to eradicate poverty, hunger, ignorance and disease. These objectives are yet to be realised and largely remain a

---

19   Hans J. Morgenthau, *Politics Among Nations,* Fourth Edition.

pipe dream to majority of Kenyans. Poverty and food security are closely linked to the politics of land, especially, the alienation of traditional land from indigenous people. The Swynnerton plan titled, _A plan to Intensify the development of African Agriculture in Kenya_ developed in 1955 was crafted by the colonial government to encourage ownership of land by Africans who could obtain credit for farming. It was intended, in part, as a response to placate blacks during the emergency.

This selective application in providing loans was the beginning of the consolidation of classes of the haves and the have nots, a macrocosm of present day society. Colin Leys observes:

> "The plan involved consolidating land fragments into single holdings and issuing registered freehold titles to individuals. The larger leaseholders would then be able to borrow from the commercial banks or from the government on the security of their titles. The political implications were quite explicit: 'Former government policy would be reversed and able, energetic or rich Africans will be able to acquire more land and bad or poor farmers less, creating a landed and landless class'…"[20]

Leys' observation, on the establishment of a class society in Kenya by the colonial authority was a divide and rule policy intended to marginalise majority blacks. This began the process of exclusion whereby alienated land was not returned to the original traditional owners, but sub-divided into small peasant holdings to settle people from outside those areas. It is the source of ethnic friction and a major component of the historical injustices at the root of intermittent ethnic clashes which have bedevilled Kenya since independence.

The land issue became one of the major long-standing injustices in the history of independent Kenya. Land, vacated by white settlers soon after independence, remains an emotive issue in Kenya having been the core grievance in the struggle for independence. The economic policies which Kenya adopted at independence consolidated the class dichotomy established by the Swynnerton plan. Although the model created a climate conducive to investment and business which gave Kenya a competitive edge over its neighbours, it also created major economic disparities between the well-to-do and poor Kenyans, and the more developed parts of the country and the less developed parts. This created a system of patronage and ethnic preferences; land allocations and close business association deals by a few at the expense of the majority who have grown poorer over the years.

---

20   Colin Leys, _Underdevelopment in Kenya._

Poverty has, thus, remained part of Kenya's socio-economic and political landscape since independence. Extreme poverty, exclusion of communities through land alienation or ethnic biases and corruption, have provided fertile ground for insecurity in the country. The policy of selective development of certain regions which was articulated in the Sessional Paper No. 10 of 1965, in the hope that this would trickle down to the least endowed regions, actually caused imbalances which exacerbated tensions and conflict. The high cost of living and the inability of the economy to create adequate job opportunities led to high unemployment among the youths. These internal contradictions affect the ability of the country to develop and strengthen its capacity to project its power on the international stage.

Coastal problem: Threat of insurgence

The coastal problem has its origins in the ten-mile strip along the coast of Kenya which was under the Sultanate of Zanzibar before Kenya's independence. Its status was settled through exchange of Diplomatic Notes between Prime Minister Jomo Kenyatta and the Sultan of Zanzibar at Kenya's independence to become Kenyan territory. Subsequent land grab by Kenyans who were allocated most of the land to the annoyance of the indigenous local inhabitants who have formed protest groups like the Mombasa Republican Council (MRC) to agitate for secession from the rest of the country. The MRC threat to secede threatens Kenya's sovereignty and territorial integrity.

Kenya must deal with grievances of its coastal population who regard themselves as marginalised from ownership of land to which they lay traditional claim, but which they regard as having been grabbed by speculators. How the state manages these grievances will to a large extent help contain the threat of insurgency by separatist groups like the MRC. Acquisition of land by people alienated the indigenous coastal residents and Arab population which has turned into a major dispute as an historical injustice. The rise of groups such as the MRC is a response to these developments. Similarly, Islamic militant groups such as Al-Shabaab and Al-Qaeda use the grievances as an excuse to recruit disgruntled youths at the coast into their ranks.

CHAPTER 5

Jomo Kenyatta Presidency, 1963-1978

Mzee Jomo Kenyatta was released from detention in 1961 after nine years. He was given a hero's welcome at an airstrip in Ruiru after being flown from Maralal. The manner of his reception was the first evidence that the British finally conceded that Jomo Kenyatta would be the future leader of Kenya. Jomo Kenyatta was transformed from a prisoner to a statesman with a new car (registration number KHA 001), bought by the colonial authorities and a re-constructed house in Gatundu. The registration of the car "KHA" was an acronym for Kenyatta Home Again. The prefix letter "K" was later to be adopted for all civilian vehicle registration in Kenya, to date.

Jomo Kenyatta became prime minister from, 1st June, 1963 to 12th December, 1964 when he became president after Kenya became a republic. Jomo Kenyatta was faced with the challenge of consolidating the newly established state from an entity to a nation that embraced diverse cultures and ethnic groups. His government formulated Kenya's Foreign Policy, during his tenure as prime minister and later president. State departments were established for all activities of the state, including defence of Kenya's sovereignty and territorial integrity, national security and economic affairs.

Jomo Kenyatta was conscious of the task of building a nation out of a multiplicity of ethnic groups with diverse interests. Duncan Ndegwa[21] observes that Jomo Kenyatta moved quickly to establish institutions of the state with a mandate to define the path Kenya was to take and formulate appropriate domestic and foreign policies, for the country to meet the aspirations and expectations of its people.

Early years of Kenya's Foreign Policy
The independence Constitution and the KANU manifesto informed the government's economic and foreign policies, which defined the political and economic direction for Kenya. It was a challenge for the founding president who wanted Kenya to emerge from a brutal war of independence to a respected and responsible country on the world stage. In his first Madaraka Day speech on 1st June, 1963, Jomo Kenyatta declared that

---

21   Duncan Ndegwa, *Walking in Kenyatta's Struggles, My Story.*

Kenya would pursue a non-aligned Foreign Policy. A segment of his speech is reproduced from Kenya News Agency (KNA) by Gideon-Cyrus Mutiso and S. W. Rohio:

> "Kenya shall remain firm and resolute in its declared stand of positive non-alignment. We shall be firm in pursuing our goals to bring our people food, education, medicine, and a better standard of life". On relations with East, he said; "It is naive to think that there is no danger of imperialism from the East. In world politics, the East has as much design as the West and would like us to serve their own interests. This is why we reject communism. It is in fact the reason why we have chosen for ourselves the policy of non-alignment and African Socialism. To us communism is as bad as imperialism. What we want is 'Kenyan nationalism' which helped us to win the struggle against imperialism. It is sad to think that you can get more food, more hospitals or schools by crying 'Communism'."[22]

Jomo Kenyatta's long stay in Europe intensified his strong support for Pan-Africanism, and non-alignment. His policy statement on non-alignment enhanced Kenya's nationalistic approach in determining its domestic and foreign policies. It was clear that Jomo Kenyatta's vision for Kenya was to borrow what was good for the country from the East and the West, which he hoped would insulate the young nation from bad policies from either the West or the East. In reality though, Jomo Kenyatta intelligently used non-alignment and a look West policy to distance Kenya from communism. It was the beginning of the ideological differences between him and Oginga Odinga, the first Vice President.

Kenya adopted a liberal economic system, attracted foreign investment and encouraged considerable support from its traditional western partners. Coupled with prudent economic management, this ensured dynamism and handsome economic growth rates in the 1960s and 1970s. Jomo Kenyatta was interested in a country which was responsive to the aspirations of the independence struggle. He chose *"Harambee"* (pulling together) which he used as a rallying call for national unity. This was in sharp contrast with its neighbours who opted for a socialist model flowered with slogans. Tanzania pursued *"Ujamaa na kujitegemea"* (Socialism and self-reliance), and Uganda, the Common Man's Charter. Kenya was the first country in East Africa to take its first major post-independence policy initiative when it adopted Sessional Paper No. 10, of 1965 on *African Socialism and its*

---

22   *Readings in African Political Thought*, Edited by Gideon-Cyrus Mutiso and S. W. Rohio.

Application to Planning in Kenya. The blueprint defined Kenya's economic policy as well as the orientation of its Foreign Policy. For an early document of its kind, the policy positions agreed upon in the blueprint were useful in defining the country's economic, political and diplomatic direction.

Major policy differences emerged between President Jomo Kenyatta and Vice President Jaramogi Oginga Odinga, over the policy direction for the country. The fall out is best described by Duncan Ndegwa in his Memoirs, in which he devotes a whole chapter "*Odinga Goes East, Kenyatta Remains Home*". This ideological struggle has characterised Kenyan politics and Foreign Policy throughout the post independence period and transitioned to their respective sons, Uhuru Muigai Kenyatta and Raila Amolo Odinga.

Jomo Kenyatta surprised both friend and foe alike when he influenced Kenya to adopt a moderate, business-friendly economic policy and a non-aligned Foreign Policy. The British, particularly, welcomed Jomo Kenyatta's declaration because of their long-held view of him as a man they believed was a terrorist. Governor Sir Patrick Renison described Jomo Kenyatta as a leader who would lead Kenya to darkness and death.[23] Jomo Kenyatta surprised many when he declared that Kenya would protect private property. Jomo Kenyatta's transition from a radical nationalist to a responsible statesman helped Kenya to attract capital from developed countries including Britain and the USA.

Jomo Kenyatta's resolve and leadership in defining the agenda for Kenya earned him and the country respect in Africa from its establishment. Ndegwa observes that:

> "Kenyatta was directly responsible for the many changes that took place prior to and in the process of the formation of a central government. He was certainly aware of the fact that due to differences in culture, ethnicity and race, many people were uncertain about the future. Despite numerous contradictory observations about Mzee, it was clear in my mind that to him, the livelihood of the people came first. He boldly defended the Constitution, law and order and laboured to find what exactly could suit and favour the majority best. Above all, Kenyatta was a practical man."[24]

Jomo Kenyatta's determination to make good on the promise of independence, confounded and surprised the colonialists, who began to view him favourably. Jomo Kenyatta's change of heart did not diminish the challenges Kenya faced: to plan, formulate and execute policies which would make Kenya realise the independence dream.

23 *Sunday Nation*, 2 March 2003, online edition.
24 Duncan Ndegwa, *Walking in Kenyatta's Struggles, My Story.*

One of the most critical challenges was the development of financial and human resource capacities, needed to roll out programmes to support the enormous task of nation building. Although Kenya had a reasonable number of educated personnel, they lacked the much-needed experience in the art of governance. However, a pool of hardnosed thinkers among the leadership, examined a whole range of issues and options and embarked on designing appropriate domestic and foreign policies for the country.

Jomo Kenyatta's first cabinet comprised well-educated capable leaders, who were determined to transform Kenya from a poor to a developed country. The cabinet was backed by senior cadres of civil service staffed with a mix of well-educated indigenous Kenyans and selected former colonial civil servants who arranged crash training programmes through attachments to Commonwealth countries and the USA. The Foreign and Commonwealth Office and the USA, especially Columbia University, provided training for the first crop of Kenyan diplomats and other civil servants.

Concentration of power in the presidency

As president, Jomo Kenyatta embarked on effecting constitutional changes which systematically transferred critical departments such as the police to the Presidency, giving himself overwhelming control over the government. The dissolution of the opposition party, Kenya African Democratic Union (KADU) when it joined the ruling party, KANU, consolidated Jomo Kenyatta's authority as president when checks and balances were reduced or done away with altogether. He was able to influence the legislature and the judiciary which gained him political control over all institutions of the state. KADU's dissolution left Jomo Kenyatta's government without credible opposition.

Policy differences between Kenyatta and Odinga

Policy differences between Jomo Kenyatta and Jaramogi Oginga Odinga emerged soon after independence, partly based on ideological inclination but, to a large extent on personality and the struggle to control organs of state power. Jomo Kenyatta had an upper hand as president and proceeded to strengthen his grip on power, which increasingly isolated Oginga Odinga from decision making. The fall out exposed irreconcilable policy differences in the approach Kenya took in domestic and foreign affairs.

Jaramogi Oginga Odinga had played an important role in the independence struggle as a staunch KANU stalwart. He refused to form a government, despite prompting from the British, before Jomo Kenyatta's release from detention. Oginga Odinga's opposition to the direction the government had taken, particularly after the adoption of Sessional Paper No. 10, of 1965, led to his resignation as Vice President. In 1966, he founded the Kenya People's Union (KPU). Duncan Ndegwa describes the transformation of Oginga Odinga as baffling and goes on to observe that:

"In Odinga's view, social, political and economic justice could only come by destroying what already existed and replacing it with a new body and spirit. He envisioned the nationalisation of land and other assets, collective labour and controlled distribution of the benefits accrued so as to eliminate social classes… Kenyatta and Odinga were bound to collide, and the victor was not hard to predict. While Odinga came up with a dogmatic cut-and-dried solution which he sought to push as a lone ranger with a few lieutenants in tow, Kenyatta brought around him a caucus with a social, ethnic and racial mix to chart a common course for Kenya. Mzee had an army of loyal servants and the entire government machinery to face Odinga."[25]

The turn of events made the British warm up to Jomo Kenyatta to protect and consolidate their interests in Kenya, which did not find favour with Oginga Odinga, even though they agreed, in principle, on the policy of non-alignment. Oginga Odinga was apprehensive of the pro-west direction Jomo Kenyatta adopted for Kenya. He preferred Kenya to act independently from the West and the East for fear of being held hostage by either side at some point in the future. The stand taken by Jomo Kenyatta proved to be a pacific strategy to calm the fears of the settlers and the West. Oginga Odinga observes:

"We fought for *uhuru* so that the people may govern themselves. Direct action, not underhand diplomacy and silent intrigue by professional politicians won *uhuru,* and only popular support and popular mobilization can make it meaningful…If our aid and investment come from one source only, we can banish the prospect of pursuing an independent policy, for we shall be brought under control by the withholding of aid, or by some other economic pressure. As an African nationalist, I cannot tolerate an African regime dominated by either the 'West' or the 'East'. If non-alignment is used to justify relations with one of these worlds alone, it is not non-alignment."[26]

25   Duncan Ndegwa, *Walking in Kenyatta's Struggles, My Story.*
26   Jaramogi Oginga Odinga, *Not Yet Uhuru.*

Jomo Kenyatta's hand was strengthened by the government machinery behind him. Duncan Ndegwa further observes:

"Perhaps Odinga viewed himself as a Fidel Castro fighting an enemy who had exploited Kenya the way the United States had done Cuba. The reality was that he was not a Castro. He was a Kenyan facing problems that did not require an ideological prescription and yet he was adamant not to see it that way. It was a vision without strategy and lacking enough followers to make it national and universally acceptable. It did not have a system of values pinioned on process that people knew or could identify with, even remotely. It did not offer pragmatic solutions to the problem of there and then."[27]

Jomo Kenyatta's relationship with Jaramogi Oginga Odinga was a strategic political partnership which became untenable once Jomo Kenyatta assumed power. The struggle for independence brought them together, but once it was attained, individual convictions soon made each drift his own way on the path Kenya was to chart for itself on the domestic and international fronts. Oginga Odinga observes that:

"During 1963 and 1964, I was becoming increasingly uneasy that forces were at work trying to drive a wedge between Kenyatta and myself. The attempt to divide us and sow suspicion between us began…at the London Constitutional Conference of 1962 at which the British Government vetoed my appointment as Finance Minister in the Coalition Cabinet, and at the time of *uhuru* when my Ministry of Home Affairs had its most important departments placed directly under the control of the Prime Minister, and the powers clipped."[28]

Jomo Kenyatta and his inner circle were wary of Oginga Odinga's soft spot for China and the Soviet Union. Kenya reacted strongly to the Chinese Premier's visit to Africa in 1964 by banning Mao Zedong's red book.[29] China reciprocated by declaring one of Kenya's diplomats in Beijing, persona non-grata. It, similarly, reacted strongly against the Soviet Union in 1969, in the face of riots against President Jomo Kenyatta on a visit to Kisumu, for the official opening of the then Russia Hospital (now Jaramogi Oginga Odinga Teaching and Referral Hospital), built by the Soviet Union through Oginga Odinga's friendship. This was a few months after the assassination of Tom Mboya. Odinga writes:

---

27   Duncan Ndegwa, *Walking in Kenyatta's Struggles, My Story.*
28   Jaramogi Oginga Odinga, *Not Yet Uhuru.*
29   See *Mao's LittleRed book: A Global History,* edited by Alexander C. Cook.

"I must admit that I calculated falsely, that the merger of KADU with KANU, far from strengthening the party, introduced dangerously divisive policies and forces into KANU and made possible the dilution of KANU's policy from within. Instead of KANU's policies triumphing over KADU...I had always said that the KADU leaders and their party machine and policies were the instruments of external, settler and colonial forces; I had not foreseen that these same forces absorbed by KANU would strengthen that wing of our own party that had shown tendencies in the past to waver and to compromise on issues of Pan-African advance and real Kenyan independence."[30]

Once he had strengthened his grip on power, Jomo Kenyatta sought to transform the bitterness of the liberation struggle into reconciliation by assuring the international community about the young nation's commitment to universal principles of democracy and respect for human and ownership of property rights. He emphasised that Kenya intended to create a favourable climate, a secure and peaceful environment conducive to business, investment and tourism and that the country would be a responsible member of the international community.

Sessional Paper No. 10 of 1965
The Sessional Paper No. 10, of 1965, defined the direction Kenya took in domestic and foreign affairs. The liberal economy which it espoused helped Kenya become a strong economy in the sub-region. The paper influenced a pro-West Foreign Policy, intended to attract capital for economic growth through official economic partnerships, investment and trade. Tom Mboya, then Minister for Economic Planning, is credited with developing the paper and, indeed, led a team which drafted it. In his team were: Professor Edgar Edwards (Princeton University), economic advisor Philip Ndegwa (later Governor of the Central Bank of Kenya) and Mwai Kibaki, then Assistant Minister for Economic Planning. Kibaki later served as president of Kenya from 2002-2013.

The Sessional Paper attracted criticism from left-wing academicians who dismissed it as a US-sponsored effort to control Kenya. Barack Obama Senior, father of Barack Obama, the 44th president of the USA, then a senior civil servant, wrote a scathing critique of the paper pointing out its bias towards more developed regions of the country as contained in article 133 of the sessional paper. His view and that of Ahmed Mohiuddin (Makerere University) exposed its weaknesses to left-leaning leaders such as Jaramogi Oginga Odinga, Bildad Kaggia and Achieng Oneko, who questioned its nationalistic authenticity and ideological inclination. Nevertheless, the

---

30   Jaramogi Oginga Odinga, *Not Yet Uhuru.*

blueprint was an important milestone in the determination of domestic and foreign policies of the country.

After Kenya published the Sessional Paper No. 10, Tanzania issued the Arusha Declaration in 1967 and Uganda followed suit with the Common Man's Charter in 1969. These policy documents were as divergent as the policy platforms they espoused. The divergent policy positions played a major role in the break-up in 1977, of the first EAC.

The blueprint considered the role of Foreign Policy in the economic development of Kenya. It reads:

> "The third conditioning factor is the need to avoid making development in Kenya dependent on a satellite relationship with any country or group of countries. Such a relationship is abhorrent and a violation of the political and economic independence so close to the hearts of the people. Economic non-alignment does not mean a policy of isolation, any more than political non-alignment implies a refusal to participate in world affairs. On the contrary it means a willingness and a desire –
>
> 1. To borrow technological knowledge and proven economic methods from any country – without commitment;
>
> 2. To seek and accept technical and financial assistance without strings; and,
>
> 3. To participate fully in world trade – without political domination."[31]

This position re-affirmed the Foreign Policy orientation Kenya adopted at independence.

Kenya's early recognition of private investment in agriculture, manufacturing and the tourist sectors was critical to its development. A liberal economic model facilitated the creation of a reasonable base in these sectors for Kenya which made it surge ahead of its competitors in the region in manufacturing and trade.

Kenya's response to the wave of socialist rhetoric in Africa in the 1960s

Many independence leaders in Africa among them, Kwame Nkrumah (Ghana), Julius Nyerere (Tanzania), Modibo Keita (Mali), Ahmed Sekou Touré (Guinea) and Patrice Lumumba (Congo-Kinshasa) emerged as revolutionaries who took strong anti-imperialist positions. They all admired and embraced socialism and adopted and put into practise some of its ideals. Moderate leaders such as Léopold Sédar Senghor of Senegal adopted negritudism as an anti-imperialist stand. Jomo Kenyatta opted for

---

31 Sessional Paper No. 10, 1965, *African Socialism and its application to Planning in Kenya.*

a similar approach to that of Senghor, for Kenya as a platform to express solidarity, while maintaining its liberal economic model. This helped Kenya to avoid censure and pursue its non-confrontational diplomatic engagement which made it maintain strong partnerships with its western development partners.

Look West policy

Kenya effectively pursued a look West Foreign Policy which steered it clear from the socialist chorus. Western development partners appeared comfortable with the position taken by Kenya against the socialist crusaders and endeared it to its development partners and the Bretton Woods institutions – the International Bank for Reconstruction and Development (World Bank) and the IMF.

Kenya's adoption of internationally acceptable principles of international relations namely: peaceful co-existence, respect for sovereignty and territorial integrity, peaceful resolution of disputes, the principles of non-alignment and adherence to the Charters of the UN and the OAU, in its Foreign Policy, made it possible to realize its full economic potential.

The pursuit of friendly relations with its neighbours was critical in securing markets for its manufactured goods from them to ensure growth of its industries, in addition to creating a conducive environment for investment, and trade to realise its economic potential.

The early years of Kenya's Foreign Policy and diplomacy have become an important reference point for the country's search for a pro-active Foreign Policy as documented in the *Kenya Foreign Policy, 2014*. The policy firmly helped Kenya, a bastion of western interests in East Africa, stand against Soviet Union influence in Africa.

The Kenya Foreign Service Institute has published a book titled, *Reminisces on Kenya's Early Diplomacy*, which gives personal accounts by some of its retired ambassadors during a symposium held at the Kenya School of Government (KSG) in Nairobi. Their reflections shed light on the general theme, Kenya's Foreign Policy, and early realisation of the importance and role of economic partners, investment and trade to economic development. This posture helped Kenya consolidate its non-aligned Foreign Policy.

Early years of Kenya's role in conflict resolution

Kenya was mandated, at independence, by the OAU to chair its ad hoc Committee on the Congo-Kinshasa, which meant that Jomo Kenyatta became the chair of the OAU mediation efforts. Due to his advanced age and health challenges, he delegated the actual mediation work to Joseph Zuzarte Murumbi, then Minister of State for Foreign Affairs in the Prime Minister's office (1963-1964). Kenyatta was conscious of superpower rivalry in the Congo-Kinshasa. He was also conscious of competing international interests in the natural resources of the Congo. The USA was interested in mineral resources (platinum) to support its nuclear industry, but were not comfortable in dealing with Patrice Lumumba, the Prime Minister. Lumumba was opposed to neo-colonial dominance and plunder of Congolese resources.

However, Kenyatta was limited in how much pressure he could manage, his concentration level and capacity to sustain long sessions had weaned. He therefore delegated the responsibility. However, the big power interests in the Congo-Kinshasa gave little chance for Kenya to succeed in mediation. Therefore, Kenyatta did not register great success in mediation and conflict resolution partly due to his advanced age and fragile health.

In 1975, Jomo Kenyatta also made unsuccessful attempts to mediate between the warring Angolan leaders: Agostino Neto, Holden Roberto and Jonas Savimbi. He chaired meetings in Nakuru, Nairobi and Mombasa which did not yield any results due to irreconcilable personal differences between the leaders and the interests of their backers. Kenya never followed it up.

Jomo Kenyatta's Foreign Policy legacy

Jomo Kenyatta assumed office at an advanced age and not in particularly good health. However, he will be remembered for the decision he took to adopt a non-aligned Foreign Policy and a liberal economic development model, which promoted trade and investment from Kenya's western development partners.

Jomo Kenyatta will, similarly, be remembered for securing Kenya's right to host UNEP and the UN-HABITAT headquarters in Nairobi. The two world bodies have since been brought under the umbrella of the United Nations Office at Nairobi (UNON) as the fourth largest UN headquarters in the world, and the only one in the developing world.

Jomo Kenyatta's arrival on the scene perceived as a revolutionary quickly disappeared once he assumed power. His inner cabinet consisting of conservatives like Charles Njonjo, Mbiyu Koinange, Njoroge Mungai and Tom Mboya persuaded him to toe down into a moderate. The inner cabinet played a major role in shaping Kenya's Foreign Policy towards the liberation of southern Africa from colonialism and apartheid in South Africa.

Kenya paid its assessed annual contributions to the OAU Liberation Committee, but was not as vocal as countries like Tanzania, and Zambia, towards the liberation struggle in Southern Africa.

Kenya's support for Joshua Nkomo in Rhodesia (now Zimbabwe), over Robert Mugabe proved ill-advised on evidence of Mugabe's socialist inclination. Charles Njonjo was notorious for bad-mouthing his classmates at Fort Hare University in South Africa, where he was a student together with Dr. Munyua Waiyaki, who later became Kenya's Foreign Minister. Similar positions were taken towards Mozambique and Angola, then under Portuguese rule. Charles Njonjo's influence was visible in the policy towards these countries. It may explain why the first state visit between Kenya and South Africa took place in October, 2016, by the third president of South Africa, Jacob Zuma, twenty-two years after majority rule was achieved.

Kenya's Foreign Policy towards Zimbabwe began to change under Dr. Munyua Waiyaki, the last Foreign Minister under Jomo Kenyatta, and first under Moi, as it became clear that whether by bullet or ballot, Mugabe was going to take power in Rhodesia. It was evident that he had the numbers, the will to fight and a launching base in Mozambique after the latter attained independence in 1975.

Relations between Kenya and Zimbabwe gradually improved, but we may never know whether Mugabe ever forgave Kenya for the miscalculation. Munyua Waiyaki raised the profile of Kenya's Foreign Policy in Africa, the Non-Aligned Movement (NAM) and the UN. He was a pro-active Foreign Minister but was distracted from his diplomatic assignments and forced to look back at potential political competition by the then Mayor of Nairobi, Andrew Kimani Ngumba, who developed an interest to replace Waiyaki as Member of Parliament (MP) for Mathare Constituency in Nairobi.

Jomo Kenyatta's pre-occupation with the consolidation of independence, especially on the issue of re-settlement of the landless, seems to define him as a president who relegated the country's Foreign Policy down the ladder of his immediate national priorities. His stance underlined the basic problem of his administration – the in-fighting by his close advisers, his advanced age and failing health. It made him look like he had little enthusiasm for active participation in foreign affairs.

It explains why Jomo Kenyatta let the Vice President and the Minister for Foreign Affairs undertake international engagements. Jomo Kenyatta's approach enabled the country to conduct a quiet, non-confrontational Foreign Policy. Jomo Kenyatta, however, personally attended the EAC Authority summits which required his presence as a member of the authority, because he was able to travel to EAC meetings by road instead of travelling by air.

Kenya's Foreign Policy under Jomo Kenyatta may be considered to have been largely successful in the defence of Kenya's independence, sovereignty and territorial integrity. He successfully crushed a Kenyan-Somali rebellion in northern Kenya in the early years of independence, and fended off territorial claims on Kenya by Idi Amin of Uganda in 1971. Furthermore, the country's economy grew progressively to become the biggest economy in Eastern Africa. Kenya enjoyed an enviable international image during his presidency.

CHAPTER 6

Daniel arap Moi Presidency, 1978-2002

Daniel arap Moi assumed power on 22nd August 1978, upon Jomo Kenyatta's death. A campaign had been started in 1976 by some of Kenyatta's inner circle to stop Moi from succeeding him to the office as by law established at the time. The personalities involved in the scheme included Defence Minister Njoroge Mungai, Internal Security Minister Mbiyu Koinange and Police Commissioner Ben Gethi, among others.

However, the scheme was thwarted by the then Attorney General, Charles Mugane Njonjo. Njonjo ensured the debate came to an end when he declared that: "It is treasonable to discuss the death of the President". His intervention put the matter to rest and allowed Vice President, Daniel arap Moi, to take the reins of power when Jomo Kenyatta died.

In spite of the attempt, there was a peaceful transition from Jomo Kenyatta to Daniel arap Moi. Joseph Karimi and Philip Ochieng observe that:

> Thus, only in the sense that Moi happened to occupy the Vice-Presidential berth at the time was the 1976 movement an anti-Moi movement. Anybody in that position at the time would have been the target; and Moi's predecessors there – Jaramogi Oginga Odinga and Joseph Murumbi – only escaped a change the constitution movement of a similar magnitude because during their tenures of office not everything had been tried and failed, and Kenyatta's health had not even become such a source of daily worry to the Family.[32]

The authors' use of "family" with a capital 'F' refers to the power barons around Jomo Kenyatta, and not to members of his family. Karimi and Ochieng's observation points to Vice President Daniel arap Moi as the target of the plot to stop him from succeeding Jomo Kenyatta in accordance with the Constitution. Moi's assumption of office ushered in a new era which marked the second phase of Kenya's Foreign Policy.

***

---

32   Joseph Karimi and Philip Ochieng, *The Kenyatta Succession*, p. 2.

Once in office, however, President Moi spent most of his first term consolidating his power. He pledged to follow in the footsteps *(Nyayo)* of Jomo Kenyatta which he progressively transformed into "*Nyayo* philosophy" as a rallying call to Kenyans to support him. The move calmed Kenyans, especially those who had been fighting to stop him from ascending to power. It provided an assurance that Moi would not fundamentally deviate from Jomo Kenyatta's domestic and foreign policies.

On the domestic front, President Moi continued with land allocation to buy allegiance and absolute loyalty from politicians. Throughout his reign, Moi escalated land alienation, extending it to include excision of the country's forest cover. By the time he left office, the forest cover had been reduced to about 1.7 per cent, far below the UN recommended 10 per cent of the land mass.

President Moi, similarly, continued with the political repression started by his predecessor and detained any person he considered to be opposed to his government or caused them to flee into exile. Most people who had dismissed Moi as a "passing cloud" were forced to eat humble pie throughout the twenty-four (24) years he was in power.

***

Kenya's Foreign Policy under President Moi was the influenced by the prevailing Cold War which lasted up to 1989, and later the post-Cold War realities from 1989 to 2002 when he left office. President Moi followed Kenyatta's footsteps, toe to toe, when he adopted his Foreign Policy on non-alignment and cordial relations with development partners.

Moi projected *Nyayo philosophy* into Kenya's Foreign Policy. At a State banquet for guests attending the 10th anniversary of the *Nyayo* era, in Nairobi on 21st November, 1989, he said:

> "We believe that there can be no meaningful development of a nation without peace among its citizens and peace with the neighbours. It is for this reason that Kenya has fostered the spirit of good neighbourliness since the beginning of our nationhood as a means of consultations on issues of common interest. We are fully committed to the policy of good neighbourliness and the amicable solution to any problems or misunderstandings between neighbours in the spirit of African brotherhood and African cooperation."[33]

Moi's application of the *Nyayo* philosophy into Foreign Policy was meant to underscore his humanist and caring view of human beings. He used it

---

33   Daniel arap Moi, during the 10th anniversary celebration of Nyayo era, 21st November, 1989.

to promote Kenya's role and objective in mediation and conflict resolution – being mindful of other people's welfare.

Politics of Moi

Moi began his political career in 1955 as North Rift representative in the Legislative Council (LEGCO). He had started out from a humble beginning as a primary school teacher in Baringo District, in the then Rift Valley Province. Moi was a member of KADU in the run up to independence. He was part of the delegation to the Lancaster House negotiations on a new constitution which led to independence in 1963.

Moi was elected MP for Baringo on a KADU ticket but joined KANU when KADU was dissolved in 1964. In 1966, Moi was appointed Vice President after the resignation of Joseph Murumbi. Murumbi had succeeded Jaramogi Oginga Odinga when he quit KANU to found the KPU.

One of Moi's most important political decisions when he became president was his declaration that he would follow Jomo Kenyatta's footsteps *(Nyayo)*. In so doing, he calmed the fears in the country which allowed him to consolidate his grip on power. Although Kenya remained peaceful under his reign, Moi remained suspicious of those around him, especially, those who had tried to stop him from succeeding Jomo Kenyatta.

***

President Moi invoked the *Nyayo philosophy* of peace, love and unity in Kenya's Foreign Policy on regional peace and security. His efforts were guided by the three pillars of the *Nyayo philosophy* which he deeply believed in. Its imprint was evident in his approach to Inter-Governmental Authority on Development (IGAD) peace processes in Sudan and Somalia and to Foreign Policy in general. In the same speech on 21st November, 1989, President Moi said that:

> "We in Kenya have a national philosophy for guiding us in the management of our political, economic and social matters. That philosophy of *Nyayo* is built on three pillars of peace, love and unity. It is a philosophy which I would recommend to other nations of the world. It is also a philosophy which, at the international level, would enormously assist all of us in building a better world for the present and future generations."[34]

---

34   Daniel arap Moi, 21st November, 1989.

1982 coup and Moi's transformation

Moi became intolerant and oppressive after an attempted coup on 1st August, 1982 by junior officers in the Kenya Air Force. President Moi established a firm grip on national politics and government for the rest of his tenure. Ironically, the coup leaders did not come from the Kikuyu community which had tried to block his ascendancy to power. Moi became suspicious of any criticism or a different point of view. He detained, without trial, leaders who opposed him.

In June 1982, President Moi had instructed Parliament to change the constitution and turn Kenya into a *de jure*, one party state. Soon after, Kenya faced integrity questions in articulating its Foreign Policy. It was seen as undemocratic and authoritarian. The speed with which he managed to change the Constitution (one day) proved that he was an imperial president singularly enjoying executive powers. He had the final word in appointing judges, ministers, ambassadors, service commanders and other senior officials who all served at his pleasure. Such executive authority on the affairs of the state diminished accountability and strategic thinking in the formulation and implementation of a sound Foreign Policy.

Raila Odinga, one of the victims of Moi's strong hand tactics, writes in his autobiography, *Raila Odinga: The Flame of Freedom* about how Moi's high handedness made development partners reluctant to engage Kenya, accusing him of running a corrupt government.[35] Moi's tactics made it difficult for Kenya to articulate a sound Foreign Policy.

Accelerated political repression after the attempted coup attracted sharp criticism from political and human rights activists locally and abroad. The international community lost confidence in the country. Kenya slowly began to face integrity questions on issues like corruption, transparency, bad governance, lack of democracy and accountability.

A queue-voting system introduced in nomination of candidates for the 1988 General Elections reversed any political gains Kenya had made over the years. It was the beginning of bad relations with its development partners and seriously damaged Kenya's international standing. Moi's personal style of leadership greatly undermined the constitutional basis of the country's Foreign Policy.

The situation was complicated by internal political challenges to Moi's authority. Opposition politicians, activists and civil society rose up to challenge the one-party state established shortly before the 1982 attempted coup. Kenya was put under scrutiny on the basis of the criteria adopted

---

35   see *Raila Odinga: The Flame of Freedom*, with Sarah Elderkin; Mountain Top Publishers, 2013

by western development partners on economic partnerships. They piled pressure on the country to the change its governance structure.

Kenya was being asked to prove its commitment to democracy, good governance, accountability, and respect for human rights by introducing reforms. Under Moi, Kenya took an economic nose dive and registered below zero Gross Domestic Product (GDP) growth for the first time since independence. A weak economy diminished Kenya's capacity to pursue a sound Foreign Policy.

Kenya's Foreign Policy after the end of the Cold War

A New World Order sprung up from the ashes of the Cold War, dominated by liberal values of the USA and its western allies. Its emphasis was on democracy, human rights, transparency, equitability, gender equality and good governance. The West made these values, conditions for economic partnerships with other countries, and effectively used them to target leaders whom they considered corrupt and undemocratic.

Moi was one of them; he failed to acknowledge that Kenya's traditional development partners now pursued their policies without the constraints of the Cold War, which had, hitherto, enabled Kenya to enjoy a strategic relationship with the West. Moi was seen as an obstacle to the values the West espoused in the New World Order. Kenya struggled to pursue its Foreign Policy after the end of the Cold War in 1989.

International dynamics changed in 1989 when the Cold War ended and the subsequent collapse of the Soviet Union, which disintegrated into fifteen independent republics. Central European countries extricated themselves from the Soviet Union sphere of influence. Furthermore, the disintegration of the Soviet Union introduced new political realities in Europe which required economic resources and political re-alignment in European affairs.

The New World Order led to the introduction of new conditionalities for global economic partnerships. Kenya was slow in its response to the changed circumstances. The seeming reluctance to acknowledge the dynamics of the New World Order proved too costly to the country. Western development partners started questioning Kenya's willingness to embrace reforms.

Focus by the West on Eastern Europe

Kenya's traditional development partners faced new challenges in Eastern Europe after the collapse of the Soviet Union. The West was concerned with the potential instability in the new republics being close to their own backyards. Furthermore, central European countries, formerly members of the Warsaw Pact, sought western economic assistance and membership in the EU and NATO. Demands by newly independent countries in eastern and central Europe drew the attention of western countries away from far flung countries like Kenya. Therefore, the dynamics of the New World Order made it difficult for Kenya to pursue its Foreign Policy.

Decades of lost opportunities

Moi's resistance to change led to Kenya's isolation by its development partners. Their decision resulted in decades of lost opportunities which led to unemployment, poverty and insecurity in the country. The deterioration of the country's economic performance, its poor political record and Moi's repression, progressively made Kenya lose opportunities to transform its economy throughout his tenure. Opportunity costs of these vices to the country were very high. Moi's failure to acknowledge the impact of the realities of the New World Order damaged Kenya's international image.

Political developments in Kenya were not unique to the country. Agitation for political reforms was evident in many African countries. Those who failed to acknowledge the realities of the New World Order paid dearly. Kenya was among the countries punished because of its resistance to implement political reforms. The dramatic changes which took place in Europe in 1989 accelerated the pace of agitation for change. Moi became increasingly isolated both at home and abroad. His intransigent stand greatly harmed Kenya's image. In a nutshell, there was dire need for a fresh evaluation of the circumstances and a different strategy to move Kenya forward.

Rise to power of progressive leaders in Africa

Developments after the end of the Cold War took a new turn in Africa. New leaders with a progressive vision for Africa rose to power in a number of countries on the continent. Among them was Yoweri Kaguta Museveni (Uganda), Meles Zenawi (Ethiopia), Nelson Mandela (South Africa), and Paul Kagame (Rwanda).

President Museveni took power in Uganda in 1986, a few days after he had signed a peace agreement in Nairobi with Gen. Tito Okello. Museveni overran Kampala and overthrew the military junta led by Gen. Tito Okello and installed the National Resistance Movement (NRM) government. The agreement between the two leaders had been negotiated under the chairmanship of President Moi. The rejection of the peace agreement stunned Moi. It was to later characterise Moi's lukewarm relations with Museveni until his (Moi's) retirement from politics.

Once in power, Museveni embarked on efforts to re-build Uganda. He emerged among progressive leaders in the region to whom western countries focussed their attention to in Africa.

In 1991, Meles Zenawi took the reins of power in Ethiopia after a bitter struggle to topple the autocratic military government of Mengistu Haile Mariam. Meles Zenawi fought alongside Isaias Afwerki of Eritrea whose participation was motivated by the promise of Eritrean independence after the overthrow of Mengistu Haile Mariam. Mengistu had earlier requested Moi's intervention before he was overthrown, when he realised that the rebels were poised to win. Meles Zenawi became Prime Minister of Ethiopia while Isaias Afwerki became the President of Eritrea – through Moi's mediation. The ascendancy of the duo to power marked the beginning of fundamental political re-alignments in Africa.

Further south, Nelson Mandela's release from twenty-seven years in jail in 1990, added to the woes of established leaders like Moi who suddenly looked tired and increasingly irrelevant to the West. Mandela had an instant towering presence on the continent, as well as worldwide. His election as the first black South African president propelled him to a position where he was able to attract international attention and respect, which left long serving leaders gasping for attention. A democratic South Africa became a major player at the regional and international levels.

African countries that failed to acknowledge the new realities found it difficult to adjust to the demands of the New World Order. Kenya was among the countries which still glorified the past in the faint hope that they would remain as attractive as before. Political developments on the continent, and in the world at large, had transformed the political landscape beyond recognition.

President Clinton's visit to Africa exposed Kenya's isolation
USA President Bill Clinton visited Africa in 1997 to underline USA's support for countries which, in its assessment, practised democracy and good governance. In West Africa, he visited Ghana and Nigeria which had emerged from military rule. In southern Africa, he visited South Africa, which had transitioned from a minority apartheid regime to black majority rule, and Botswana which was hailed for establishing a democratic system of government.

In East Africa, President Clinton visited Rwanda which had survived from genocide to socio-economic and political stability. Kenya's missing on President Clinton's itinerary made President Moi ill at ease as he realised that Kenya was no longer held in high esteem by the USA. International focus had shifted to other countries in the region due to the perception that Kenya resisted political change and seemed complacent in the war against corruption. President Clinton's choice of countries for his first historic visit to Africa drove home the point that fruitful political relations would very much depend on good governance and accountability.

President Clinton's planned meeting with leaders from the sub-region at Entebbe, Uganda irritated President Moi. He perceived it as a snub not just for Kenya, but for himself as he was instrumental in conflict resolution in the Horn of Africa and the Great Lakes Region. Kenya made a diplomatic intervention, invoking its role as a peacemaker and a hub for humanitarian assistance in the Horn of Africa to persuade Clinton to visit Kenya. Its attempt to make the US change its mind about Kenya did not bear fruit.

In hosting the summit in Entebbe, Uganda elevated its diplomatic profile considerably. Diplomacy is a mind game whose success is in perception, not necessarily the hard reality.

President Moi was keen to demonstrate to Kenyans that their country was important and should be included on President Clinton's itinerary. The government tried to explain the omission using the same reasons advanced by the USA: that Clinton's choice of countries to be visited was informed by what was thought to be the main object of his visit, namely; to support new democracies emerging from political instability. This official position seemed sensible, but in reality, President Moi was being punished for inaction on rampant corruption, bad governance, and resistance to implement political reforms.

Internal challenges which Moi faced after the attempted coup and the pressure by the opposition, civil society and the international community led to the repeal of Section 2A of the Constitution in 1991, to allow for multi-party politics once again. Even though, the damage to Kenya's international image during this time was immense.

Between 1992 and 2002 when President Moi retired, the government and the opposition agreed on a set of minimum reforms. The minimum changes agreed were intended to create a level playing field for political competition in the country as a way of returning sanity to the country's political landscape. The reforms agreed to were, among other changes, two five-year presidential term limits, to presidential tenure. The change constitutionally barred President Moi from seeking a further term in the 2002 presidential elections.

The Inter-Parties Parliamentary Group (IPPG) representing opposition and ruling party Members of Parliament (MPs) also proposed a complete review of the Constitution to guarantee a political level playing field and ensure democracy and accountability for posterity.

Clamour for a new Constitution

By the early 1990s, international pressure combined with domestic political activism made President Moi realise that change was inevitable. He finally gave in to demands for a new Constitution. He created the CRCK under the chairmanship of Prof. Yash Pal Ghai, a prominent Kenyan constitutional lawyer, who was recalled from Hong Kong to chair the Commission. As the Commission was nearing the end of the exercise, Moi disbanded it.

The dissolution of the Commission demonstrated that Moi was not committed to a new Constitution as it would have reduced the immense powers he exercised as president.

Kenya had lost the attraction and respect it had enjoyed in the years after independence due to abuse of powers of the presidency which had weakened other arms of government – the judiciary and parliament, resulting in lack of transparency, accountability and bad governance.

Moi left office before a new Constitution was approved.

Moi's Foreign Policy legacy

Moi's tenure was marred with internal conflicts which kept international attention focused on Kenya. Whereas Moi was faced with the clamour for political reforms, he still maintained interest in peace efforts in the Horn of Africa and the Great Lakes Region. Kenya's focus on peace in its Foreign Policy remained a major agenda. Moi was active in Kenya's Foreign Policy especially in conflict resolution at regional and international levels.

Moi played a major role in mediation and the signing of the following agreements:

- Comprehensive Peace Agreement (CPA) in 2005 between the government of Sudan and the Sudan People's Liberation Movement/ Army (SPLM/A) which led to the birth of South Sudan in 2011
- the conflict in the DRC
- Uganda after the second overthrow of President Milton Obote
- Somalia after the overthrow of Siad Barre, 1991
- Ethiopia after the overthrow of Mengistu Haile Mariam

- Mozambique between Mozambique National Resistance Movement (RENAMO) and Front for Liberation of Mozambique (FRELIMO) under President Joachim Chissano.

- Chad

Kenya was very active in pursuing its Foreign Policy on environment under President Moi. It participated in diplomatic conferences on climate change in New York, Stockholm and Rio de Janeiro. Kenya's participation underlined the importance it attaches on hosting UNEP and UN-HABITAT headquarters in Nairobi.

President Moi will be remembered as the only president to chair the OAU for two consecutive years (1981-1983).[36] In 1982, member-states were supposed to meet in Tripoli, Libya, to elect Colonel Muammar Gaddafi as chairman to replace Moi. However, many members were unwilling to elect Colonel Gaddafi, due to his anti-Western stance. Fearing reprisals from the superpowers, many members stayed away and so, without quorum, the meeting was postponed.

Kenya took advantage of the position to engage in mediation in Chad during Moi's tenure as chairman of the OAU. Kenya was likewise engaged in the Mozambique peace process on invitation by President Chissano. Others were: the Sudan and Somalia peace processes under IGAD and AU mandates, respectively. Kenya was also active in international efforts in the Great Lakes Region, which eventually led to the deployment of the biggest UN peacekeeping mission in the DRC.

---

36   https://www.upi.com/Archives/1982/11/26/OAU-summit-collapses/8961407134800/

CHAPTER 7

Mwai Kibaki Presidency, 2002-2013

Mwai Kibaki was elected president at a time when the country's international standing was at its lowest since independence. Kenya faced isolation from its traditional development partners who demanded good governance, accountability and a concerted fight against corruption. His rise to power, through rare unity by the opposition, was seen as a turning point for Kenya, after decades of wasted opportunities during the KANU regime. At the time he ascended to power, the economy was under-performing due to inadequate injection of capital through investments owing to bad governance and corruption. The 2002 elections which brought Kibaki to power were viewed as the birth of the second republic by many Kenyans.

Kenya's Foreign Policy under Kibaki focussed on strengthening those elements of Kenya's national interest which had been weakened during Moi's presidency. Top among them was the ruined economy and the reluctance to adjust to the dynamics of international relations after the end of the Cold War. The second was the quality of government. Public confidence in the democratic and legal systems was at an all-time low. The third priority was re-statement of the values, beliefs and aspirations which had been lost through weakened institutions, especially, parliament and the judiciary, which had been interfered with to a point where they were unable to effectively deal with vices like corruption in the public service.

Kibaki's contribution in revitalising the economy made a huge impact on a core element of the national interest. Among the planning blueprints developed under his direction were the Economic Recovery Strategy on Poverty Eradication and Employment Creation (ERSPEEC) in 2004, and Vision 2030 in 2007. Its implementation is expected to transform Kenya into a middle-income country by 2030.

In 2014, though, the World Bank, the International Monetary Fund (IMF) and the Kenya National Bureau of Statistics (KNBS) analysed and rebased the economy taking into account all its sectors, both formal and informal, and concluded that it was bigger than previously assessed. The size of the economy, valued at about US$ 53 billion GDP, classifies Kenya as a middle-income country.

This rating indicated the dominance of Kenya's economy at more than fifty percent of the GDP of all the other EAC partner states put together. Kenya's Foreign Policy must be aggressively pursued to sustain a regional climate conducive to stable markets for its goods and services as its primary objective.

The transition from Moi to Kibaki faced challenges of a deeply divided and polarised country. Moi's failure to acknowledge change as demanded by of majority Kenyans, contributed to the overwhelming defeat his party, KANU, suffered in the 2002 general elections that brought the National Alliance Rainbow Coalition (NARC), to power. Moi handpicked Uhuru Kenyatta as his preferred successor in KANU. However, a political wave for change across Kenya swept Moi's choice and KANU out of power in an election which was hailed as free and fair and endorsed by the international community.

Kenya's hopes of burying the past were dashed when the newly installed NARC government did not seem willing to move away from ethnic conflicts and personal loyalties which had characterised past regimes. It somewhat neutralised the feel-good factor that had been generated by the outcome of the elections. In spite of a huge majority in Parliament, it soon became clear that internal struggles for power over-shadowed one of their electoral pledges – enactment of a new Constitution within one hundred days of their ascending to power. Disagreement among the coalition parties arose out of an apparent Memorandum of Understanding (MoU) which had been reached earlier, on sharing power in the new government, if they won the election.

The fall-out over the MoU sharply divided NARC on the issue of a new Constitution. A conservative wing comprising parties allied to President Kibaki's National Alliance Party of Kenya (NAK) preferred to retain the status quo and developed a draft constitution which was radically different from the proposals from the Bomas draft by the Yash Pal Ghai led Constitutional Review Commission of Kenya (CRCK) before its disbandment by Moi. The progressive wing comprising of parties allied to Raila Odinga's Liberal Democratic Party (LDP) refused to play ball and campaigned against it when it was put up to a referendum. The conservative faction was led by President Mwai Kibaki while the other was led by Raila Odinga, then Minister for Roads and Physical Planning.

The draft constitution which was presented at the plebiscite was an amended version (referred to as the Kilifi draft) of the Bomas draft by the defunct CRCK. The triumphant side in the referendum represented by an orange as its symbol, constituted itself into ODM led by Raila Odinga. The other side of the coalition led by Mwai Kibaki represented in the referendum by a banana as its symbol, suffered the proverbial tug of the banana republic in the referendum.

Initiative to publish Kenya's Foreign Policy

President Kibaki lived up to his pledge to improve Kenya's international image during his first term in office when he directed that Kenya should publish its Foreign Policy. In his view, the policy was to map out a clear direction to support the efforts on reviving the economy. He directed the Ministry of Foreign Affairs to prepare a Foreign Policy blueprint for the country.

The idea was not new; it had first been mooted under Moi by the late Dr. Bonaya Godana when he was Foreign Affairs Minister (1998–2000). Dr. Godana believed that Kenya had a story to tell the world. He understood the potential which Kenya could exploit to influence events in the sub-region in pursuit of its national interest. Unfortunately, Dr Godana's short stint at the Ministry was not enough to oversee publication of Kenya's Foreign Policy. He was transferred from the Ministry barely three years into his tenure.

The preparation and writing of *Kenya Foreign Policy, 2014* was no mean task. In 2005, the author, as the Permanent Secretary in the Ministry of Foreign Affairs, took steps to actualise this vision mooted in 2004 by the Kenya bi-annual Ambassadors and High Commissioners' conference held in August, 2004 in Mombasa.

The workshop, which took place in Naivasha, was attended by senior officers of the MOFA. The PS formally tabled the recommendations of the conference at the workshop for discussion. The purpose was to come up with a draft Foreign Policy for Kenya.

The recommendations included examination of the evolution of Kenya's Foreign Policy since independence, an evaluation of its strengths and weaknesses, and pointing out specific critical elements of Kenya's Foreign Policy. Among the critical elements was a scrutiny of the country's diplomatic engagement and dynamics of international relations which influenced Kenya's relations with its development partners and other actors in the international system.

It was an opportune time to discuss Kenya's Foreign Policy after the 2002 general elections, dubbed as the second liberation. Its significance to the process was immeasurable. The feel-good factor was evidently high.

Kenyans were proud to demonstrate a sense of belonging and a desire to promote, project and defend the image of the country. This feeling formed a good basis for evaluating the status of the country's Foreign Policy and diplomacy. The changed political landscape in the country after the successful 2002 general elections helped promote the values, beliefs and aspirations which the Foreign Policy would articulate. The NARC manifesto was added to the list of sources of the Foreign Policy.

The objective of the exercise in totality was to produce a draft Kenya Foreign Policy for discussion with other stakeholders before approval by the cabinet and Parliament for publication.

The four-day workshop produced a raw draft which emphasised pursuit of economic diplomacy to meet the challenges of globalisation and international cooperation. The draft defined the national interest and the principles of Foreign Policy to guide its pursuit. The draft acknowledged the challenges Kenya faced from the region on infrastructure and political stability in neighbouring states. It acknowledged that the discovery of new resources such as oil in Uganda and gas in Tanzania would give them economic strength they did not have before. Kenya had to improve its image and economic performance to remain competitive. At this point, the author left the Ministry of Foreign Affairs.

The workshop recommended further review of the draft through consultations with stakeholders – the national assembly, government ministries and the public. The Parliamentary committee on foreign affairs and defence reviewed the draft twice and submitted their recommendations which were incorporated in the draft.

***

The draft was also circulated to all government ministries and departments for their input. There recommendations too were included in a final draft. Kenya must define how to deal with international public opinion on issues of governance, democracy and human rights, including humanitarian and refugee questions. Its Foreign Policy should project the image of a responsible state. It has the necessary resources and infrastructure to engage other states. Critical hardware issues of infrastructure such as physical facilities, buildings, diplomatic missions, communication equipment, vehicles and finances are largely in place. It must regularly upgrade its software issues including human resource capacity and technology. Both the hardware and software must be deployed in a productive manner.

President Kibaki finished his second term before the Kenya Foreign Policy could be completed and published, largely due to constant changes in senior personnel during his tenure.

2007/2008 post-election violence

Kenyans went to the polls on 27th December, 2007, full of expectations and hope to consolidate the democratic gains made after the 2002 elections, hailed as free and fair. The voters were upbeat in the run up to the elections, believing that the elections will bring about fundamental political change. The feel-good factor generated by the 2002 defeat of KANU, the peaceful hand-over of power from Moi to Kibaki, and an improving economy, underlined the feeling of confidence among Kenyans who voted enthusiastically.

President Mwai Kibaki was running for a second and final term on the PNU ticket which had been hurriedly formed after the final fallout in NARC. His main challenger in the race, Raila Odinga, was running on an ODM party ticket. Kalonzo Musyoka was the third main contender running on an Orange Democratic Movement-Kenya (ODM-Kenya) party ticket.

However, the hopes and expectations of ODM supporters were dashed when President Kibaki was announced as the winner and hurriedly sworn in for a second term. The announcement by Samuel Kivuitu, then Chairman of the Electoral Commission of Kenya (ECK) sparked off violence in Nairobi, Nyanza, Western Kenya and the Rift Valley as the opposition cried foul.

The international community was alarmed by the unexpected turn of events and the post-election violence. The crisis immediately attracted intervention from the AU. The AU despatched its then Chairman, President Kufuor of Ghana to mediate between President Kibaki and Raila Odinga. Kofi Annan, former UN Secretary General, was appointed chief mediator. He led a group of eminent persons including Benjamin William Mkapa, former president of Tanzania, and Graca Machel, former First Lady of Mozambique, and later wife of Nelson Mandela.

International mediation resulted in the National Accord and Reconciliation Act, 2008 which constitutionally provided for power sharing between PNU of Kibaki and ODM of Raila Odinga. They formed a Grand Coalition Government in which Kibaki remained president while Raila became prime minister.

The Grand Coalition Government was a product of the National Accord and Reconciliation Act, 2008. It was a compromise between the PNU and ODM parties after international mediation.

They further agreed on how to address historical issues deemed to have caused ethnic conflict at every general election, since independence. Two commissions of inquiry were formed to inquire into the matters. The first one was the Independent Review Commission chaired by Justice Kriegler, a South African. It was mandated to ascertain details of the 2007 general elections with particular emphasis on presidential election. Its report concluded that it was not possible to determine who had won the presidential election.

The second was the Commission of Inquiry on Post-Election Violence chaired by Justice Phillip Waki. This commission was mandated to investigate and recommend for prosecution the perpetrators of any crimes committed during the post-election violence. It recommended further investigation into the conduct of certain individuals during the elections.

The Constitution of Kenya, 2010

Throughout the period of clamour for political reforms, there were false starts to the review of the Constitution to address long standing problems on land, corruption, governance and democratic participation. Attempts to enact a new Constitution during Kibaki's first term had collapsed in November, 2005 when the government lost a referendum to a faction of the ruling coalition led by Raila Odinga.

It took the Grand Coalition government to agree on the outline of the new Constitution. Under the National Accord, the two parties agreed on an agenda which included the process for a new Constitution before the next elections due at the end of the Grand Coalition Government. It created a platform for dialogue and negotiations, and a political settlement on a new Constitution.

A new Constitution was approved at a referendum on 4th August, 2010 and came into force on 27th August, 2010. The new supreme law has provisions which devolve power away from the presidency to other arms of government, giving independence to the Judiciary and oversight powers to Parliament and other constitutional and independent commissions. Parliament now has powers to vet appointees to constitutional offices such as Cabinet Secretaries, Principal Secretaries, Ambassadors and High Commissioners, among others.

The distribution of powers hitherto vested in the presidency was expected to strengthen checks and balances in the system of governance and shield public officers from undue influence from the executive. One of its immediate tasks was to introduce reforms to address historical injustices Kenyans had faced for decades. The Kenya Constitution, 2010, through Chapter 4, restored and entrenched fundamental human rights.

The Constitution of Kenya, 2010, provides a legal mechanism to resolve the historical injustices at the root of the post-election violence which undermined Kenya's claim to peace, tranquillity and tarnished its international image. The violence attracted an immediate response by the international community.

The 2013 presidential election dispute was settled by the Supreme Court. Its 2013 decision confirmed Uhuru Kenyatta as duly elected president of Kenya.

The underlying political issues which led to the 2007/2008 post-election violence require collective attention by all stakeholders. It emerged that there are issues which remain unresolved because of lack of political will to do so. Over the duration of the Grand Coalition, the country underwent considerable political changes intended to safeguard against election malpractices to ensure that there was no repeat of election violence. Kenya does not seem to have learnt a lesson. In spite of the comprehensive and progressive Constitution, old habits die hard.

In addition, the constitution provides for checks and balances to guarantee good governance, respect for human rights and spreads the benefits of independence equitably across the country.

In 2017, the Supreme Court nullified the 8th August, 2017, presidential election results in a ruling delivered on 1st September, 2017. The experience of 2017 elections is hardly inspiring.

Impact of the violence on Kenya's Foreign Policy
Kenya has experienced political violence after every general election, but the 2007/2008 post-election violence was well beyond any past experience. Kenya witnessed an outburst of political expression never seen in the country before since independence. The most affected areas were Nairobi, the Rift Valley, Nyanza and the Western part of the country. These areas happen to be the strong holds of the opposition, ODM.

The quick reaction by the international community confirmed Kenya's position as a beacon of peace in a politically volatile region, and a major economic power in East Africa. Still, the violence and insecurity caused disruption, and, in many cases, complete shutdown of transportation and other economic activities. The NCTS which is the main artery for external trade serving hinterland countries such as Uganda, Rwanda, Burundi, and eastern DRC, was completely shut down for several days. The shutdown forced Uganda, Rwanda and Burundi to seek alternative routes via Tanzania.

The post-election violence dented Kenya's image as a peaceful, stable and tolerant country. Its previous success as an anchor for humanitarian assistance in the Horn of Africa and the Great Lakes Region, and the host of the Fourth UN headquarters was brought into question.

The violence is likely to have long-term influence on strategic economic interests of Kenya's trading partners. Some are likely to secure alternative routes for their external trade just in case such violence recurs. It dominates the consideration for the construction of the SGR and the oil pipeline from Uganda. Kenya must take these factors into consideration in its Foreign Policy in the region.

Kenya's Foreign Policy under the Grand Coalition Government

The Grand Coalition Government had a huge task of improving the image of Kenya after the violence. Power sharing arrangement in the coalition had been hailed as a solution to the political stalemate to avoid bloodshed caused by election disputes. In 2011, the Kenyan model was replicated in Zimbabwe when rivals President Robert Mugabe and Movement for Democratic Change (MDC) leader Morgan Tsvangirai agreed to share power after a disputed election.

Kenya's Power sharing arrangement was, similarly, cited in the compromise arrangements in Afghanistan between the two rivals for the Afghan presidency, Ashraf Ghani and Abdullah Abdullah, when they signed a power-sharing agreement. These are the attributes which the country's Foreign Policy should articulate. The power sharing model, however, raised some doubts as a political solution to controversial elections. It seems to perpetuate impunity by incumbents.

After the 2007/2008 crisis, the report by the Waki Commission of Inquiry recommended six people for further investigation and possible prosecution for their role in the violence. Among them was Uhuru Kenyatta, then Deputy Prime Minister and Minister for Finance, Francis Muthaura, then Head of Civil Service and Secretary to the Cabinet, and Major General Hussein Mohamed Ali, then Commissioner of Police, from the PNU-government side.

From the ODM side of the coalition, the Waki report recommended prosecution of Agriculture Minister William Ruto, Industrialisation Minister Henry Kosgey, and radio journalist Joshua arap Sang. They were all accused of perpetrating crimes against humanity.

The cases were taken to the ICC when Kenya failed to establish a local judicial mechanism to try the suspected perpetrators of the violence.

Kenya considered pulling out of the Rome Statute under which the ICC is established, arguing that it is too intrusive in the internal affairs of the country.

The Grand Coalition Government tried to address the international public on the issue of justice for the victims but lacked the consensus to make any significant progress due to power struggles and entrenched ethnic interests which influenced decision-making.

The lack of political goodwill hampered the coalition's ability to articulate a coherent Foreign Policy. The situation was not helped by Kibaki's low profile interest in Foreign Policy where he left most decisions to his ministers to make. Instead, the president and prime minister competed for limelight and influence in domestic and foreign affairs.

The new Constitution provides Kenya with the opportunity to develop capacity and re-brand afresh to effectively compete on the international stage. Its provisions on Kenya's international obligations on treaties and conventions, the removal of immunity from prosecution for a sitting president, its regulations on democracy, good governance and provisions on citizen's freedoms and human rights, should make Kenya a country of envy to other states. However, from that, Kenya's image improved tremendously during the Grand Coalition Government, especially in relations with development partners.

It reached out to new partners whose investment in the country has made a huge difference in infrastructure development.

Kibaki made a mark with a state visit to China in the autumn of 2005, which attracted Chinese collaboration in road and the SGR construction from Mombasa to Nairobi.

Diplomatic miscalculation

Kenya's Foreign Policy and diplomacy should portray the country at its best and fight for it during difficult times. It should define its interests and use its diplomacy to advance them. This is possible when Kenya respects the Vienna Convention on Diplomatic and Consular Relations and other treaties to which it is party.

In 2006, then Senator Barack Obama voiced his concerns about rampant corruption in the country at a public lecture at the University of Nairobi on a visit to Kenya. The remarks were not taken kindly by the government which unleashed its officials to admonish Obama, describing him as "a junior Senator" who was not qualified to talk about Kenya. They also issued veiled threats of retribution against Obama urging him to keep off the internal matters of Kenya.

Furthermore, the then newly appointed Kenyan Ambassador to Washington DC, protested in the media about Obama's remarks in breach of accepted practice for envoys before presentation of Letters of Credence. The ambassador had not presented his letters of credence to the then US President George W. Bush. Courtesy demands that an unaccredited envoy presents his/her Letters of Credence to the head of state before he/she can issue press statements or give interviews in media in the country of accreditation. This was a clear breach of international protocol.

When Barack Obama was elected the 44th President of the USA on 4th November, 2008, Kenya celebrated his victory as if he was its own president. This was barely two years after Obama's speech at the University of Nairobi. His election was received with nostalgia in Kenya and hailed as a national achievement.

Obama's father, Barack Obama Snr, a Kenyan, was a senior civil servant in the government of Jomo Kenyatta from the 1960s up to his death in 1982. So, President Kibaki declared a national holiday the day after the elections to allow Kenyans to savour Obama's election victory. One of Kenya's embassies hosted a diplomatic reception to celebrate the victory. Yet the USA itself did not close shop to celebrate even though history had been made to elect the first African-American president of the country.

In his inaugural address on 20th January, 2009, Obama made it clear that the United States would watch carefully what other countries did or failed to do with respect to democracy and good governance. He made specific reference to Kenya when he said in his words: "those who steal elections, those who are corrupt everywhere, including from the remotest part of the world where my father was born," in reference to the disputed 2007 presidential election results in Kenya which were perceived to have been won by Raila Odinga.[37]

Obama must have had in mind Kenya's reaction to his speech in 2006 alluded to above. Any illusion about using Obama's election to re-energise

---

37   See https://www.nation.co.ke/news/politics/Raila-won-2007-elections--says-Macharia/1064-3506012-q12oic/index.html

relations with the USA seemed to have been miscalculated. Kenyan leaders seemed to have forgotten Obama's comments in 2006, and his message during his inauguration. As US president, Barack Obama represented, first and foremost, the interests of the USA.

The nostalgia about Obama's election made Kenya's foreign minister undertake a trip to the USA ostensibly to attend his inauguration. US protocol classifies the inauguration of a new president as an internal matter. Any foreign participation is usually limited to accredited ambassadors and specifically invited foreign dignitaries. Kenya's intention may have been to seize the moment to improve bilateral relations which had taken a nose dive in the years after the end of the Cold War.

The zeal exhibited by Kenya seemed to suggest that, at last, "a messiah" had arrived to lift the country from its difficult relations with the West. It was clear that the nostalgia with which Kenyans celebrated Obama's election was most unmissably beyond expectation for a president of another country. Kenyans may be excused for celebrating his election.

Eventually President Obama visited Kenya in 2015. His visit attracted more Americans to Kenya and led to greater interest in Kenya for business opportunities and tourism.

Kibaki's Foreign Policy legacy

Mwai Kibaki noticeably shifted Kenya's Foreign Policy towards the East and attracted China which dominates infrastructure development projects in Kenya and across Africa. His state visit to China in 2005 drew the attention of the USA and the UK. The visit firmly anchored China as one of the most important development partners of Kenya. The rehabilitation of the dilapidated infrastructure, initiatives contained in planning blueprints developed during his presidency, contributed to the economic development of the country and significantly secured its national interest.

Kibaki's legacy includes presiding over the 2007 elections whose presidential results were disputed which nearly plunged the country into chaos and dented Kenya's image as a peaceful, stable and secure country. The economic gains from initiatives like the Vision 2030, intended to transform Kenya into a middle-income country, received a severe blow. Some of the projects Kibaki conceived such as the construction of the SGR and the expansion and modernisation of the port of Mombasa were taken up by Uhuru Kenyatta when he became president in 2013. Kibaki's initiative to publish the *Kenya Foreign Policy, 2014* was a major contribution to an understanding of the country's Foreign Policy orientation.

CHAPTER 8

Uhuru Kenyatta Presidency, from 2013

Uhuru Kenyatta was the first president to be elected under the Constitution of Kenya, 2010. He was bound to face challenges of implementing a Constitution he half-heartedly supported.[38] Uhuru Kenyatta was perceived to be ambivalent to the process between those for it, symbolised by *green* (yes), and those against it, symbolised by *red* (no). Deputy President, William Ruto (then Minister for Agriculture) outrightly voted against the new Constitution. The stewardship of the country under the new constitutional dispensation lies in the hands of people who were, at best, lukewarm to it in addition to having been indicted by the International Criminal Court at The Hague, for crimes against humanity committed during the 2007/2008 post-election violence.

During the 2013 presidential campaigns for office, Uhuru Kenyatta and William Ruto promised Kenyans that, if elected, they would separate their respective personal trials at The Hague from execution of their duties as president and deputy president, respectively. In the middle of the campaign, Johnnie Carson, then US Assistant Secretary of State for African Affairs and former ambassador to Kenya, made remarks which seemed to advise Kenyans not to vote for Uhuru and Ruto. He said in a radio interview that warned Kenyans that:

> "Kenyans had a right to elect their leaders but choices have consequences."[39]

Uhuru and Ruto capitalised on Carson's implied threat and galvanised support for their ticket, to full effect, arguing that the USA was interfering with the internal affairs of Kenya. They won the elections.

Uhuru Kenyatta's Foreign Policy challenge over the ICC was unprecedented in Kenya's history. For the first time, the president of Kenya faced trial in an international court. Once in power, Uhuru Kenyatta's government embarked on shuttle diplomacy led by Deputy President William Ruto, and later the Cabinet Secretary for foreign affairs Amina Mohammed, to persuade the AU to take a stand against their trial at the ICC. Kenya deployed considerable

---

38   See https://edaily.co.ke/entertainment/president-kenyatta-i-was-labeled-a-watermel-on-for-consulting-ruto-120481/enews/ekenyan/
39   Former US Ambassador to Kenya, Johnnie Carson on the 2013 elections in Kenya.

resources to influence African countries to support its case. However, the AU is not party to the Rome Statute and, therefore, its resolutions amounted only to political declarations of support. The UN Security Council advised Kenya to engage the Assembly of State Parties (ASP) to the Rome Statute to deliberate and decide on the issue at its meeting in October, 2013, at The Hague.[40]

Kenya's Foreign Policy and diplomacy should address the issues surrounding the ICC and not try to run away from them. Section (4) of Article 143, of the Constitution of Kenya, 2010, has removed immunity from prosecution of a sitting president for crimes against humanity. It states:

> "The immunity of the president under this Article shall not extend to
> a crime for which the President may be prosecuted under any treaty to
> which Kenya is party and which prohibits such immunity."[41]

This limitation applied to the proceedings at the ICC against Uhuru Kenyatta. Chapter 1, Article 2, sections 5 and 6 of the Constitution make international treaties and conventions Kenya is party to, part of the law of Kenya and obligates Kenya to respect and uphold them by honouring their provisions. In the context of these provisions, the AU could not have been of much assistance on the issue even though it provided political support through declaratory resolutions.

Uhuru Kenyatta's historic decision to attend the status conference at the ICC enabled him avoid breaching the Constitution. On this score, he demonstrated his commitment to respect and uphold the Constitution which he swore to defend and protect upon assumption of office. Above all, it assuaged the judges about his commitment to the rule of law.

Uhuru Kenyatta, to use his own words, declared that he would *"attend the status conference in a personal capacity"*, because the charges did not cover his actions as Head of State.[42] His action, he argued, enabled him to avoid bringing into disrepute the sovereignty of the country and people of Kenya. The president's action was an affirmation of the supremacy of the Constitution and Kenya's recognition of the ICC with jurisdiction on crimes against humanity on which Uhuru Kenyatta's charges were based. The case against Uhuru Kenyatta collapsed in 2014 and the one against William Ruto in 2015 for lack of sufficient evidence to proceed with the prosecution.

---

40   See https://asp.icc-cpi.int/en_menus/asp/sessions/documentation/12th-session/
     Pages/default.aspx
41   The Constitution of Kenya, 2010.
42   See http://www.theeastafrican.co.ke/news/Uhuru-Kenyatta-to-go-to-Hague-court-
     in-personal-capacity/2558-2477790-4ijo1qz/index.html

The 2007/2008 post-election violence remains a major headache for the country. The plight of the victims of the violence has not been resolved. Kenya must address the issue of justice for victims of the violence quite apart from re-settlement and compensation for survivors. Kenya must convince the public and the world that it understands its obligations to the citizens through unravelling the deep-rooted contradictions and historical injustices its people have suffered since independence. The collapse of trials at the ICC paved the way for US President Barack Obama's visit to Kenya in 2015, two years into Uhuru's tenure and seven years into Obama's presidency which brought Kenya out of the diplomatic cold.

Uhuru Kenyatta's indictment at the Hague presented a major Foreign Policy dilemma for the president and Kenya. It was a challenge to his authority as a sitting president and Kenya's international standing. After the discharge of their cases, Uhuru Kenyatta has visited the USA, China, the EU, Nigeria and hosted many heads of state. President Obama's visit in 2015, combined a State visit with participation in the International Entrepreneurship Forum on business innovation. Other world leaders who visited Kenya included Prime Minister Narendra Modi of India, President Xi Jinping of China and Jacob Zuma of South Africa, among others. Uhuru Kenyatta's focus has been on economic diplomacy. Kenya hosted the United Nations Conference on Trade and Development (UNCTAD) and the Tokyo International Conference on Africa's Development (TICAD), in succession, which re-affirmed it as an important international conference venue.

Uhuru Kenyatta's first term

Under President Uhuru Kenyatta, Kenya's Foreign Policy and diplomacy was initially defined by its relationship with the ICC. His election as president while still facing indictment at the ICC complicated Kenya's international relations. As President, he sought to influence domestic and international public opinion in his favour.[43] However, his exercise of power was limited by the Constitution of Kenya, 2010, which has considerable checks and balances. This was evidenced by the attempt by the National Assembly to precipitate Kenya's withdrawal from the Rome Statute. The attempt hit a snag because effecting fundamental amendments to the constitution requires a referendum.

Issues such as democracy, good governance, corruption and human rights which were previously regarded as internal affairs of states have become major issues of interest in Foreign Policy. The Constitution of Kenya, 2010, envisages consensus through consultations on governance.

---

43   https://www.nation.co.ke/news/politics/Uhuru--ICC-trial-no-longer-a-personal-obligation/1064-2031568-snv0jrz/index.html

This presumption has reinforced the values, beliefs and aspirations which both the domestic and foreign policies should articulate.

Uhuru Kenyatta's 2013 election was challenged in the Supreme Court. The court's ruling in favour of Uhuru Kenyatta helped avert violence once the opposition accepted it. It was a vindication that political reforms, which had culminated in the adoption of a new Constitution, had mechanisms for conflict resolution in electoral disputes.

President Uhuru faced a similar experience in the 2017 presidential elections when the results were challenged in the Supreme Court again. This time, the court nullified the presidential election and ordered a repeat within 60 days under Section 140 of the Constitution. With the nullification of the election, Kenya became the fourth country in the world where presidential elections have been overturned. It joined a handful of the others namely, Maldives (2012), Ukraine (2013) and Austria (2016).

The Supreme Court's nullification of the presidential election was a landmark decision in electoral jurisprudence in Kenya, a rare experience in Africa and probably in the world. Chief Justice David Maraga in reading the Supreme Court majority ruling, observed that:

"The greatness of a nation is found in its respect for the law and its fear of God."[44]

The Supreme Court's decision received international acclaim and underlined constitutional development and growing strength of the rule of law in Kenya. Its impact in Kenya may be likened to the experience Kenya went through after the 2002 elections when KANU was swept out of power.

***

The 8th August, 2017 presidential elections pitted Uhuru Kenyatta and his running mate William Ruto of Jubilee Alliance Party (JAP) against Raila Odinga and Kalonzo Musyoka of the NASA Coalition. The results gave Uhuru Kenyatta a win which was successfully challenged by NASA at the Supreme Court. The IEBC was ordered to conduct a repeat poll within 60 days. The IEBC scheduled the repeat poll on 17th October, 2017 but moved the date to 26th October, 2017 due to inadequate time to print ballot papers. NASA boycotted the repeat election claiming that there was no level playing field without electoral reforms.[45]

44   The Supreme Court decision, 1st September, 2017.
45   https://www.aljazeera.com/news/2017/10/kenya-raila-odinga-withdraws-election-run-171010135516759.html

President Uhuru Kenyatta was declared the winner, running against fringe party candidates.[46] The election was largely viewed as flawed.[47] The electoral victory was upheld by the Supreme Court. What followed was violence and resistance by NASA which said it would not recognise Uhuru's presidency.[48]

Consequently, Uhuru Kenyatta's second term in 2017 began in greater controversy. That raised doubts about its fairness and credibility.[49] Kenyans believed that issues which caused conflict, suspicion and exclusivity in the country had been overcome through implementation of the Constitution of Kenya, 2010.

Issues which arose from the Supreme Court rulings in 2013, and 2017, should inform how citizens appreciate the democratic and governance process in the country. Elections are expected to usher into office leaders chosen by voters through a free, fair and credible process. If the electoral process cannot be trusted, citizens lose confidence in the process and the leadership which emerges from it. Free, fair and credible elections should reflect the free sovereign will of the people. What happened in 2013, and 2017, raised doubts on this question. If there is lack of confidence in the two elections, the conclusion one may draw is that there is a steady decline of state institutions – the executive, the National Police Service (NPS), the Independent Electoral and Boundaries Commission (IEBC) and the Judiciary, which could lead to the failure of the state.

Kenya faces multiple challenges with regard to democracy, governance, security, and observance of human rights which impact negatively on its international image. It is critical for it to overcome these challenges, so as to articulate a successful Foreign Policy and claim a leadership role in East Africa.

Kenya must overcome its internal differences and set aside sufficient financial and human resources to support an elaborate diplomatic infrastructure so as to consolidate its voice at the regional and international levels. A clear line should be drawn between internal infighting and consolidating national efforts to focus its attention on achieving its Foreign Policy goals. The experience in peaceful transfer of power from one president to another in 2002, and the adoption of the Constitution of

46   See https://www.nation.co.ke/news/Uhuru-Kenyatta-Kenya-election-win-next-steps-/1056-4162938-qukcgu/index.html

47   https://www.nation.co.ke/news/politics/Live-blog-Oct-26/1064-4156294-1sk0pm/index.html

48   http://www.theeastafrican.co.ke/business/Kenya-opposition-boycott-Safaricom-Brookside-Bidco/2560-4172060-jjn3ec/index.html

49   https://www.bbc.com/news/world-africa-41757612

Kenya, 2010, are two positive developments which Kenya can use to market itself to the international community. It must avoid the systemic threat to the sovereign will of the people at every election.

The *Diaspora Policy,* the Ministry of Foreign Affairs *Web Portal* and *Kenya Foreign Policy, 2014,* were published in 2014, during Uhuru Kenyatta's tenure. These were major milestones in the evolution of Kenya's Foreign Policy, even though not all aspects of the country's Foreign Policy were covered. More needs to be done in the pursuit of SMART Foreign Policy objectives.

The *Kenya Foreign Policy, 2014,* rightly assigns a role for Kenyans in the diaspora but grossly errors by naming them as one of the pillars of Kenya's Foreign Policy. Kenyans in the diaspora cannot be regarded as a pillar of its Foreign Policy on account of dual citizenship. Dual citizenship is a compromise on loyalty to the country of choice as well as of birth. Many of the people in the diaspora make decisions to invest in Kenya for personal and family, but not nationalistic reasons. They are generally a mix of diverse and sophisticated groups to mobilise; they only congregate to promote their interests. Kenyans in the diaspora should be regarded as an important target group of the Foreign Policy and urged to invest in their country of birth.

Kenya's Foreign Policy articulates respect for sovereignty and territorial integrity of other states, good neighbourliness, peaceful co-existence, economic diplomacy, environmental diplomacy and Kenyans in the diaspora. The strategy envisioned in the Kenya Foreign Policy should contain a clear understanding of the country's national interest whose elements drive its Foreign Policy. Such an understanding must inform the areas in which the Foreign Policy aims to influence and/or selected actors considered critical to Kenya's national interest. A multi-pronged approach is best suited to such a strategy on a case by case basis. The country needs to agree on specific targets with clear objectives to sustain a consistent Foreign Policy. The credibility of its government will enable Kenya to consolidate its role and place at the regional and international levels.

Challenges ahead

In 2015, Uhuru Kenyatta personally acknowledged that corruption is a threat to national security and needed to be tackled head on.[50] But, he did very little in actual practice to curb the vice. The public expected him to take concrete measures in line with his pronouncements.

---

50   See https://www.standardmedia.co.ke/ureport/story/2000195444/corruption-is-a-national-security-threat

After being sworn in for the second and final term, President Kenyatta's legitimacy was questioned by NASA who threatened a matching swearing in for their candidate, Raila Odinga, in the election. This sharply divided the country between Jubilee and NASA supporters. The threat was actualised at Uhuru Park on 30th January 2018, when Raila Odinga pronounced himself "the People's President". The relations were frosty, giving the country a bad image.

On 9th March, 2018, both Uhuru and Raila appeared at the steps of Harambee House and declared that they had signed an agreement to work together. The handshake later become famous and improved their relations tremendously and brought tranquillity to the country. After the "handshake", Uhuru's pronouncements on corruption led to arrests of culprits linked to corruption scandals. Only time will tell the extent of this success. His Foreign Policy legacy will, therefore, depend on his government's ability to deal with the problems facing the country, especially corruption.

Uhuru Kenyatta's Foreign Policy legacy

Uhuru Kenyatta fended off the ICC trial quite successfully in his first term, but remains mired in intractable local issues mainly governance, corruption, and ethnicity. The 50-50 distribution of cabinet posts between his party, The National Alliance (TNA) and William Ruto's United Republican Party (URP) was viewed by many people against the spirit of the Constitution which anticipates public appointments to reflect the face of Kenya.

In response to his ICC trial, he made many foreign trips to rebuild his image and that of the country. The choices of his destinations among them, China, India, Russia and the United Arab Emirates, demonstrate his approach to Kenya's international engagement and desire to balance Kenya's economic partnerships. He further visited the USA and the EU Headquarters in Brussels, Belgium.

President Barack Obama made a state visit in 2015 which completed Kenya's return to international respectability. President Obama's return in July 2018 after leaving office, to launch the Sauti Kuu, an NGO in K'Ogelo, western Kenya, sponsored by Dr. Auma Obama – his step-sister – once again put Kenya in the limelight.

Other leaders who visited Kenya during Uhuru's reign included Prime Minister Narendra Modi of India, President Xi Jinping of China, Jacob Zuma of South Africa, John Pombe Magufuli of Tanzania, King Abdullah of Jordan and Prime Minister Benjamin Netanyahu of Israel. Uhuru Kenyatta's Foreign Policy legacy will be determined by how he observes transparency, accountability and respect for the rule of law. It is what will cement Kenya's Foreign Policy and diplomacy during his presidency.

PART III

REGIONAL RELATIONS, SECURITY CHALLENGES, MEDIATION AND CONFLICT RESOLUTION

This Part examines how Kenya has managed regional relations, security challenges, mediation and conflict resolution since independence, which defined its Foreign Policy in the region. The objective of Kenya's Foreign Policy and diplomacy in the region has been peaceful co-existence and good neighbourliness to secure markets for its products.

It also focuses on regional relations and security challenges which have shaped Kenya's Foreign Policy on mediation and conflict resolution, particularly, through IGAD. This has made Kenya incur heavy financial and diplomatic capital in mediation and conflict resolution. This is because it values peace as a pre-requisite for economic development. As a result, Kenya has played a role in peace processes in the Horn of Africa and the Great Lakes Region, through regional and international collective action or directly.

CHAPTER 9

Regional Relations and security challenges for Kenya

Kenya's geographical location shapes its policy on conflict resolution and mediation. It is surrounded by countries which experience insecurity and political instability. Kenya's desire was to establish peace and stability to promote regional economic development. The main focus was to secure markets for its goods and investment opportunities. Throughout its existence, Kenya has largely remained peaceful, save for periodic inter-ethnic clashes around its elections. The region, and the international community in general, found it expedient to coordinate peace processes in the Sudan and Somalia from Kenya. This was supported by a reasonably functional economy and actively willing political leadership. Furthermore, Kenya is the main transit country for the external trade of Uganda, Rwanda, eastern DRC, Burundi and South Sudan using the NCTS to the port of Mombasa. Both factors help consolidate Kenya's strategic importance in East Africa.

Kenya's location is, therefore, critical to understanding its Foreign Policy on conflict, insecurity and political instability in the Horn of Africa and the Great Lakes Region. The volatile political situations in these countries have forced Kenya to adopt an active role in the search for peace to promote stability, economic development and to safeguard its national security interests. Kenya's security concerns stem from political instability caused by conflicts in neighbouring countries. They manifest themselves through trans-boundary security issues, inflow of refugees, proliferation of SALW, international terrorism and threats to its territory by some of its neighbours.

Threats to Kenya's territorial integrity
Kenya has faced threats to its territorial integrity from her neighbours as follows: Somalia in the 1960s (Greater Somalia Policy); Uganda during Amin's rule in the 1970s and also its claim on Migingo Islands in Lake Victoria; and South Sudan over the territory between Nadapal in Turkana County and the border at Nakodok. SPLM/A sought Kenya's help to build a staging post for its humanitarian assistance programmes into the

then Southern Sudan during its liberation war against the government of Sudan. Kenya also has a maritime border dispute with Somalia before the International Court of Arbitration at The Hague.

Territorial and other threats from Somalia since the 1960s

Somalia has been at the heart of complex security challenges facing Kenya since independence. Its policy of Greater Somalia adopted at independence was responsible for the initial challenge on territorial claim of the areas occupied by ethnic Somali Kenyans. Throughout the early years, Somalia pursued a nationalist policy which was intended to consolidate all territories occupied by Somali speaking people into one Somali nation, leading to insurrection by ethnic Somalis in Kenya in the 1960s. The Greater Somalia policy targeted the then Northern Frontier District (NFD) comprising current Garissa, Wajir and Mandera counties. The Shifta insurgence took place after the referendum held in 1963 for the Kenyan-Somali who voted overwhelmingly to join Somalia.

Kenya took decisive military action to crush the insurrection to safeguard the sovereignty and territorial integrity of the country as provided for in the Charters of the OAU, and the UN, which at independence adopted colonial boundaries to be the international boundaries of African countries. Kenya's decision to neutralise the Shifta insurrection made it review the capacity of its military to respond to such threats and act as a deterrent to further trouble. For many years, an uncomfortable bilateral calm existed between Kenya and Somalia due to internal strife in Somalia, which persisted in varying degrees until the 1991 overthrow of Siad Barre when Somalia exploded into outright civil war.

Terrorist groups based in Somalia

Siad Barre's overthrow in 1991, precipitated the free fall of the country into a failed state. The turmoil he left behind when he fled to Nigeria via Kenya destroyed Somalia when its central government collapsed and, in its place, warlords curved the country into spheres of influence. The warlords engaged in a fierce competition for power and control over large chunks of the country and their resources. The absence of a central government caused insecurity, out of which emerged terror groups such as Al-Qaeda, Al-Shabaab, and pirates who established their bases in the country. The breakdown of law and order further led to uncontrolled ownership of guns that is the main source of the proliferation of SALW in the Horn of Africa.

Kenya has been a victim of the menace due to the porous border, which is difficult to patrol and the tough terrain and hostile climate. It is exacerbated by close family and clan loyalties in both countries. The rise of groups such as the ICU, Al-Shabaab, and maritime piracy groups pose a major problem from Somalia, which shares a 684-kilometre border with Kenya. The border runs from the Indian Ocean through arid and semi-arid terrain to the Ethiopian border. The border is, particularly, difficult to effectively secure without joint efforts by Kenya, and in the absence of an effective central government in Somalia. Given that international terrorism has become a major global problem, groups like Al-Qaeda and Al-Shabaab and their backers take advantage of weak states in which they hide, plan and execute their operations. Kenya needs to be on the lookout and be prepared to deal with security challenges from such groups in Somalia and beyond to collectively use international mechanisms to confront security threats emanating from outside its territory.

The security challenges which Kenya has encountered since its independence define its Foreign Policy in the region. Its role in the Sudan and Somalia peace processes was to establish peace and stability in these countries, to allow for meaningful economic development in the Horn of Africa. Kenya's priority in Somalia was to establish the TFG to embark on the re-establishment of institutions of state to return Somalia to normalcy.

Al-Shabaab attacks

Al-Shabaab is a branch of Al-Qaeda which has established itself in Somalia from where it operates. It has attacked government buildings, civilians and AMISOM troops in Somalia. It has also carried out attacks in Uganda, Ethiopia and Kenya. Most of its operations in Kenya have been in Nairobi, Garissa, Wajir, Mandera and at the coast. In 2011, Al-Shabaab abducted British and French tourists from Lamu and aid workers from Dadaab refugee camp into Somalia. The abduction presented two challenges to Kenya; first, Dadaab camp, the largest refugee camp in the world, is the face of Kenya's humanitarian efforts in support of refugees from neighbouring countries, most of who come from Somalia. Second, Al-Shabaab targeted the tourist industry which is a vital economic sector for the country. Kenya took action to protect its interests against Al-Shabaab with the approval of the TFG of Somalia and as part of international war on terrorism.

Kenya could not remain indifferent to Al-Shabaab's provocation. It took swift action, notwithstanding the established agreement on direct military intervention in member countries of IGAD and the AU. Somalia's approval provided the legitimacy Kenya needed to avoid contravening the regional understanding in military intervention in each other's territory. The intervention helped the TFG to extend its control over more territory and gave it a chance to establish itself and consolidate its authority in the country.

Kenya's intervention in Somalia did not stop Al-Shabaab from escalating attacks against its interests. Al-Shabaab claimed responsibility for attacks on the up-market Westgate Mall in Nairobi, in September 2013, with the loss of sixty-seven lives and millions of shillings in property damage. It, similarly, claimed responsibility for the attack on Garissa University College in April, 2015, with the loss of one hundred and forty-eight lives, most of them students; and for attacks on a bus in Mandera with a loss of thirty-eight lives; followed by another attack on quarry workers with a loss of over thirty lives. The presence of Al-Shabaab in Somalia and its ability to attack targets in Kenya is undoubtedly one of the major security challenges facing the country. Kenya must continue to collaborate with other countries in order to eliminate this threat to ensure its security and save the economy.

Al-Shabaab escalated attacks on Kenya's interests with a daring attack on a KDF base in southern Somalia near the border with Kenya on 15th January, 2016, with a loss of about two hundred soldiers. It was baffling to many as to why the attack was so lethal, considering that the camp is situated close to a Somalia army base. Kenya found it difficult to explain how its forces could not have mounted a proper defence to foil the attack which exposed major weaknesses within AMISOM. It was evident that there were problems of coordination and command between troop contributing countries and the AMISOM headquarters in Mogadishu. Decisions appear to be driven by national interests of contributing countries and self-interest among AMISOM leadership. There have been demands by some elements in Somalia for the withdrawal of KDF from Somalia. Kenya should deploy sufficient resources to address the problem.

Piracy: Threats to maritime commercial shipping

The disruption of international commercial shipping routes in the Indian Ocean threatens Kenya's international trade. The area affected runs from the Red Sea along the African coast to South Africa. Pirates found a haven in Somalia due to its inability to respond to security and coordinate state activities on its territory. The pirates thrived well in the chaotic situations; they hijacked merchant ships, took hostages and demanded ransom for their release. Since 1991, the lawlessness in Somalia, warlords and absence of a central authority created fertile ground and hideouts for terrorists and pirates. They attacked, maimed and killed innocent people and caused untold damage to property.

Somalia's weak institutions enable pirates to operate from its territory. Pirates have engaged in blackmail, torture and sometimes execution of hostages. It is faceless, inhuman, brutal and unforgiving. Piracy off the coast of Somalia is, therefore, an international problem and its threat to trade routes impacts negatively on the global economy and must be tackled by all nations. China, the EU and the USA have deployed warships to protect the trade route.

The piracy threat exists for Kenya and hinterland countries of Uganda, Rwanda, Burundi, eastern DRC and South Sudan, which use the port of Mombasa for their international trade. Piracy is not a major economic and Foreign Policy issue to Kenya alone, but to the sub-region as a whole.

As a frontline state, Kenya must take the lead as a coastal country and participate in international efforts to eliminate the threat. Kenya's Foreign Policy towards Somalia and the Horn of Africa should target a collective approach through collaboration with other regional and international organisations. Kenyans expect the country's Foreign Policy to seek and secure peace and stability in the Horn of Africa to facilitate trade, investment, tourism and foster economic development.

Territorial threats from Uganda

As part of British East Africa, Kenya was considered to be a transit territory to Uganda which the white settler community preferred for its climate and fertile land. The naming of the railway line constructed from Mombasa to Kisumu as Uganda Railway, emphasised the white settlers' perception that Uganda was more central to the region, hence their preferred destination. The railway was named after Uganda and underlined the colonialists' preference. When Kenya was established as a state, it effectively landlocked Uganda, making it imperative for the latter to agree on transit arrangements with Kenya. The colonial bonds translated into strong economic links to both countries.

Uganda's dependence on Kenya for is external trade has made it Kenya's largest trading partner. Whereas relations are warm and cordial, territorial claims and disputes have from time to time characterised exchanges between the two countries.[51] It began with Idi Amin's claim of Kenyan territory up to Naivasha on the eastern side of the Rift Valley in 1976. Kenya's President, Jomo Kenyatta, responded by modernising Kenya's armed forces, especially buying F5s jet fighters to confront the threat. Amin backed off.

The second territorial claim by Uganda on Kenyan territory regards the dispute over the rocky Migingo Islands in Lake Victoria. The cause of the

---

51   https://www.nation.co.ke/lifestyle/dn2/Diplomatic-fights-that-shaped-foreign-policy/957860-2086360-ii7kqtz/index.html

dispute is the fight to control economic resources around it such as fish and potential minerals. The dispute should be resolved through diplomatic negotiations for a sustainable solution based on the OAU and the UN legal instruments on international boundaries.

The NCTS from Mombasa runs through Kenya to Uganda, Rwanda, Burundi and eastern DRC and South Sudan. Its significance was acutely felt during the 2007/2008 post-election violence which brought business to a halt in Kenya. Rwanda and Burundi sent delegations to Dar es Salaam, Tanzania to conclude agreements on alternative trade routes via Dar es Salaam. Political turmoil quickly turned a viable economic resource into waste within a short time. Kenya's inability to peacefully manage its political process was responsible for the impasse, and probably behind the strategic decision by Uganda to re-route its oil pipeline through Tanzania.

Kenya needs to work together with its neighbours to protect the arteries of economic activity for the region. Plans to upgrade road and railway infrastructure from Mombasa to Malaba and the development of Lamu port and other infrastructure through northern Kenya to South Sudan and Ethiopia, should help address this problem. Completion of these projects will strengthen Kenya's position as an anchor economy in East Africa. As an economic power house and a regional hub for air transport and tourism, Kenya should play a leading role in the sub-region. Kenya should be alert to competition from its coastline neighbours like Tanzania, which is keen to develop the Central Corridor Transport System (CCTS). The CCTS will run from Dar es Salaam through Kigoma to Rwanda, Burundi, Uganda and eastern DRC. Furthermore, Kenya has to invest heavily in the security of the country and its people.

Uganda initially expressed interest in the development of the LAPSSET transport system, which involves the construction of an oil pipeline, the SGR and an optic fibre internet infrastructure. The idea was to link the pipeline to its oil fields in western Uganda. The pipeline will provide South Sudan with an alternative export route for its oil. Kenya plans to develop LAPSSET through Garissa, Isiolo to Turkana to serve northern Kenya, South Sudan and Ethiopia. The objective is to create a regional transport corridor to complement the NCTS from Mombasa through Nairobi to Uganda, Rwanda, Burundi and eastern DRC. Security concerns appear to have convinced Uganda to develop its oil pipeline through Tanzania, a significantly longer route than through Kenya, for fear of insecurity via northern Kenya.

Threats from political instability in South Sudan

South Sudan's independence in 2011 was a product of Kenya's Foreign Policy on peace and its role in the conclusion of the CPA in 2005. Kenya invested financial and diplomatic capital in the peace process. South Sudan's application and subsequent membership to the EAC pointed to the development of positive relations. South Sudan's degeneration into internal political power struggle threatens to turn it into a failed state and a source of refugees into Kenya.

Kenya and South Sudan do not appear to agree on the boundary between the border of the two countries, which could present a potential source of conflict in the future. SPLM/A leadership sought Kenya's humanitarian assistance for its people during the struggle for self-determination from Sudan, which Kenya facilitated through the South Sudan Relief and Rehabilitation Assistance (SRRA). The SRRA is an NGO then based in Nairobi but acted as the development arm of SPLM/A charged with all governance, administrative and humanitarian functions of the SPLM.

It coordinated all humanitarian activities in secured areas by the SPLM/A in South Sudan. This was done in conjunction with the Operation Lifeline Sudan (OLS), a UN humanitarian assistance programme coordinated by UNICEF to ensure relief and other humanitarian assistance reached the people of South Sudan. Part of this relief was transported by road via Lodwar and Lokichogio to Kapoeta in South Sudan. The border crossing at Nakodok proved to be a major barrier as snipers hiding in the hills overlooking the border point killed lorry personnel, looted or destroyed the goods. To address this problem, SPLM/A requested Kenya to temporarily move the border point 8 km into Kenya territory at Nadapal to allow the SPLM to effectively secure the route for the transporters to cross safely. The stretch of land along the border is a potential territorial dispute area for the two countries.

Kenya went further and allowed Germany to assist the SPLM/A fighters fish at the northern tip of Lake Turkana to supplement their food ratios and for other vulnerable people. The dispute thus runs along the whole international border from the Uganda border to the Ethiopian border. Kenya should deploy its human resources, including those privy to the understanding between the SPLM/A and Kenya, to resolve the problem before it escalates into a major international dispute.

Threats to strategic economic interests

Kenya faces threats to its economy from a variety of sources within the Horn of Africa and the Great Lakes Region. Its more developed and vibrant agricultural, manufacturing and service sectors are vulnerable to disruption caused by instability and conflict within the neighbouring states. Kenya's geographical location makes it imperative for it to be alert to the political and security developments in the region. Kenya has generally shied away from intervention, consistently upholding the principle of non-interference in the internal affairs of other states. Terrorist and piracy threats to its economic interests shifted its stand from being defensive from within its borders to confronting threats without hesitation. Its action against Al-Shabaab demonstrates the political will and military readiness for such action.

Trans-boundary security management
Kenya's Foreign Policy and diplomacy in the Horn of Africa and the Great Lakes Region is defined by security threats to the country. The problem is caused by instability and conflict in the neighbouring countries which encircle Kenya from Somalia in the east, Ethiopia in the north, South Sudan in the north west and Uganda, Rwanda and the DRC in the west. Ethiopia, Uganda and Rwanda have largely improved internal political situations, but potential for relapse into chaos remains high.

Kenya must work with its neighbours to contain insecurity along Kenya's borders through effective border security mechanisms. The umbrella instrument is the Joint Commission usually organised by ministries of foreign affairs to deal with bilateral issues under specific sectoral committees. Kenya has local trans-boundary security committees with its immediate neighbours to deal with security issues. The committees are critical in the management of trans-boundary community security between the following:

- The Somali ethnic group astride the entire length of Kenya/Somalia border and also Ethiopia at Mandera
- The Borana and Oromo across the Kenya/Ethiopia border
- The Turkana and Toposa across the Kenya/South Sudan border
- The Turkana and Pokot with Karamojong in Uganda
- The Bukusu, Sabaoti, Teso and Samia with Bagisu across the Kenya/Uganda border.

The others include the Luo groups astride the Kenya/Uganda border, the Kuria and Maasai and Taita and Chagga across the Kenya/Tanzania border. The list indicates across border population mix which has the potential for conflict over economic resources. Trans-boundary security is critical to the principle of good neighbourliness and non-interference in the internal affairs of other states.

Joint border security committees

Joint border security committees are useful diplomatic tools deployed to deal with local issues to maintain peace and allow for local economic relations among border communities along its borders with Ethiopia, Uganda, South Sudan and Tanzania. The committees fall under Joint Ministerial Commissions under the Ministries of Foreign Affairs and constitute the basic diplomatic engagement between the respective countries. Joint Commissions provide the forum for negotiating bilateral engagement in all areas of cooperation.

Trans-boundary security committees deal with all issues which promote peaceful co-existence between communities along common borders. The committees are expected to develop early warning systems to identify and contain situations before they degenerate into conflict. Most common problems include competition for resources – land, pasture and water. Disputes over grazing fields between Karamojong in Uganda and Turkana in Kenya and between Maasai in Kenya and Maasai in Tanzania are quite common. Kenya must make an effort to contain cross-border incursions by cooperating with its neighbours, through mechanisms for peaceful resolution of disputes. Joint Border Security Committees (JBSCs) exist with Ethiopia, Uganda and Tanzania.

Joint Border Security Committees constitute the most rudimentary diplomatic engagement of modern times – a kind of devolved diplomatic practice that is people-centred, transparent and effective. Consultations take place at local levels and do not invoke traditional diplomacy as defined under the Vienna Convention on Diplomatic Relations, unless the severity of specific situations requires a full Joint Commission (JC) under whose general mandate they function. Many delicate situations have been resolved between Kenya and Ethiopia through the mechanism.

Kenya/Ethiopia defence pact

Kenya and Ethiopia signed an MoU on defence soon after Kenya's independence, in response to the threat posed by Somali's Greater Somalia policy as discussed in Chapter 10. The territorial threat contained in the policy led to the Shifta insurrection in Kenya in the 1960s and caused the Ogaden war in Ethiopia in 1973. Ethiopia survived the overthrow of Emperor Haile Selassie in 1974 and Mengistu Haile Mariam in 1991. Mengistu's ascendance to power in Ethiopia, in 1974, put a strain on Kenya/Ethiopia relations in the initial stages of his dictatorship. Jomo Kenyatta did not forgive Mengistu for the overthrow of the Emperor and the manner in which he (the Emperor) was killed, until his (Kenyatta's) own death in 1978.

Kenya and Ethiopia agreed to develop infrastructure linking the two countries to open up their semi-arid and arid regions to economic development, with the objective of improving trade ties and security along the common border. Whereas Ethiopia completed its side of the road from Addis Ababa to Moyale, Kenya did nothing on its side for two reasons. First, the Shifta insurrection put on hold any development in the NFD. Second, its priority as spelt out in Sessional Paper No. 10 of 1965 was to develop the NCTS. The NCTS was considered economically viable and more strategic than the Nairobi-Moyale road. However, Kenya completed the road in 2017 under President Uhuru Kenyatta.

Management of security along the Kenya/Ethiopia border
In concluding discussion on Joint Border Security Committees, it may be helpful to study how Kenya and Ethiopia manage their border security. Both countries have agreed on comprehensive early warning mechanism to avert potential conflicts and how to deal with them should they explode. Under the MoU on defence, they agreed to come to the defence of each other in the event of an attack from a common enemy. The pact, which was concluded in response to the threat by Somali's Greater Somalia policy, was not invoked either during the Shifta rebellion in Kenya or the Ogaden war between Ethiopia and Somalia. The MoU outlived successive regimes and remains one of the most enduring understandings between Kenya and Ethiopia.

Significantly, the two countries have, through international arbitration, demarcated and agreed on the common border and have established an early warning mechanism to alert authorities on either side to any security flare-ups along the border. Kenya needs to maintain a balance between its security and economic development agenda. The need for markets for its established manufacturing sector demands a peaceful and stable environment, conducive to trade among its neighbours and beyond. Kenya's Foreign Policy must therefore be focussed to effectively deal with external threats over which the country has no direct control. The country's security is directly affected by conflicts in the neighbouring countries from where refugees run away from.

Kenya's pursuit of its Foreign Policy of peaceful co-existence is driven by security consideration as a fundamental principle. David J. Francis explains the nexus between peace and development in Africa as follows:

"Peace and development have proved far more difficult and complex to achieve than the Afro-optimists envisaged in the immediate post-independence period, owing to a range of domestic and external factors. Two contrasting iconic images have dominated the public, if not the global, perception of Africa. First, the image of the dangerous and mysterious Africa as represented by perennial violent wars and bloody conflicts, perpetual political instability, unrelenting economic crises, famine, disease and poverty – all symbolising 'the hopeless continent' and the African predicament."[52]

Francis' observation provides an important insight into the underlying issues in economic and Foreign Policy strategies. Kenya has been a peaceful country since its independence. There are however, lingering territorial disputes with its neighbours which must be dealt with to guarantee peaceful co-existence.

Other security challenges include territorial threats, international terrorism, proliferation of SALW, influx of refugees, famine and international economic crises, taking into account the impact of globalisation to fragile economies such as Kenya's. The challenges must be dealt with through intensive regional and international engagement. Economic challenges include: food security, poverty, ignorance and emerging diseases. Similarly, Kenya needs to address the uneven levels of development among the 47 counties to consolidate its economic power as a major element of its national interest.

Refugee problem

Kenya has hosted large numbers of refugees from Somalia and Sudan, Ethiopia, Uganda, Rwanda, Burundi and the DRC who fled into Kenya in fear of persecution in their own countries. The refugees pose a threat to Kenya's economy and its internal security. Kenya must find a solution to managing the large numbers of refugees in the country. The Tripartite Agreement with Somalia and the United Nations High Commissioner for Refugees (UNHCR) on the return of Somalia refugees back to their country is likely to ease the burden, if it is implemented in accordance with its provisions.[53] It is feared that some of the refugee camps, notably Dadaab, may harbour terrorist elements who may target critical sectors such as academic institutions, transport, commercial ventures and the security infrastructure and other activities. Kenya's decision to close the Dadaab refugee camp has been informed by these challenges.

---

52   David J. Francis, *Peace and Conflict in Africa*.
53   www.refworld.org/pdfid/5285e0294.pdf

Proliferation of Small Arms and Light Weapons

Political instability, insecurity and conflict have led to unregulated ownership and proliferation of Small Arms and Light Weapons (SALW) in the Horn of Africa and the Great Lakes Region. This is a major security issue for Kenya. In a major Foreign Policy initiative in 1999, Kenya took a bold step when it convened the first regional conference to examine the impact of proliferation of SALW in eastern Africa.[54]

Dr. Bonaya Godana, then Foreign Affairs Minister, convened a Sub-Regional Inter-Ministerial meeting of Ministers for Foreign Affairs to consider and propose a way forward in combating the problem. Kenya despatched Special envoys to Tanzania, Ethiopia, Djibouti, Eritrea, Sudan, Uganda, Rwanda, Burundi, and the DRC to explain the objective and invite its counterparts to participate in a conference in Nairobi from 17th to 19th of April, 2000.

The Conference findings startled many observers from the sub-region. Kenya then established a regional Secretariat for small arms in Nairobi to analyse, document and make recommendations on the nature and scope of the problem in the Horn of Africa and the Great Lakes Region. It was agreed that the findings and conclusions of the conference be forwarded to the AU and the UN for discussions at continental and global levels. The UN's role was considered to be crucial to any plan of action in tackling the problem. It was discussed as a special item at the UN General Assembly in September, 2000. Kenya took lead on the issue, which in turn consolidated its efforts in the peace negotiations in Somalia and the CPA in Sudan.

Signs of conflict in Somalia were evident from its independence. Somalia was created out of two systems – a British system in Somaliland and an Italian system in the rest of Somalia. This was compounded by strong loyalty to clan interests and power struggle, which culminated in the coup d'état in Somalia in 1991 that ousted Siad Barre. The disintegration of Somalia state into fiefdoms controlled by warlords directly led to Somalia's descent into a failed state. State institutions collapsed, which made it impossible for it to provide security for its citizens to carry out meaningful economic activities and enjoy their freedoms and human rights. Daron Acemoglu and James Robinson observe that:

> "Nations fail today because their extractive economic institutions do not create the incentives needed for people to save, invest and innovate. Extractive political institutions support these economic institutions by cementing the power of those who benefit from the extraction.

54   http://erepository.uonbi.ac.ke/bitstream/handle/11295/101690/GABRIEL%20%20 SAMIA%20%20LENENGWEZI.pdf?sequence=1&isAllowed=y

Extractive economic and political institutions, though their details vary under different circumstances, are always at the root cause of the failure."[55]

Although Somalia is a homogeneous nation of one people, one culture and one religion, the inability of the state institutions to function inevitably led to its failure to operate as a state. This led to major security repercussions for its neighbours. Kenya has suffered the most from refugees, proliferation of SALW, piracy and international terrorism. The suffering is because of the Kenya/Somalia border that cuts through some of the most hostile desert terrain on the continent. The threats remain real for Kenya today as they have been always.

The influx of large numbers of refugees and their plight was not only humanitarian; it imposed a heavy burden to the economy and posed serious security challenges through proliferation of SALW. Northern Kenya, which is inhabited mostly by nomadic pastoral communities is, particularly, susceptible to the proliferation due to the fragile security situation, dire economic deprivation and, therefore, high levels of poverty.

The spate of robberies in and around Nairobi and other major towns in Kenya were fuelled by easily available firearms. The fight over resources, compounded by the lifestyle of pastoral communities, each claiming rights to all livestock, often results in intense cattle rustling, pitting one community against another, usually with fatal consequences. Given the sparsely populated expansive areas occupied by pastoral communities and their nomadic lifestyles, it becomes difficult for state institutions to provide adequate security or interventions.

---

55   Daron Acemoglu and James Robinson, *Why Nations Fail.*

CHAPTER 10

Mediation, Peace Efforts and Conflict Resolution

Mediation is the process of seeking a compromise between two or more protagonists to resolve a conflict. The beginning of any mediation process is very challenging. The first difficulty relates to acceptance of the mediator by the parties, without which the process cannot begin. Second, agreeing on a venue for the process; the security for both parties must be guaranteed. Third, logistics and recognition of each other as legitimate partners. Fourth, the mediator must be seen and perceived as independent from the influence of both parties to the conflict. Martti Ahtisaari observes that:

> "The independence of mediation is important for the integrity and credibility of the process."[56]

Specific peace processes which Kenya has either spearheaded or participated in had to religiously follow the above methods to take place and proceed to conclusion.

Kenya's Foreign Policy on mediation and peace efforts has been informed by its location in East Africa. Unstable neighbours to the east, the north and the west pose serious security problems, which undermine Kenya's potential and ability to consolidate its independence, undertake its economic development and chart a path for its Foreign Policy. This realisation influenced formulation of Kenya's Foreign Policy to focus on peaceful co-existence with its neighbours. It faced the biggest challenge of how to strike a balance between peace and security, and its policy on non-interference in the internal affairs of its neighbours, to enable it undertake its economic development and nation-building.

Kenya was recognised as a revolutionary state when it joined the OAU in 1963. Jomo Kenyatta, its founding prime minister, was recognised as a Pan-Africanist. This vote of confidence persuaded the OAU to appoint Jomo Kenyatta as the mediator in the Congo and Angola crises.[57]

---

56   Martti Ahtisaari, *Conversations with Ahtisaari*.
57   https://www.tandfonline.com/doi/full/10.1080/07075332.2016.1189951?src=recsys

Unfortunately, Jomo Kenyatta assumed power at an advanced age which constrained his efforts in the two crises. Kenya's engagement with the protagonists in the two crises did not produce tangible fruits on that account.

Kenya's role in conflict resolution

Kenya intensified its role in conflict resolution during Moi's presidency from 1978-2002. President Moi's tenure as Chairman of the OAU from 1981-1983 gave him a first-hand overview of conflicts in Africa and what needed to be done to resolve them. It became clear to him that the most affected sub-regions were the Horn of Africa and the Great Lakes Region. Kenya adopted a free market economic model which encourages public and private sector participation. This helped its economy to expand at a faster pace than those of its neighbours. The development required a balance between regional peace and internal security; both were pre-requisites for the stability and economic development of the country. The unfolding scenario made Kenya adopt a non-confrontational diplomatic style in its relations with its neighbours. The approach later became instrumental in its mediation efforts in the region. The real objective of Kenya's Foreign Policy was to secure markets for its agricultural and manufactured goods and services.

Mediation as an instrument of Kenya's Foreign Policy

Mediation is an art. It is a mechanism of making two or more protagonists to negotiate a solution to a conflict through compromise. It would be impossible for protagonists to agree on the way forward if each stuck to his/her hard-line position. Mediation is a mechanism by which disputes may be resolved between two or more protagonists through negotiations. The approach to such negotiations depends on their nature and type. There is need for recognition of the government in power by the opposing party before the peace talks can begin. If one of the protagonists contested the constitutionality of the authority in power, the chances of a negotiated settlement diminish.

Moi learnt this art when he deputised for Jomo Kenyatta for twelve years as Vice President. When he took over as president, conflict raged in Kenya's neighbouring countries. Moi recognised the need to engage the main protagonists in the conflicts. The aim was not only to secure peace, security and political stability, but also to stem the inflow into Kenya of refugees and SALW. In the end, Kenya could reap the peace dividend by securing regional markets for its goods and services.

Mediation demands attention to details of the cause of conflict, the protagonists' views and understanding of the same and sensitivity to their views and interests. Sometimes, family issues may be brought on board as a negotiating strategy. If such issues are not properly handled, they could hold the process to ransom. Mediators should be tactful yet honest; they must win the confidence of both sides in the conflict to make progress. Peace making requires considerable financial and human resources.

When Kenya assumed a major role in conflict resolution under the auspices of IGAD, it had to be prepared for the challenges ahead. One of the most difficult challenges was how to balance diplomatic relations with the respective neighbouring countries against the interests of their opponents, but remain objective. This aspect was particularly thorny in the Sudan peace process; Sudan commonly accused Kenya of supporting SPLM/A. Kenya could not have sided with one party and still maintain objectivity in the negotiations to the end. If Sudan did not have confidence in Kenya's ability to carry on with the negotiations, the CPA could not have been concluded.

Kenya invested its diplomatic capacity and financial capital in the search for solutions to conflicts in the Sudan, Somalia, Ethiopia and Uganda. It made it clear that its Foreign Policy objective was peace, security and political stability in the interest of countries in the Horn of Africa and the Great Lakes Region. Moi's overview of conflict resolution efforts across Africa crystallised during his time as the OAU Chairman from 1981-1983. This period earned him respect among his peers in the OAU and IGAD.

IGAD is a small and relatively financially weak organisation which requires considerable resources to carry out its mandate. Its focus on food security, environmental issues far outweigh the resources available to it through assessed annual contributions by member states. Conflict resolution requires much more. Member states concluded from the beginning that IGAD provides the best vehicle to tackle political issues in the Horn of Africa. Member states should honour their financial obligations to support peace initiatives. Kenya is among the countries which regularly meet their obligations on the assessed contributions to IGAD.

As pointed out in discussions on specific peace processes, a team of negotiators was appointed for each peace process to initiate contacts with the protagonists. Their brief included initial meetings at venues acceptable to them, assurance of their safety and the intentions of their counterparts in government. This had to be done before any arrangements were made for any travel. Kenya has, through its involvement in different peace processes, developed a pool of experienced negotiators which can be called upon to support mediation and peace efforts in the region. In addition, Kenya should establish post-conflict reconstruction mechanisms which it can deploy to assist countries emerging from conflict situations, to implement peace agreements.

Conflict resolution is costly, dangerous and unpredictable. Kenya should establish a fund to provide technical assistance for countries emerging from conflict in the region to give peace a chance. Such a fund should, together with private sector participation, consolidate Kenya's role in conflict resolution and peace-making. This is bound to strengthen Kenya's Foreign Policy on the promotion of peace, security and political stability to enhance cooperative relations in the sub-region. A successful Foreign Policy in this area will help the country to address political and security issues to secure its national interest.

International focus on the Horn of Africa
The Horn of Africa has come under sharp focus from the international community. Most countries in the sub-region have experienced political turmoil. The major upheavals include insecurity, political instability, internal conflicts, refugees, proliferation of SALW and terrorism. Unlike its neighbours, Kenya has been relatively peaceful; except for occasional ethnic clashes around its general elections cycle.

On the contrary, conflicts have arisen in Somalia, Ethiopia, Sudan, Uganda, South Sudan and the DRC. The circumstances prevailing in these countries have from time to time attracted the attention of the international community which is wary of protracted conflicts. Some conflicts have been running for decades. Kenya is genuinely concerned with instability among its neighbours because it becomes difficult for its citizens to engage in meaningful economic activities with the affected countries in the sub-region.

The Horn of Africa attracted intensive attention from the international community, specifically the West, after the terrorist attacks on the World Trade Centre (WTC) and the Pentagon on 11th September, 2001, in the USA. Woodward observes:

> "11 September, 2001 was to add to the claim that liberal states faced serious new and growing threats, and that intervention, including outright invasion, would not only liberate the peoples of at least some countries, but make the world safer for liberal democracies as a whole. It was to herald what was seen by some as a potential revolution to international relations, including a consolidation of the power of

Western liberal democracies led by the USA. In a speech at Chicago in 1999, on the 'Doctrine of the International Community' Britain's Tony Blair questioned the sanctity of national sovereignty, which seemed to justify Britain's role in the invasion of Afghanistan and then Iraq, he was to contribute to debates about 'the right to protect,' often abbreviated R2P."[58]

The international attention on the Horn of Africa and the Great Lakes Region was based on the threats by terrorist groups that they would target USA and British interests in the region. There were renewed calls for pro-active regional engagement to address longstanding insecurity, and political instability that made it easy for terrorists to carry out attacks. Some effort has been made in the Horn of Africa (through IGAD) and in the Great Lakes Region (through the International Conference on the Great Lakes Region).

However, more must be done to solicit the needed international assistance to deal with the security problem. Kenya should monitor developments among its trading partners in the sub-region and intervene where its interests are threatened, or just to be part of efforts to create peace or thwart any threats to peace in the two sub-regions. Kenya's Foreign Policy should take full advantage of its economic advantage to back up the country's position as a regional economic hub. The peace processes which Kenya has been directly involved in include: Ethiopia, Somalia, Uganda, Sudan, South Sudan and the DRC, in varying degrees.

Sudan peace process

Conflict in the Sudan between the Arabs in the north and blacks in the South may be traced to the conquest of Mohamed Ali, the Viceroy of Egypt, in the first quarter of the 19th century. At the time, Sudan did not exist as an entity. Abel Alier observes:

> "The Sudanic kingdoms of Sennar and Darfur between them controlled much of what is now called the Northern Sudan (current Republic of Sudan), but the Southern waterways of the Bahr el Ghazal, White Nile, and Sobat were occupied and dominated by the Dinka, Shilluk, Anuak and Nuer; four of the largest groups of Southern Sudanese peoples.... Mohamed Ali sought gold and slaves in the Sudan in order to establish autonomy from the Ottoman Sultan...The Sudan's gold was too little to meet Mohamed Ali's needs, and its population too small to provide

---

58   Peter Woodward, *Crisis in The Horn of Africa*.

the slaves for the army. It was a combination of these which drove the Turco-Egyptian administration further south to open lands which had previously lain beyond the reach of the old Sudanese kingdoms. And in this effort the Turco-Egyptian colonial power enlisted the support of the Northern Sudanese subjects, many of whom not only wanted to be relieved of the harsh demands now placed on them, but also saw an opportunity to make their fortunes in the new lands."[59]

The historical dimension of the conflict provides an insight into its complexity from the time of the Turco-Egyptian conquest through the colonial period to the CPA signed in 2005. The CPA was negotiated to end exploitation and marginalisation of majority blacks by the Arabs who controlled the levers of power in Khartoum and made it impossible for the people of the south to freely enjoy equal rights with them.

The struggle for self-determination began immediately after the independence of Sudan in 1956. The Anyanya I and Anyanya II peace agreements between the government of Sudan and southern Sudan collapsed because of their failure to address segregation, subjugation and exploitation committed by the Arab north against the predominantly Christian south.

The collapse of the Anyanya I and Anyanya II peace agreements strengthened the case for self-determination by the people of the south who then embarked on the fight for their liberation in 1983. That is the year when Colonel Dr. John Garang de Mabior, defected to found the SPLM/A while on a mission to quell rebellion in the south. He decided to fight against these injustices and other human rights violations. Dr. Garang was a highly-trained and respected military officer in the Sudanese army. Initially, Garang's primary intention was to win the argument for change in Sudan to allow for the respect for human rights for the people of Southern Sudan. Progressively, however, the issue of independence for South Sudan gained momentum on realising that the Arab north was not ready to change its mind-set.

Kenya became involved in the search for peace in Sudan for two reasons. First, to execute the mandate of IGAD. Kenya believed in making a contribution to the peace agenda in Africa and therefore, to the maintenance of international peace and security. Second, it did so in its national interest. Kenya took cognisance of its interests in a peaceful Sudan in the context of the use of the Nile waters and as a market for its goods. The primary objective in both circumstances was to secure peace, security and political

---

59   Abel Aller, *Southern Sudan: Too Many Agreements Dishonoured.*

stability and create an environment conducive for constructive economic engagement, investment and trade.

Dr. Garang deserted the Sudanese army because he was convinced that freedom and equality for the people of southern Sudan would be achieved through military means. However, IGAD, notably its member states of Kenya, Uganda, and Ethiopia prevailed on Dr. Garang and the SPLM/A to seek a negotiated settlement. Dr. Garang consulted a number of African countries such as Nigeria and Egypt. The latter played a role in these efforts which enabled him to secure their sympathy, understanding and support in negotiations with the Government of Sudan on the future of the people of Southern Sudan. IGAD appointed Kenya to lead the peace process.

Negotiations for a new agreement

IGAD's resolution arose out of its realisation that the conflict in Sudan would present serious security problems to the region, which would hamper the development of infrastructure and promotion of trade. It was aware of a possible dilemma for Kenya, a member of IGAD with which they maintained bilateral diplomatic relations and an immediate neighbour, leading the peace process. Kenya, however, was the best bet, given its relative economic strength and an anchor of humanitarian assistance to conflict states in its membership. It was critical to secure the agreement of the government of Sudan, which it did, to facilitate Kenya's search for a breakthrough in the conflict.

Kenya faced major obstacles in starting the Sudan peace process. It needed to strike a balance between the interests of the protagonists, guarantee the security of Dr. Garang, leader of the SPLM/A and his colleagues, and sustain its diplomatic relations with Sudan. The challenge was witnessed when agents linked to Libya made an attempt on Dr. Garang's life in 1986, as he was about to leave Uganda for his base in Southern Sudan.[60] The incident led to frosty relations and a major fallout between Dr. Garang and President Museveni for many years. It made Dr. Garang become suspicious of everybody. Kenya committed itself and worked around the clock to provide him with a safe house, which enabled him to re-locate his young family to Kenya. Kenya re-assured him and made him focus on the peace process. That opened the way for Dr. Garang to make international contacts, which became pivotal to the SPLM's ability to engage outside actors.

Once the personal security issue was settled, the Government of Sudan became suspicious of the level and nature of support for SPLM/A

---

60   https://paanluelwel.com/2011/08/08/biography-of-the-late-dr-john-garang-de-mabior/

by neighbouring countries, notably, Kenya and Ethiopia, which share long borders with Sudan. Kenya re-assured Sudan that its interest was to make peace and not help prosecute war. Although Sudan was not entirely satisfied, its position did not threaten the peace process. By the early 1990s, the Government of Sudan (GoS) and SPLM/A were in a position to deal with specific aspects of the conflict. Garang's diplomatic exposure gave him the confidence to tackle the real issues of the conflict. Kenya's strategy was to get the two parties to negotiate and agree on the DoP without which the CPA would never have been concluded.

Declaration of Principles

President Moi's behind the scenes team did outstanding work to endear Dr. Garang to Kenya. It enabled Dr. Garang to formally name a negotiating delegation to the mediation sessions under the then Minister for Foreign Affairs, Dr. Zachary Onyonka and Ambassador Bethwel Kiplagat, then Permanent Secretary in the same ministry, who helped negotiate the DoP. President Moi named Lt. General Lazarus Sumbeiywo, Chief negotiator for the peace process. Dr. Onyonka successfully negotiated eight of the ten items of the DoP which formed the pillars of the CPA. The most difficult issues namely, state and religion and self-determination for the people of southern Sudan, were negotiated under the chairmanship of Kalonzo Musyoka as Kenya's Minister for Foreign Affairs assisted by Lt. General Lazarus Sumbeiywo, a former Kenya Army Commander.

Lt. General Sumbeiywo's military background and training proved invaluable in re-assuring the protagonists than it would have been with traditional diplomats. Lt. General Sumbeiywo describes the complexity of the Sudan peace talks in a series of lectures on the Sudan peace process. He observes:

> "The essence of negotiations is for the parties to work together to solve a problem. Negotiations are a continuation of war in a different theatre of operations. It is not possible to switch off the war and then start the negotiations. War continues in a different theatre, in a different field."[61]

Signs of a breakthrough began to surface after complex negotiations between the GoS and the SPLM/A when they agreed on a set of principles dubbed Declaration of Principles (DoP) in 1994. The DoP formed the basis of the CPA, which both parties signed in 2005. The parties recognised that the root cause of the conflict was firmly anchored in the separation of

---

61   Lazarus Sumbeiywo, *To be A Negotiator: Strategies and Tactics*, published by the Centre for Security Studies (CSS), Swiss Federal Institute of Technology, ETH Zurich.

religion from the state and the economic marginalisation of the south by the north. It further brought out the issue of racism implicit in the policy of the Khartoum government to Arabize the south.

Kenya was tactful in handling SPLM/A while maintaining its relations with Sudan. The difficulty was how to ensure SPLM/A's confidence in the process in order to maintain their cooperation and participation. Dr. Garang undertook many diplomatic engagements with several African and world leaders, on recommendation from mediators or on his own initiative. He used the meetings to explain why southern Sudanese had resorted to armed struggle. He participated in meetings in Nairobi, Addis Ababa, Abuja, New York, and Washington DC, among many others. In one of the meetings, after the breakup of the Soviet Union, he was asked by an American diplomat in Nairobi whether he foresaw the breakup of Sudan after which the South could declare independence. Dr. Garang firmly rejected the idea of a breakup, observing that nothing momentous had happened in Sudan to justify such development. This was a clever way of fending off Sudanese government charges that he was seeking the disintegration of the country.

Towards the end of his reign, Moi pushed hard for the resolution of the problem. The CPA was, however, signed in 2005 under President Mwai Kibaki's watch, three years after Moi had left office. The CPA provided for a referendum after a six-year transition period, for the people of Southern Sudan to decide on separation with the north or stay together as one country. The referendum took place on 9th January, 2011 in which over 98% of the people of Southern Sudan voted for secession. South Sudan ultimately declared its independence from Sudan on the 9th July, 2011 under the terms of the CPA.

Unfortunately, Dr. John Garang did not live to usher South Sudan to independence. After leading the SPLM/A for twenty-one years, he was killed in June 2005, in a helicopter crash only twenty-one days after being sworn in as First Vice President of Sudan, under which he shared power with President Omar al-Bashir under the CPA – and also as President of Southern Sudan. Commander Salva Kiir Mayadit, then Dr. Garang's deputy, took over from Dr. Garang in both positions.

Death of Dr. John Garang

Dr. Garang's death was a major setback not only to South Sudan, but to the whole sub-region in general. The instability, ethnic tensions and power struggle erupted early in South Sudan's independence.

Dr. Garang's experience in managing the SPLM/A provided the inspiration and engagements; in the issues about the South Sudan/Kenya border, it might have helped find a solution to the 8 km disputed territory with Kenya between Nadapal and Napotpot River. The Nadapal post was constructed inside Kenya so that humanitarian and relief operations could be coordinated and despatched from there to Southern Sudan, during the liberation war against the government of Sudan.

South Sudan's power struggle strains relations with its neighbours

South Sudan was established and recognised as a state on 9th July 2011, on the implementation of the CPA between the government of Sudan and the SPLM/A. It came as a welcome relief to a region known for conflict, insecurity and political instability. Two years into its independence, a fierce power struggle erupted between President Salva Kiir Mayadit and Vice President Dr. Riek Machar, which overshadowed resolution of the remaining outstanding issues with Sudan over Abyei and South Kordofan boundary, and the export of South Sudan's oil through Sudan. South Sudan's expected role in the region's politics and diplomacy as a new player dissipated. Instead, IGAD's efforts were thrown back to deal with the internal power struggle, which quickly degenerated into ethnic infighting, principally between the Dinka and the Nuer, to which Salva Kiir and Riek Machar belong, respectively. The ethnic rivalry has engulfed other groups in the country. Some have deserted the government of Salva Kiir to pursue their own interests under ethnic cover.

South Sudan applied for and was admitted as the sixth member of the EAC in 2015. Its membership to the EAC confirmed its intention to cooperate more with its southern neighbours, than with Sudan in the north. Its diplomatic trajectory to the south enjoined it with the Nile waters riparian states of Kenya, Uganda and Ethiopia in battle with Sudan and Egypt in seeking a solution to the use of the Nile waters. The 1929 Nile Treaty signed by the UK, Egypt and Sudan, gave the two countries a disproportionate right to the waters of the Nile. Apart from the politics of the Nile waters, the expectations that South Sudan would consolidate its independence by focussing on economic and social programmes to bring about change in the lives of its people, were dashed by the political turmoil, which broke out in 2013.

South Sudan faces unresolved border issues with Kenya to the south and Sudan to the north. Its border with Kenya includes the Elemi Triangle which has been under Kenya's administrative control since the 1930s.

This was when two former colonial British Governors in Khartoum and Nairobi agreed that Nairobi should look after the Elemi Triangle because the area was too remote to control from Khartoum. The status quo was maintained by the independent governments in Sudan and Kenya. Previous attempts to resolve the matter never took off because of the conflict in Sudan between the north and south.

The second unresolved border issue between South Sudan and Kenya relates to the remainder of the border with Kenya, up to the border with Uganda. The international border lies about thirty kilometres north, parallel to Nadapal at Nakodok. The post at Nadapal was constructed to assist the SPLM/A coordinate the distribution of humanitarian assistance to its people in southern Sudan. Kenya and South Sudan understand the situation very well. It should be possible to reach an agreement to delineate the border, install beacons and secure it in the interest of both countries, now that South Sudan has gained its independence. Resolution of the border issues will facilitate meaningful bilateral relations and consolidate regional security and stability.

Impact of South Sudan power struggle on regional economies

South Sudan faced potential post-independence conflict from the beginning. The power struggle within the ruling SPLM/A characterised its evolution since it was founded in 1983, into the political and military machine that brought the government of Sudan to the negotiating table. The movement comprises groups of militia armies which came together to fight a common enemy – the government of Sudan, whose policies alienated South Sudanese on racial and religious grounds. Riek Machar was one of its leaders who flirted with Khartoum on many occasions. Dr. Garang managed to contain him. Competing ethnic interests fuelled by fierce personal struggle for power by South Sudan's senior politicians must be resolved in a power-sharing arrangement to give peace a chance, in order to unleash South Sudan's enormous potential for economic development.

The conflict and struggle for power in South Sudan revolves around personal egos of the principal actors fighting for supremacy and control of the party and country. In the early years of the struggle against Khartoum, Dr. Riek Machar was among politicians from the south who broke away from mainstream SPLM to form SPLM–Nasr. He negotiated with President Omar al-Bashir to join the government in Khartoum. He was appointed as an advisor.

The other rebel leader was Dr. Lam Akol, the first black Foreign Affairs Minister of Sudan during the transition period. He was courted by Khartoum to divide and weaken the liberation struggle. Khartoum's intention was to direct attention away from injustices at the heart of the rebellion namely: the ideological war against economic deprivation, marginalisation and racial and religious segregation by the Arab north against the people of Southern Sudan, whom the north referred to in derogatory terms.

The rivalry between President Salva Kiir and Dr. Riek Machar is vicious and deadly for South Sudan. President Salva Kiir is simply a soldier who rose to the top under Dr. John Garang; and probably did not cultivate leadership qualities until Garang's death. Dr. Riek Machar considers himself an intellectual who had leadership ambitions from the beginning. Salva Kiir, however, believes that Riek Machar has little or no regard for him; he looks down upon him. The fight for supremacy between them thrust the country back into conflict with significant impact on regional peace and stability.

The conflict came at a time when border issues with Sudan, specifically on oil rich Abyei and North Kordofan, had not been resolved. IGAD, which negotiated the CPA, was once again called into action to save South Sudan from this unnecessary internecine struggle. A peace agreement signed by the two leaders provided a road map for an inclusive government, but effectively ended when the two fell out in 2013. It was blown apart with events which started in December, 2014, when government troops stormed Dr. Machar's house on suspicion of spearheading a military take-over.

The countries in East Africa, the Horn of Africa and the Great Lakes Region worry about instability in South Sudan because of its implications on peace and security in the sub-regions. It was expected that the independence of South Sudan would usher in a period of peace and tranquillity to allow its economy to recover from years of neglect and deprivation. The move by South Sudan to join the EAC, which Kenya supported right from the beginning, might have been in vain if South Sudan remains mired in conflict and political turmoil.

Instability in South Sudan could deal a severe blow to the realisation of the proposed construction of the LAPSSET transport corridor. The development of Lamu port, rail, road and optic fibre cable connection via Isiolo to Juba, and Addis Ababa is now in jeopardy. LAPSSET, however, promises huge economic benefits for Kenya, South Sudan and Ethiopia. South Sudan and Ethiopia are potentially huge markets for Kenyan products.

South Sudan was interested in LAPSSET after independence, a viable commercial venture and important contribution to overall infrastructure development in East Africa. Its link to Ethiopia would be important in addressing some of the communication obstacles in the Horn of Africa, as well as lifting the hopes of populations which have felt marginalised for years.

President Salva Kiir's and Dr. Riek Machar's forces' clash in July 2016, at the Presidential palace in Juba, complicated the situation even further. Dr. Machar fled to the DRC from where he proceeded to Khartoum, Sudan. Salva Kiir sacked and replaced him, effectively side-lining Machar from the political process agreed to under IGAD. The disruption led to further displacement of the population and put into question the role of the UN peace-keeping force in Juba. In response, the UN Secretary General sacked the Kenyan Commander of the force, prompting Kenya to pull out its contingent from South Sudan. The decision to withdraw Kenyan troops reached between the UN Secretary General and Kenya reflects the acknowledgement of Kenya's role as a central player in peace efforts in South Sudan. As a country, which has invested in peace in South Sudan, the withdrawal served no useful purpose in Kenya's long-term strategic Foreign Policy objectives in the region.

Kenya's interest in the peace efforts in South Sudan has always been to guarantee security and political stability in the region for its long term economic interests in trade and investment. This will help consolidate South Sudan's membership to the EAC and commitment to integration as a means of realising its own development objectives.

Uganda peace process

Uganda lies to the west of Kenya. It is the most direct hinterland country linked to the Mombasa port via the NCTS. Uganda's significance to modern Kenya may be traced to the first railway line built by the British in 1901, linking present day Kenya and Uganda from Mombasa to Lake Victoria. It was named the Uganda Railway. As part of British East Africa, Kenya was considered a transit territory by the British who preferred the climatic conditions in Uganda, which they regarded as the most fertile part of British East Africa. These historical links turned Uganda into the automatic and number one trading partner for Kenya. Kenya carefully watched any developments in Uganda because of the strategic economic relations between the two countries.

Uganda attained its independence from British rule in 1962. Soon after its independence, signs of potential conflict began to emerge over the role of the Kabaka of Buganda, and other kingdoms, in relation to the central government. Four years later, in 1966, Milton Obote the then Prime Minister, abolished the Kingdom of Buganda. He later stormed the palace, forcing Kabaka Muteesa II into exile the same year. This situation created tension, mistrust and hostility which Idi Amin, the then Armed Forces commander, later took advantage of, and overthrew Obote in 1971. Although Obote's overthrow by Idi Amin was initially welcomed in Uganda, it plunged the country into turmoil, turning Uganda hitherto referred as the "pearl" of Africa into a pariah state with a dysfunctional government.

Amin's military take-over presented Kenya with a very difficult Foreign Policy choice at a bilateral level and within the EAC. Amin's rule was anathema to Kenya, it created serious complications for the country from having to defend its position of recognising Amin's rule, to fending off territorial claims on the country and ensuring the functioning of the authority of the then EAC. Kenya's ambivalence led some pundits to conclude that Kenya did not have a clear Foreign Policy or even a Foreign Policy at all. Comparisons were made with Tanzania, whose President Julius Nyerere, denounced Amin's coup and refused to deal with him thereby paralysing the authority of the EAC.

Kenya's position on Amin's take-over of power in Uganda was dictated by the extensive economic ties between the two countries. The umbilical connections between Kenya and Uganda made it impossible for the former to give a harsh verdict on the coup. Amin's reign was characterised by high drama. His wild territorial claims on Kenya forced President Jomo Kenyatta to modernise its armed forces to neutralise the problem.

Kenya's ambivalent position ensured continuity in trade as well as a guaranteed trade route for Burundi, Rwanda and eastern DRC. Although Kenya tried to justify its policy under the guise that it recognised *countries,* not *governments,* the position made it appear insensitive to the plight of Ugandans under Amin's brutal dictatorship. Throughout Amin's rule, Uganda probably experienced the darkest period in its independence history. It was a period when many prominent Ugandan professionals, intellectuals, and businessmen were either killed or forced into exile in droves, depriving the country of skilled manpower and leading to the collapse of institutions, organisations and businesses. The country's economy spiralled downwards. Although a lot has been done to revive the economy since President Yoweri Museveni assumed power in 1986, Uganda continues to nurse the scars of Amin's and Obote's rules.

Amin made a fundamental error of judgement when he made wild territorial claims on Tanzania, like he had done to Kenya and went on to invade the north-western part of the country. We may never know his calculation. Perhaps he felt that Tanzania would not react with equal force as Kenya had done. It was the straw that broke the camel's back; President Nyerere mobilised public support, and, riding on international opinion, against Amin, proceeded to invade, and ultimately drove him out of power in 1979, into exile in Libya and later Saudi Arabia, where he died on 16th August, 2003.

Milton Obote, the long-time friend and comrade of Nyerere, returned to power, courtesy of Tanzania's invasion. It soon became clear that Obote had learnt nothing from his first tenure. The second tenure of Obote (1979-1984) was marred by gross human rights violations and assassinations, which isolated him from even his close friend and mentor, President Julius Nyerere. He was deposed in a military coup in 1984 and fled into exile in Zambia where he died on 10th October, 2005.

When Moi succeeded Jomo Kenyatta in 1978, Kenya shifted gear to become pro-actively engaged in peace initiatives, out of the realisation that political stability in the sub-region was vital for its own economic development. Kenya's involvement in peace efforts in Uganda were based on Uganda being, by far, the largest single market for Kenya's products in the world and has been for a long time, ahead of Tanzania in the sub-region and the UK.[62] Uganda links Kenya to Rwanda, Burundi and eastern DRC, which are important markets for Kenya, and depend on the NCTS for their external trade.

After the overthrow of Obote while in his second reign, a period of an uncertain transition took place in Uganda with a turnover of three presidents in quick succession between 1985 and 1986 when Yoweri Museveni overran Kampala and took over the reins of power; before the ink on a peace agreement brokered by Moi a month earlier had dried. The peace agreement with the Okello government sought a cease-fire and a coalition government in Uganda. Museveni assumed control of the country, forcing Okello to flee north into Sudan.[63] Moi considered this development as a slap in the face for all the effort he had made in the search for a political solution. This was later to be a factor in the frosty personal relations between Museveni and Moi who kept a respectful, but polite distance from Museveni throughout his tenure.[64]

---

62   https://www.businessdailyafrica.com/economy/Uganda-overtakes-South-Africa-in-Kenya-exports/3946234-4291772-fbd3idz/index.html

63   http://www.monitor.co.ug/OpEd/columnists/CharlesOnyangoObbo/Flashback-1985-Nairobi--peace-jokes--Museveni-is-older/878504-3260634-6pe5f9/index.html

64   https://www.standardmedia.co.ke/article/2000002115/moi-and-museveni-s-love-hate-relationship

Most public policies are, in general, compromises. The framework of each policy determines the position Kenya takes on any issue at home or abroad. The dynamics, such as economic and strategic considerations, define the pursuit of specific policy objectives. It is not surprising that some of the Foreign Policy decisions Kenya has made have left mixed interpretations on what it really stands for. Its decision to continue normal business with Uganda after Amin's military take-over stood out as ill-advised when Amin's brutality became evident. In its defence, Kenya used one of the OAU's cardinal principles of non-interference in the internal affairs of other member countries to justify its stand. This position enabled Kenya to turn a blind eye to Amin and the atrocities he committed against the people of Uganda. But this stand denied it the moral authority to deal with the wayward leadership in Uganda, which was out of tune with democratic principles to which Kenya subscribed.

Territorial claims by Uganda on the rocky Migingo Islands were initially made during Kibaki's presidency; coming long after similar claims on Kenyan territory by Amin in the 1970s. The purpose of Uganda's claim was to control resources around the island. Coincidentally, the claim came at a time when there was political divide and power struggle in Kenya. Such internal feuds had greatly weakened state institutions, reducing their capacity to act quickly against such threats. Kenya opted for a diplomatic solution to the problem and made it known that it would not go to war over the matter. Both sides claim to be making progress, but Migingo is likely to remain a potential source of conflict between the two countries.

Uganda's calculation may underline its decision to construct an oil pipeline through Tanzania, an obviously longer route, and to de-prioritise the construction of the SGR to link Rwanda to Mombasa port.[65] The dynamics in relations between Kenya and Uganda point to a review by the latter of its total dependence on Kenya for its external trade. There are closer consultations with Tanzania on the development of infrastructure projects intended to diversify Uganda's access to international markets via alternative routes. Kenya's Foreign Policy should address issues behind Uganda's policy towards Kenya. As staunch members of the EAC, IGAD and the Common Market for East and Southern African Countries (COMESA), Kenya and Uganda have the potential to grow by leaps in the years to come by working together.

---

65   https://observer.ug/news/headlines/57627-uganda-tanzania-set-new-fast-track-deadline-for-oil-pipeline.html

Ethiopia peace process

Kenya's Foreign Policy towards Ethiopia has overcome many obstacles since Kenya's independence. Founding President Jomo Kenyatta sustained very cordial relations with Emperor Haile Selassie until he was overthrown by Mengistu Haile Mariam in 1974. Jomo Kenyatta refused to warm up to Mengistu and was, particularly, upset by the brutal murder of the emperor. Mengistu's reign ushered Ethiopia into a period of turmoil and instability. Moi took a pragmatic view of relations between Kenya and Ethiopia and decided to engage with Mengistu. Resistance at home to Mengistu grew until Mengistu realised that he would not win. He turned to Kenya for mediation.

Kenya was invited to mediate in the Ethiopian crisis by Mengistu who sought Moi's intervention when the port of Massawa was taken by the Eritrean People's Liberation Front (EPLF) and the Tigrinya People's Liberation Front (TPLF). The loss of Massawa paralysed Ethiopia's external trade, which forced it to shift to Djibouti. Mengistu had developed close relations with Moi for unexpected reasons. Mengistu agreed with Moi's defence of black people, alongside Kaunda of Zambia, Mobutu Sese Seko of Zaire (now the DRC) and Abdu Diouf of Senegal. All believed that the black person was despised, exploited, marginalised and disrespected everywhere in the world. This view held them together even though each pursued completely different political philosophies.

Moi lent diplomatic support to both Isaias Afwerki under the EPLF and the TPLF under Meles Zenawi to negotiate the latter's secession once they captured power in Addis Ababa. When Mengistu was overthrown, it was Moi he turned to for safe transit arrangements to exile in Zimbabwe. Mengistu's down fall created the conditions for a negotiated settlement. Meles Zenawi and Isaias Afwerki were able to agree on Eritrea's independence in fulfilment of their strategy to overthrow, first the Emperor and later Mengistu. President Moi's role did not have IGAD or the AU's mandate. But, its success must go down as another contribution by Kenya to peace in Africa. Eritrea had fought for more than 30 years to break away from what it described as Ethiopian colonialism under Emperor Haile Selassie and Mengistu Haile Mariam. Its transition to an independent country was made possible through the Moi facilitated negotiations.

Relations between Ethiopia and Eritrea deteriorated in the 1990s when the then Ethiopian Prime Minister, Meles Zenawi fell out with Eritrean President, Isaias Afwerki over territorial dispute which culminated in a boundary war and severance of diplomatic relations, air, road and rail links between the two countries. The stalemate lasted for 20 years (until May 2018) when Ethiopia accepted the UN Tribunal's decision on its boundary with Eritrea. Resumption of bilateral relations are likely to reduce the cost of Ethiopia's external trade through the port of Massawa in Eritrea, and improve chances of establishing durable peace in the Horn of Africa since the two countries ended military hostilities in 1998.

In November, 2018, the UN Security Council, through a resolution, removed the sanctions it had imposed on Eritrea in 2007. The decision has made it possible for Eritrea to resume full exercise of its rights, duties and responsibilities as a normal state.

Somalia reconciliation process

Kenya's Foreign Policy on Somalia takes into account its (Kenya's) ethnic-Somali population which occupies a large part of the territory along Kenya's border with Somalia. The geographical location of its Somali population was the target of Somalia's Greater Somalia Policy, which it declared at its independence in 1960. The policy was conceived to address the consequences of Somalia's double British and Italian colonial heritage under which the British controlled Somaliland and the Italians controlled the rest of Somalia. The two heritages offered contrasting colonial administrations. Somalia's independent leaders resolved to bring all Somali-speaking people under one flag, which they designed to incorporate five stars representing the geographical location and spread of Somali speaking people namely; Somalia (Italian), Somaliland (British), Djibouti (French), Ogaden (Ethiopia) and Northern Frontier District (Kenya).

Somalia stated at independence that it intended to have all Somalis into one country, which informed its Greater Somalia policy. The policy was symbolised by five stars on its flag, which referred to two stars representing Somali population in Somalia itself – (formerly under Italian and British colonial administrations respectively) and a star each for the populations in Djibouti, Ethiopia and Kenya. Somaliland was under the British rule while the rest of Somalia was under Italian rule. Their separate colonial heritages played a big role in Somaliland's desire to break away from the rest of Somalia in its quest to become independent.

The Greater Somalia policy caused problems to Kenya, which led to the Shifta insurrection; and to Ethiopia, which caused the Ogaden war in the 1960s and 1970s respectively.[66] Somali citizens in Somaliland were never quite comfortable in Somalia. They believed that the state favoured

---

66   https://www.standardmedia.co.ke/article/2000041423/kenya-s-first-secessionist-war

the former Italian-controlled part of the country. Somalis are one people who speak one language, share one culture, and predominantly profess the Islamic faith. But clan loyalties among them are extremely strong and override most considerations when it comes to clan interests.

Somalia does not appear to be willing to enter into negotiations towards Somaliland's independence. Somaliland will continue to agitate for full independence and recognition by the IGAD, AU and the UN. It remains unrecognised because Somalia has refused to entertain such a prospect. Somalia itself needs to work hard to contain the other regions of Puntland and Jubaland as building blocks to save Somalia from disintegration. Somaliland appears to be better organised than the rest of Somalia.

Peter Woodward has written about developments in the run up to Somalia's independence in 1960, where he shows a strong nationalist movement among Somali youths. Its objective was to bring all Somali speaking people under one flag. It targeted Somali people who straddle the common borders and in essence constituted territorial claims on those countries. He observes that:

> "After World War II the Somalis showed the beginnings of a nationalist movement, similar to those growing in so many areas still under European rulers. The movement known as the Somalia Youth League (SYL) began in 1943 and spread such that it eventually led towards democracy, encouraged by the UN. Following elections in 1959, Britain and Italy encouraged their respective territories to come together in one state that became fully independent in 1960. There were hopes that with one language, culture and religion Somalia might be well placed to forge a new nation. However, from the outset, the new government was keen to remind the international community that there were still many Somalis in the neighbouring territories of Ethiopia, Djibouti and Kenya. Only two points on the five-pointed star of the new country's national flag had come together, and irredentist impulses were strong."[67]

The nationalist approach adopted at independence under the guise of the Greater Somalia Policy ran into problems of clan supremacy with fierce competition for resources and control of the authority at the centre. Somalia embarked on a dangerous mission to secure its Greater Somalia policy, through support for the Shifta rebellion in the then NFD of Kenya; and the Ogaden War with Ethiopia to expand Somalia to incorporate the Somali populations outside Somalia. Kenya was well aware of Somalia's strategy at independence and was fully appraised about the potential for

---

67   Peter Woodward, *Crisis in the Horn of Africa.*

political instability from that end. It was evident from the beginning that the internal political situation in Somalia itself was precarious and showed signs of deterioration from the early days of its independence.

Ever since the Shifta insurgence, relations between Kenya and Somalia never blossomed as is expected of neighbouring countries. President Moi made the first state visit to Somalia by a Kenyan head of state in 1979, a year into his presidency. Moi's objective for the state visit was to find ways to neutralise the anxiety of ethnic Somalis in Kenya about their citizenship in the context of Somalia's policy of Greater Somalia. No joint communiqué` was issued at the end of the visit, which indicates that there was no agreement on any bilateral issue. It showed that President Siad Barre was not ready to be seen publicly as having compromised on the policy of Greater Somalia.

Moi began to promote Kenyan-ethnic Somalis to senior positions in government to demonstrate inclusiveness in the Kenyan society as a way of addressing their grievances. Many rose through the ranks in the civil service to hold senior positions while others were appointed to political positions, including to the cabinet. General Mahmoud Mohamed rose through military ranks and was appointed Chief of General Staff of the armed forces of Kenya in 1986, taking over from the long serving Major General Jackson Mulinge.

President Siad Barre's overthrow in 1991 exacerbated the conflict in Somalia, leading to the breakdown of law and order. Since then, the situation in Somalia remains the biggest security challenge and threat to Kenya. The clan differences and competition saw Somalia disintegrate into a failed state. The vacuum created at the centre destroyed any capacity Somalia may have had to manage its affairs. The clan warlords balkanised Somalia into spheres of influence and power which paralysed its government, worsened insecurity and brought about political instability.

Kenya was requested to lead IGAD efforts to resolve Somalia's problem. It hosted the main warlords for exploratory peace talks, many of whom were hostile to each other. Kenya believed that an all-inclusive approach was best suited for Somalia. Sessions were held variously in Nairobi and Eldoret in the hope of a break through, but these efforts encountered the traditional obstacles of clan competition and confrontation. The venues for the sessions were carefully chosen with a view to confining the delegates in one place in an attempt to make them bond and possibly begin to develop a common view of their country. It was a daring attempt, given the explosive tempers exhibited by Somalia delegations. After many months of haggling, eating together, completely cut off from the rest of the world, they began to see themselves, at least superficially, as Somalis with a common destiny.

A break-through occurred in 2004, in Nairobi, Kenya, when the warlords signed on to transitional arrangements, which led to the formation of the TFG of Somalia in which different clans agreed to share power. Abdullahi Yusuf from the Darod clan was appointed President, Prof. Mohamed Ghedi from Hawiye clan as Prime Minister and Sharif Hassan Sheik Adan from Majaritan clan as Speaker in a 4-4-1 formula, which took into account numerical strengths of the clans. In general, clan balance is essential to political organisation in Somalia as it can make or break any alliance, if the representation is seen as skewed. Furthermore, regional balance must be taken care of within the federal context when designing a roadmap for a resolution of the stalemate in Somalia. The regional interests of breakaway regions such as Puntland and Galmudug must be considered. Somaliland did not participate in the process. Clan interests must be taken into account to bring everyone on board before securing sustainable peace.

Implementation of the TFG became possible after an agreement was signed with the Somalia Reconciliation and Restoration Council (SRRC) which had opposed its formation. The agreement based on the power-sharing formula by the clans provided inclusive participation by the various clans and agreed to establish Transitional Federal Institutions which included a Transitional Parliament comprising 275 members, a Transitional Government headed by a President with a mandate to appoint a Council of Ministers including the Prime Minister, and a Transitional Charter, which would form the basis of a new Federal Constitution.

Kenya agreed to host the TFG and Somalia's transitional parliament in Nairobi due to the prevailing security situation in Mogadishu, provided it would relocate to Somalia at the earliest opportune time. It was clear to all that the date for the relocation of the TFG and other state institutions to Mogadishu was impossible to predict. The longer the relocation took, the more difficult it became to sustain the relief and general satisfaction generated at the formation of the TFG. It required dramatic measures to facilitate their relocation. Kenya was apprehensive that the TFG would become irrelevant to Somalia before it took its seat in Mogadishu.

Kenya faced a dilemma of appearing to have two presidents, its own and the Somalia one, that is, the longer Somalia's president stayed in Nairobi. Pictures of Somalia Members of Parliament seen fighting during their sessions in Nairobi seemed to show lack of respect for their hosts. The Kenyan public was not amused with such indiscipline. Mogadishu increasingly became marginalised with the President of Somalia exercising his functions on Kenyan, rather than on Somalia territory. Somalia MPs, sitting in Nairobi, became unruly and uncontrollable. Many of their sessions degenerated into physical fights with heavy exchange of blows. This culture was alien to Kenya, whose politics was generally confrontational but did not degenerate into such physical fights.

A year after the formation of the TFG, Kenya engineered the relocation of both the TFG and the Parliament to Mogadishu. Kenya reached this conclusion when it became clear that relocation to Mogadishu was becoming increasingly difficult, and was in danger of not taking place at all. The TFG was free to relocate to any other place in Somalia. The message was communicated to President Abdullahi Yusuf Ahmed that arrangements would be made for him, at a mutually acceptable time, to call on President Kibaki and bid him farewell, and then relocate his government to Somalia territory.

For the first time since President Siad Barre, a President of Somalia inspected a guard of honour mounted by the Armed forces of Kenya, after which President Yusuf took off ostensibly for Somalia. He flew instead to Djibouti where he stayed for some time before he eventually proceeded to Somalia after appropriate arrangements had been made for his stay. The TFG eventually established itself in Mogadishu within a year and began the process of taking control of areas occupied by different warlords. This process has been hampered by terrorist groups which established bases in the country because of its weak institutions. The most violent of them all is Al-Shabaab.

Kenya's Foreign Policy on Tanzania

Kenya's Foreign Policy on Tanzania is founded on peaceful co-existence and non-interference in each other's internal affairs. Kenya seeks friendship and markets for its goods and services. Its economic development model spurred faster growth than was the case in Tanzania, which opted for a socialist economic model. In the 1970s, President Nyerere closed the common border with Kenya citing Kenya's interference in Tanzania's internal affairs.[68] The real reason was the contrast in the economic performance between the two countries. Kenya enjoyed robust economic growth with a thriving public and private sector through partnerships, while Tanzania's socialist-oriented economy stagnated with severe commodity shortages. The closure of the border crossing point did not restrict people-people cultural relationships. The economic activities continued along the rest of the border throughout the period.

---

68   https://www.washingtonpost.com/archive/politics/1977/04/27/kenya-tanzania-border-tension-rises/3d85043b-bddb-4aaa-8265-659c40b56ec6/?noredirect=on&utm_term=.7867cfbcb154

Tanzania is the only country among Kenya's neighbours to have escaped internal political instability. As the second largest market for Kenyan exports in Africa after Uganda, and the leading investment destination for Kenya, Tanzania is an important Foreign Policy focus for Kenya. It is among the top five countries Kenyans have invested in. The main areas of investments include: manufacturing, agriculture and services such as banking, insurance and security. Tanzania's traditional suspicions about Kenya at a bilateral level and within the EAC is bound to affect the pace of integration, as the two countries are the leading economies within the community.

Bilateral issues of concern can be solved through negotiations at local or national levels. The ban on Kenyan-registered tourist vehicles from operating on Tanzanian roads;[69] confiscation and auction of cattle owned by Kenyan-Maasai seeking green pastures in Tanzania[70] in keeping with age old tradition, and the destruction of day-old chicks, in September, 2017, bought in Kenya for breeding, need not attract customs penalties.[71] Both countries would advance the course of cooperation and integration in East Africa, if they collaborated in addressing trans-boundary security issues to promote meaningful economic activities along the common border. The regular suspicion, mistrust and tit for tat actions undermine the agreed road map for integration under the EAC Treaty.

Tanzania's role in the 2007 election crisis in Kenya

Tanzania played a leading role in resolving the 2007/2008 post-election crisis in Kenya through both retired President Benjamin Mkapa and President Jakaya Mrisho Kikwete. Tanzania was drafted in the team with the task of returning peace to Kenya under the auspices of the AU. Retired President Mkapa was a member of the African eminent persons alongside Graca Machel, who assisted Kofi Annan to negotiate the Kenya National Accord.[72] President Kikwete witnessed the signing of the agreement at the time. This role made Tanzania assume a high diplomatic profile in the region.

---

69 https://www.google.com/search?ei=hldTW_PuOc-DsAfFsr_QC
w&q=ban+on+Kenya+registered+tourist+vehicles+&oq=ban+on
1l2.5330.5330.0.7070.1.1.0.0.0.0.299.299.2-1.1.0....0...1.2.64.psy-ab..0.1.299....0.-2VG_
M1NVFg

70 https://www.the-star.co.ke/news/2017/10/21/vacate-or-we-auction-your-cattle-tanzania-tells-maasai-pastoralists_c1656127

71 https://www.nation.co.ke/news/Tanzania-destroys-another-5-000-chicks/1056-4303090-r1idwuz/index.html

72 http://www.klrc.go.ke/index.php/mandate/national-accord-and-agenda-four-commissions

Tanzania harbours an ambition of becoming the first port of call in East Africa. In a space of less than five years, Tanzania hosted two sitting US presidents in quick succession – George W. Bush in 2007 and Barack Obama in 2010. President Obama's visit took place at a time when Kenya faced serious governance issues with its development partners. But more specifically, President Uhuru Kenyatta still faced trial at the ICC. President George W. Bush announced US contribution to the Global Fund for Africa in Tanzania.[73]

Barack Obama's visit to Tanzania during his first term in office was, particularly, painful to many Kenyans who had hoped that he would visit the country of his father's roots before any other in the region. That is when Kenyans appreciated that Obama was first, the president of the USA who was elected to serve US interests. Nostalgic feelings and demands from the country of his father's birth were a side issue.

Mozambique peace process

Political disagreements which led to military confrontation between the Front for the Liberation of Mozambique (FRELIMO) and the RENAMO were ideological.[74] FRELIMO fought for the independence of Mozambique, heavily supported by the Soviet Union while RENAMO was a creation of apartheid South Africa, which wanted to help install friendly regimes around it for self-preservation. RENAMO received military and financial support from the apartheid regime to pursue its objectives. FRELIMO, on the other hand, was supported by frontline independent African states such as Tanzania, Zambia, Angola and Zimbabwe (after its independence in 1980). Zimbabwe had a direct interest in peace in Mozambique because the port of Beira in Mozambique was critical for its external trade.

When President Chissano concluded that the conflict had reached a stalemate, he invited Kenya and Zimbabwe in 1989 through recommendation by some African leaders, including Abdu Diouf of Senegal, Kenneth Kaunda of Zambia, Robert Mugabe of Zimbabwe and Mobutu Sese Seko of the then Zaire. Similar recommendations came from religious and philanthropic groups which had great respect for Kenya's humanitarian efforts in Southern Sudan. Kenya saw the opportunity to project itself on the world stage after the end of the Cold War, which had somewhat side-lined it from its position as a major player on the continent to the periphery. Kenya was considered a beacon of peace in a

---

73   https://georgewbush-whitehouse.archives.gov/infocus/africa/trip2008/
74   RENAMO was fighting against FRELIMO's attewmpts to establish a socialist one-party state.

politically volatile region, fraught with insecurity, conflict and political instability.

President Moi's participation in the Tripartite Summit and eventual involvement in the Mozambique peace process elicited mixed reactions from Zimbabwe, due to its direct transit interests through Mozambique. Moi's experience in peace initiatives in the Sudan, Somalia, Uganda and Zaire (now the DRC) was a major factor which compensated for any misgivings on Kenya's interest in the matter. After consultations, President Mugabe decided that it would be better for Kenya to lead the efforts rather than Zimbabwe because it was in a more neutral position. Zimbabwe on the contrary was an immediate neighbour with direct interest in transport through Mozambique for its external trade. Mugabe argued that Zimbabwe's proximity to Mozambique was too close for the comfort of RENAMO. A perception that Zimbabwe was not neutral would have been counter-productive. But he promised to assist the process in whatever way possible. President Chissano's choice of Moi was vindicated when RENAMO's leaders more readily accepted Moi than would have been the case with a socialist-leaning leader.

Kenya made great efforts to bring together the protagonists since they were not particularly known to Kenyan officials. Initial contacts with the protagonists were facilitated by four religious leaders namely: the Anglican Archbishop Sengulane, Cardinal Dos Santos, Rev. Mochache and Archbishop Gonzales of Beira who later brought on board St. Egidio Catholic order in Rome, Italy, in the final phase of the peace process. Involvement of church leaders in the peace process came as a huge relief to both FRELIMO and RENAMO leaders and the negotiators.

Kenya overcame many obstacles to balance the interests of Mozambique and RENAMO, a rebel movement financed by apartheid South Africa. Mozambique was convinced that South Africa was responsible for the death of its first president, Samora Moisés Machel in a mysterious air crash on its (South Africa's) territory. South Africa was clearly fearful of a domino effect in the increasing number of leftist governments opposed to its regime. Its support for RENAMO was not accidental, but was intended to destabilise the new government in Maputo and possibly overthrow it. Zimbabwe, supported FRELIMO as an appreciation of its support in the final onslaught on the Ian Smith illegal regime. International interests at play in Mozambique were overwhelming. Tiny Rowland, whose company, London Rhodesia (Lonrho), had mining interests in Mozambique and harboured Cecil Rhodes' colonial dream of linking Cape town to Cairo, was an active player.

President Chissano's decision to opt for a negotiated solution meant that grievances which made RENAMO take up arms could be addressed. He acknowledged RENAMO's opposition to the Marxist system advocated by FRELIMO. Mozambique's apprehension about the support RENAMO was getting from South Africa in turn attracted western support as a front against communist expansion in Africa. It was critical for the Mozambican government to recognise RENAMO as a legitimate political player for the negotiations to start and move the peace process forward. That would mean guaranteeing safe passage for RENAMO leaders once arrangements had been made to take them out from the forest in Mozambique for negotiation meetings. President Mugabe's decision to allow Zimbabwe to step aside in favour of Kenya removed what would have become a potentially explosive cross-border misunderstanding and strengthened Kenya's role as a neutral broker.

Mozambique's flexibility proved helpful in the logistics of securing safe passage for RENAMO leaders to and from their base at Gorongosa. President Chissano agreed to this arrangement on condition that his government was informed of any such movements. Kenya's delegation left Maputo trying to figure out how to reach out to RENAMO to assure them of the government of Mozambique's sincerity and willingness to negotiate a settlement. The safe passage of RENAMO's leaders was the biggest challenge to overcome. It was a challenge to select a third country, acceptable to both the government of Mozambique and RENAMO which RENAMO leaders could transit through.

It took extensive consultations with leaders in the three probable countries and church leaders to persuade RENAMO leader Afonso Dhlakama and his group to venture outside Mozambique. In the end, only two countries were considered for transit – Tanzania and Malawi. Tanzania was ruled out on account of the strong bonds of friendship between Tanzanian leaders and FRELIMO leaders dating back to the Mozambican liberation years. RENAMO leaders settled on Malawi, arguing that Tanzania's vast territory was too insecure due to its difficult terrain and poor flight connections.

Afonso Dhlakama agreed to transit through Malawi because of the common ideological persuasion with its president, Dr. Kamuzu Banda. Both leaders were opposed to socialism, which FRELIMO espoused in Mozambique. Furthermore, Malawi itself received considerable support from white South Africa – including planning and construction of its capital, Lilongwe. Another factor in favour of Malawi as transit route was its proximity to Manicaland province of Mozambique which RENAMO controlled. It was more practical for its leaders to get out of Mozambique and back without facing too much danger.

Kenya accepted to play a role in the peace talks without any pre-conditions. It was, however, conscious of the enormous financial and diplomatic capital it would invest in the process. Kenya did not use a structured method of engagement through its Ministry of Foreign Affairs. Instead, the process was organised around personalities in government at the behest of President Moi, headed by Ambassador Bethwel A. Kiplagat, then Permanent Secretary in the ministry. Kenya employed shuttle diplomacy, dispatching special envoys between Mozambique and Malawi, to agree on logistics for the movement of the rebel leaders for consideration and consensus.

Mozambique's agreement with Malawi on the transport arrangements signalled the first sign of movement forward. RENAMO was difficult to bring on board because they needed to be assured of safe passage, bearing in mind that their leaders were on the run from the Mozambique government. This required quiet diplomacy to deal with the logistics as well as keep Zimbabwe on board, even when it considered RENAMO as fighting a proxy war of destabilisation against frontline states on behalf of Apartheid South Africa.

Like in other peace processes in which the movement of rebel leaders is a challenge, so was it with moving RENAMO's leader Afonso Dhlakama, out of Manicaland in Mozambique to meetings and back safely. He was afraid that he could be captured; he doubted the sincerity of those involved, particularly, the government of Mozambique which he was at war with. Dhlakama genuinely thought that the whole idea of peace talks was a ploy to get him arrested. He refused to move from his hideout unless Kenya sent an emissary to accompany him to Nairobi. Dhlakama was extremely sensitive to people whom he did not know or trust. He, however, agreed to travel to Nairobi on condition that Kenya would send a special envoy to accompany him. Ambassador Kiplagat went to fetch him.

The commencement of any peace process is difficult, treacherous and uncertain. Nothing could be left to chance. This was especially challenging because the leader of RENAMO was totally unknown outside his own organisation. Archbishop Sengulane, of the Anglican church and Cardinal Dos Santos of the Catholic Church in Mozambique assured him that Kenya's special envoy was an honest man who was working for peace in Mozambique and was working for a peaceful resolution to the conflict.

Dhlakama's acceptance paved the way for putting in place logistics, which included transport means and travel documents for him and his delegation to Kenya.

Preparations for the first trip for Dhlakama out of Mozambique were complex and fraught with risks to him and his delegation on one side and to the special envoy sent to get him out of his base at Gorongosa, in central Mozambique. Kenya worked out the logistics, taking into account security concerns of RENAMO's leader and the location of his base. It was of utmost importance to demonstrate to both parties that Kenya was, indeed, an honest broker in the peace process. RENAMO still harboured suspicions about the real intentions of President Chissano. Chissano in turn blamed RENAMO for paralysing infrastructure and for making large parts of the countryside ungovernable.

Dhlakama landed in Nairobi on one cold and rainy evening, a pitiful sight, confused and lost in thought. He was expected to stay for only a few days. Dhlakama was dressed in jungle uniform and looked so terrified that the sound of a cough made him shudder as if a shot had been fired. He did not speak English. It was difficult to imagine that he was someone one could engage in serious negotiations.

Kenya's challenge was to prepare Dhlakama for the task ahead. Dhlakama remained suspicious that a trap might have been hatched by Chissano and executed with the complicity of Moi to have him arrested and handed over to the government of Mozambique for trial, whose outcome would be obvious. It took a huge amount of effort and time to convince him that Kenya would not allow itself to be complicit in a scheme to kill him or destroy his organisation at the behest of anybody. He was advised to invite some of his top lieutenants to Nairobi to be part of the initial efforts in the search for a political settlement. Dhlakama cautiously agreed to give it a try. A number of meetings were arranged between different leaders and Dhlakama and his delegation. First and foremost was for him to call on President Moi who assured him of protection. The re-assurance gave Dhlakama hope and a fresh impetus to move on with peace efforts. Dhlakama began to see President Moi as a father figure, which concretised his trust and confidence in him.

Kenya managed to transform Dhlakama from a guerrilla into a negotiator. It even convinced him to stay for two months continuously. During that time, he was mostly confined to the hotel where he took intensive coaching lessons in English language. Before he left Kenya for Mozambique, Dhlakama had held meetings with a number of people who helped him understand the importance of a negotiated, all-inclusive settlement in which RENAMO would be recognised as a legitimate partner. His effort and ability to speak English progressively enhanced his confidence and personality to a level where he began to feel comfortable in discussions. He realised that war was not the only means which he could apply to achieve his objective. Dhlakama's stay in Nairobi was instrumental in moving forward subsequent talks about talks before the actual negotiations started.

Dhlakama's safe return to Mozambique opened up subsequent travel on condition that he was accompanied by an official of the government of Kenya, on a Kenya Airways flight to and from Lilongwe, Malawi, from where he would be whisked across the border into Mozambique. His safe return was a boost for the peace process. Dhlakama felt safe under Kenyan protection and gradually accepted that Kenya genuinely wanted peace for the people of Mozambique. Dhlakama's stay in Nairobi helped him understand the importance of what Kenya was trying to do in efforts to find a peaceful solution to the conflict. He also realised that without a way forward, their struggle had reached a stalemate.

Dhlakama took time to come to terms with being away from his base on peace missions, for prolonged periods in fear of an insurrection against him. He was, particularly wary of a Raul Domingos, in charge of strategic planning and operations in the organisation. Arrival of some of his lieutenants including Domingos, improved the atmosphere considerably. Dhlakama was able to consult his group easily, which made a big difference in facilitating talks with persons and groups willing to help in the peace process and agreed to dialogue with the government of Mozambique. RENAMO stressed the need for the government of Mozambique to halt hostilities to allow for dialogue in addition to an assurance that its members with families outside Mozambique had to be brought to Nairobi where the negotiations were taking place. The Mozambican delegation insisted that no negotiations would take place unless RENAMO stopped attacks on the infrastructure, especially, the railway line linking Zimbabwe to the port of Beira. Such attacks amounted to economic sabotage. RENAMO read mischief in the statement. Kenya worked hard to persuade them to abandon their hard-line positions and concentrate on how they could achieve peace for the interest of the people of Mozambique.

By the time the negotiations moved to St. Egidio, Rome, Italy, in 1992, Dhlakama and his team had transformed from diehard bush fighters to partners and sophisticated peace negotiators. Kenya's role in bringing together the protagonists cemented confidence between RENAMO and the government delegation. It helped create an enabling environment conducive to the peace process, which hitherto had largely been unsuccessful. RENAMO had requested that the final stages of the negotiations to take place in St. Egidio, Rome, Italy, for fear of a possible government of Mozambique interference in the outcome, if the negotiations were concluded in Nairobi. By the time the General Peace Agreement (GPA) was signed in 1992, the civil war had claimed more than a million people after sixteen years of conflict.

RENAMO went on to contest in two general elections with Dhlakama as its flag bearer and came second to FRELIMO. It operated as the official opposition party until disagreements within it, and with the government, became overwhelming, forcing it back to rebellion, once again. Afonso Dhlakama died of a heart attack in May 2018.

Instability in the Great Lakes Region

The Great Lakes Region straddles five Regional Economic Communities (RECs) of the EAC, IGAD, COMESA, Southern African Development Community (SADC) and the Central African Economic Cooperation. It has huge economic potential, most of which has not been tapped. It has considerable deposits of minerals and other resources. It is home to the second largest rainy forest in the world, after the Amazon in Brazil. It includes countries from four linguistic groups of the AU – English, French, Portuguese and Arabic. Kiswahili, the fifth language, is spoken across the four linguistic groups.

The Great Lakes Region is strategic to Kenya for trade and investment. Eastern DRC, Burundi, Rwanda and Uganda conduct their external trade via Kenya and Tanzania. The higher percentage of trade is through Kenya. When turmoil broke out in the DRC (then Zaire) in the 1990s, President Mobutu Sese Seko invited Moi, with whom he shared great passion for negritude, to intervene and help end the rebellion started by Laurent Kabila in the east of the country. This was an opportunity for Kenya to influence events in the DRC to its advantage.

In addition to trade, the DRC is constructing a major hydro-electric dam at Inga on River Congo, which has the capacity to supply power to most sub-Saharan countries for many years. Kenya should tap into this resource to make up for its shortfall in power generation to support its drive to become a middle-income country by 2030.

Kenya's involvement in the DRC provided a road map for the adoption of the Lomé resolution by the OAU which led the UN Security Council resolution on the deployment of a UN peacekeeping mission in the country. Countries in the region agreed to the International Conference on the Great Lakes Region to spearhead peace efforts in the region. The efforts did not save Mobutu's original intentions to save his presidency. Laurent Kabila's forces overran Kinshasa forcing him to flee to Morocco where he died in exile.

Conflict in Eastern Democratic Republic of Congo

The DRC is a huge country (the size of Western Europe) with vast resources. The DRC has a long history of political instability since its independence on 30th June, 1960. Major powers compete for influence to control its resources. Soon after its independence, at the height of the Cold War, its socialist prime minister Patrice Lumumba was killed and Joseph Desire Mobutu (later Mobutu Sese Seko) installed as president by western powers in their proxy war with the Soviet Union. Although the country had a semblance of stability under Mobuto, it was badly managed with most areas remaining undeveloped.

The DRC is surrounded by unstable countries including the Central African Republic (CAR), South Sudan and Burundi. Uganda, Rwanda and Angola have emerged from political turmoil. Its stable neighbours include Tanzania, Zambia and Congo-Brazzaville. Instability in the DRC was aggravated by the genocide in Rwanda in 1994. This was sparked off by the death of President Juvenile Habyarimana of Rwanda and Cyprian Ntanyirira of Burundi, when the plane on which they were travelling was shot down in unclear circumstances on approach to Kigali International Airport from a regional Summit in Dar es Salaam, Tanzania. It triggered the Rwanda genocide in 1994.[75]

The population in eastern DRC includes the Banyamulenge, a Tutsi ethnic group also found in both Rwanda and Burundi. Rwanda is reported to use them as proxy to deal with the Interahamwe renegade soldiers from the defeated Habyarimana army. Generals Nkunda and Ntaganda who served in the DRC army, but defected to lead uprisings against the government in Congo-Kinshasa belong to Banyamulenge. General Nkunda is reported to be under house arrest in Rwanda while General Ntaganda handed himself to the ICC where he is facing charges for crimes against humanity.

The DRC occupies a fundamental position in the Great Lakes Region. Its stability is critical to peace and security which should enhance trade and investment in eastern Africa. Conflict in the DRC quickly engulfs neighbouring countries with its negative consequences on security and trade in eastern Africa.

---

75   https://www.history.com/topics/rwandan-genocide

PART IV

REGIONAL AND MULTILATERAL DIPLOMACY

Kenya's regional and international Foreign Policy and diplomacy is two pronged. At the regional level, it seeks to promote and maintain good neighbourliness to facilitate trade and investment. It further seeks to secure peace, security and stability. Consequently, Kenya has maintained cordial relations with its neighbours to achieve the two objectives. It has been an active member of IGAD, the EAC, COMESA, and the AU.

At the international level, Kenya promotes good relations with other states to support its economic development goals through beneficial partnerships and to collaborate with the international community in combating terrorism, human and drug trafficking, illicit trade in endangered species, among other global issues, and enable Kenya to contribute to the maintenance of international peace and security. Kenya's non-aligned Foreign Policy has enabled it to cooperate with the Group of 77 (G77) plus China, the Commonwealth and the UN. Kenya's choice of this policy at independence was in response to the dynamics of the Cold War. Since then, Kenya has been an active participant in international meetings on issues such as environment and climate change, the law of the sea and international justice system.

In the post-Cold War period, Kenya re-oriented its Foreign Policy to the East in response to the changing realities of the international politics and to diversify its economic development partnerships and potential. The new international dynamics are likely to influence Kenya's Foreign Policy in future with the aim of maintaining beneficial relations with other states and actors across the globe.

CHAPTER 11

Regional Diplomacy

Kenya was the last of the original founding members of the defunct East African Community (EAC) to become independent. Shortly before Tanganyika's independence, Nyerere had declared his willingness to delay it so that the three East African countries could attain independence together. It did not materialise. Instead, Tanganyika became independent in 1961, Uganda in 1962, and Kenya in 1963. Kenya's process of independence was completed on 12th December, 1964 when it became a republic. President Nyerere was able to control the date of Tanganyika's independence because he was assured of its freedom as a protectorate of the UN. After the three countries became independent, the founding fathers, Julius Nyerere, Milton Obote and Jomo Kenyatta agreed on a framework for regional cooperation. They adopted the colonial framework and replaced the East African Common Services Organisation (EACSO) by the EAC.

Origins of regional cooperation in East Africa

Regional cooperation in East Africa can be traced to the colonial era when the British constructed the Uganda railway, towards the end of the 19th century, to serve white settlers in Uganda. As already stated, it was named the Uganda railway, although its entire length traversed through Kenya. Both Kenya and Uganda were part of British East Africa. In 1900, colonial authorities established the East African High Command (EAHC) between Uganda and Kenya to consolidate colonial interests in British East Africa. It was later replaced with the EACSO which became the basis of regional cooperation for Kenya, Uganda and Tanganyika in the early 1960s, after their independence.

These early efforts supported the white colonial settler community in Uganda, whose climate was favourable to white settler interests such as farming. The whites further liked Uganda because of historical nostalgia for Lake Victoria named after Queen Victoria. Tanganyika joined the High Command in 1922 after it became a British Trustee territory under the League of Nations when Germany, the colonial power, was defeated in World War I in 1918.

The EACSO coordinated services among the three states. The Secretariat was based in Nairobi, Kenya. Under this arrangement, each East African state was assigned to host specific functions. The East African Harbours (EAH) were given to Tanganyika, while both the East African Airways (EAA) and the East African Railways (EAR) were given to Kenya. On the other hand, The East African Posts and Telecommunications (EAP&T) and the East African Development Bank (EADB) were given to Uganda. East Africa's experience with regional cooperation and integration, therefore, began long before the independence of the founding members of the communit: Kenya, Uganda and Tanganyika. Founding leaders saw merit in the arrangement and adopted it to foster economic development in East Africa after independence.

Before and in the early years of Tanganyika's independence in 1962, Julius Nyerere was more passionate about the community than either Jomo Kenyatta or Milton Obote. He observes:

> "The East African Treaty of Co-operation marks an important step for Uganda, Kenya and ourselves. We have now agreed on a thorough and complete reform of the arrangements for economic co-operation which we inherited from our ex-colonial masters, and really effective instruments of joint economic services."[76]

The regional cooperation was a noble idea for Kenya, Uganda and Tanzania after emerging from British colonialism. They shared same colonial heritage and semblance of common approach to development of services and infrastructure. But their paths to independence were totally different. Whereas Kenya waged a bitter struggle to win its independence, Uganda was a beneficiary of the hopelessness the British acknowledged in Kenya's war of independence. In Tanzania's case, it could choose the date of its independence given that it was a trustee territory under the mandate of the UN. Perhaps this was a pointer to the difficulties the three countries faced in nurturing economic cooperation from the beginning. Each country seemed to have different expectations from the others. While all the ingredients for a strong mechanism for cooperation were evident, internal political dynamics in each state were in conflict to those of the others.

Potential conflict became evident because of the different economic models adopted by the three countries. Kenya adopted Sessional Paper No. 10 of 1965 which espoused a mixed economy model, Tanzania the Arusha Declaration in 1967, on socialism and self-reliance and Uganda the Common Man's Charter in 1969, on socialism, which pointed towards an imminent dysfunction and possible collapse of the Community.

---

76   Julius Nyerere, *Freedom and Unity.*

Each member, therefore, defined its Foreign Policy orientation on the basis of the economic policies adopted. The Community further ran into internal opposition from within the three countries who preferred to enjoy their independence. Jomo Kenyatta and Milton Obote focused their attention to internal political dynamics. Of the three leaders, Julius Nyerere, more or less remained the lone advocate for economic integration in East Africa. Tanganyika became Tanzania in 1964, after the merger with Zanzibar.

In the early years of Uganda's independence, President Obote faced a serious power struggle with King Fredrick Muteesa II of Buganda. President Jomo Kenyatta was on his part pre-occupied with consolidation of his power internally, and in part addressing the land issue which was at the heart of the struggle for independence. Nyerere focused his country's Foreign Policy on anti-colonialism in southern Africa. In particular, he laid emphasis on abolition of apartheid in South Africa. The OAU liberation Committee was domiciled in Tanzania to coordinate its work from a front-line state. Nyerere's vision of a united Africa is reflected in the National Anthem he adopted for Tanzania, whose opening stanza begins with God bless Africa (*Mungu Ibariki Africa*), based on a composition by a South African as a rebuke to the abhorrent system of apartheid. Nyerere exerted all his political energies and his country's resources towards decolonisation and abolition of apartheid.

Kenya's choice to settle for a proactive regional engagement was directed towards securing for itself a strategic position as a commercial, investment and tourist destination in East Africa. This broad policy framework required the country to strengthen its vital national assets such as the port of Mombasa, the road and railway networks, telecommunications and air connectivity to support this objective. This Foreign Policy projection was aimed at hinterland neighbouring countries of Uganda, the DRC, Rwanda and Burundi which depend on Kenya for their external trade. It informed Kenya's role in peace processes in the Sudan, Somalia, Ethiopia, Uganda and the Great Lakes Region.

The East African Community
Kenya has a unique historical opportunity to pursue regional cooperation through the EAC. It is among the international organisations for integration to which Kenya belongs; the other being COMESA and the AU. Together, they provide platforms on which Kenya may define its international role based on its strategic national interest. Thus, Kenya must use the community as a springboard to its diplomatic engagement at both regional and international levels. Its Foreign Policy choices will determine its level

of influence with the other partner states in the community. Kenya should promote collective bargaining on common issues with its EAC partners to advance the community's vantage position and in the process, secure its national interest.

Kenya should be prepared to engage in collective negotiations on specific issues to enlist other partners' support and cooperation and exercise responsible leadership to maximise on the comparative advantage it enjoys compared to other EAC partners. The sectors of interest could include agriculture, manufacturing, trade, and investment. Kenya is reported to account for more than half of the US$ 73 billion GDP of all the EAC Partners put together. Some member-states in the community have large mineral resources or are actively investing in the service industry to challenge Kenya's comparative advantage. Kenya's sophistication in infrastructure, financial services, manufacturing, Information, Communication Technology (ICT), legal framework and political participation makes it stand out as a leader in several fields.

One of the critical areas which Kenya needs to address urgently is governance and corruption. The 2007 disputed presidential elections brought the country to the brink of collapse. Disputes arising from the 2013, and 2017 presidential elections were successfully resolved by the Supreme Court, an institution created under the Constitution of Kenya, 2010. Suspicion and doubts on the court's credibility caused a negative perception for Kenya, hitherto regarded as an example of a young but functioning democracy. Kenya will remain under a microscope until it addresses the issues to a standard that can win international confidence necessary for investment and trade and to provide its citizens with a feel good factor. Its relatively developed economy places it in a strategic position to champion community issues. It should take the opportunity to lead in the implementation of the EAC milestones to maximise on the benefits of integration.

Kenya should engage its neighbours to deal with the historical boundary issues through agreed international legal instruments. The territorial claims by Uganda on Migingo Islands in Lake Victoria should be resolved by implementing the OAU and UN resolutions, which adopted colonial boundaries which both countries acceded to at independence. The trans-boundary security issues with neighbouring countries should be addressed through agreed local security committees, so as not to degenerate into conflict over economic resources such as pasture for animals in the dry season. As the community expands through admission of new members, the three founding members of the community remain its strong pillars.

Kenya's projection of power and influence stands out when it acts together with its partners. The collective approach vindicated the approach taken by their Permanent Representatives to the AU seeking the recognition of the EAC as a Regional Economic Community (REC) by the AU Action in February, 2005 in Abuja, Nigeria. It proved that joint action as a block carries greater weight and guarantees success. Ambassadors Msuya Mangachi of Tanzania, Wasswa Birigwa of Uganda and the author, then Permanent Representative of Kenya to the AU, worked hard to secure the approval of AU's policy organs in February, 2005, to recognise the EAC as a REC and one of the pillars for the future African Economic Community.

Political marriage in the East African Community

The original EAC was created when the East African Common Services Organisation (EACSO) was replaced by the founding fathers of Kenya, Uganda and Tanzania, at independence. However, strained relations began to emerge soon after, founded on post-independence initiatives in the form of economic blue-prints, which saw Kenya drift towards capitalism while Tanzania and Uganda drifted towards socialism. The ideological and personal differences which emerged among the leaders in the three countries increasingly became irreconcilable with time.

Further strain occurred when Obote was overthrown in 1971, which threatened the community's future, after Nyerere refused to recognise Amin, paralysing the authority of the community. At that early stage, the community was the most advanced on the continent in terms of institutional set up. It was comparable to the European Community then. The collapse of the EAC in 1977, led to fragile relations among the three countries. It became imperative to chart a new framework for regional cooperation in its place.

New East African Community

The revived community began in 1999, as East African Cooperation (EAC) when Presidents Daniel arap Moi of Kenya, Benjamin Mkapa of Tanzania and Yoweri Museveni of Uganda agreed to negotiate a new framework for economic cooperation in East Africa. The new arrangement was based on harmonisation of policies to inform the process of cooperation. This approach was designed to avoid the political pitfalls which its predecessor faced in the 1960s and 1970s. The promise of better economic prospects for Kenya, Tanzania and Uganda favoured revival of the community. It was clear that the goals for the new community required careful thinking and common approach by the three countries. The new EAC Treaty defines its vision and mission as follows:

Vision:

"...to establish a prosperous, competitive, secure and politically united East Africa."

Mission:

"....to widen and deepen economic, political, social and cultural integration in order to improve the quality of life of the people of East Africa through increased competitiveness, value added production, trade and investment."[77]

The vision and mission of the EAC provide a road map for economic and political integration in East Africa. The process has been slow and tedious, but better placed to deliver integration than the previous one. The road map is beleaguered with serious obstacles including internal political dynamics on democracy and governance, ethnic strife and fight for resources between some member states. The external security threats emanating from conflicts and territorial claims by some of the member states and countries outside the community must be overcome to focus attention on implementation of the integration process.

The Treaty has identified milestones to inform the integration process, namely, customs union, common market, common currency and a political federation. Implementation of the milestones has a direct bearing on the sovereignty of member states which are bound to restrict their sovereign actions to comply with the regional community positions. Kenya, like other member states, has chosen to coalesce on certain strategic objectives through the Community as this gives them a stronger voice on such issues through collective bargaining.

A successful community will guarantee trade and investment, which Kenya could take advantage of to position itself as a destination of choice for investors and businessmen. Negotiations for a common currency and political federation will be difficult because of the fragile internal political developments and governance issues in member states. Pre-occupation with constitutional changes in some member states, by some leaders, to abolish presidential term limits, electoral disputes and lack of respect for the rule of law could lead to decline of state institutions, which will create uncertainty, instability, insecurity, conflict, ethnic tensions, poor governance and threaten the community.

---

77   The Treaty Establishing the East African Community.

Collective bargaining capacity such as the Economic Partnership Agreement (EPA) between the EAC and the EU, the creation of a free trade area under COMESA and the tripartite negotiations between the EAC, COMESA and SADC consolidate strengths of individual member countries' capacities. It provides strengths in numbers and a collective voice as a bloc and moderates actions by member states. The East African Court of Justice rulings, for example, point towards a regional jurisprudence on the political issues within community member states in conformity with Treaty provisions. Nullification in 2006, of the election of the East African Legislative Assembly members from Kenya, forced a repeat of the election and strengthened respect for institutions of the community. Customs Union rules oblige member states to seek exemption for imports of commodities from outside the Community which member states are able to produce internally, such as rice and sugar from non-community member states. Kenya is caught up in this problem with regard to sugar imports from COMESA countries, unless it demonstrates compliance, to privatise its publicly owned sugar factories in line with COMESA policy.

The EAC member states drive to harmonise and strengthen the community's policy framework through negotiations is bound to enhance integration and maximise benefits for all. The focus on fast tracking the development of vital strategic national assets such as ports, telecommunication facilities, road and railway infrastructure, advance common objectives of the community, in facing challenges like the impact of the 2007/2008 post-election violence in Kenya. Hinterland countries which rely on the NCTS for their external trade as well as Kenya itself were completely paralysed as a result of this violence. Uganda, Rwanda and Burundi quickly rushed to Tanzania to negotiate an alternative route to the Northern Corridor for their external trade. The port of Mombasa is a national asset which should be managed efficiently to cope with increased trade from East Africa and beyond. To meet the demand, Kenya should accelerate the development of the NCTS to improve efficiency and capacity to handle large volumes of trade.

Global realities facing member states in the new EAC demand a Foreign Policy, which will embrace international economic partnerships which govern movement of investments, trade and capital. Reluctance by Uganda and Tanzania to sign the EPA is not just because of discomfort with some of its provisos, but their respective levels of development compared to Kenya. It is prudent for Kenya to deploy its diplomatic skills to have them sign the agreement without which its trade is bound to greatly suffer because of imposition of duties on its products exported to the EU.

Uganda and Tanzania will continue to export to the EU free of duty as they are considered to be HIPIC while Kenya has been re-classified as a middle-income country.

Kenya's Foreign Policy and the objectives of the community
Kenya's Foreign Policy in the community is guided by its desire to expand its economy and become an investment destination of choice and is driven by its desire to maintain a strategic position in East Africa. This is informed by the size of its budget and GDP compared to its partners put together. Kenya's 2016 budget was US$17 billion, Tanzania, US$7 billion, US$5 Uganda billion, and Rwanda US$3 billon. Tanzania, Uganda and Rwanda budgets put together were less than Kenya's by a large margin and confirmed it as the leading economy in the Community.

Kenya has pursued a Foreign Policy geared towards expanding markets for its goods and services. The Community offers the best chance for Kenya's trade prospects. Kenya's support for the admission of Rwanda and Burundi was part of this Foreign Policy drive. The purpose is to consolidate opportunities for trade and investment in the region of over 140 million people. As a leading economy in the region, Kenya is in a strong position to further strengthen its economic status. It must take a lead in consolidating the integration process to strengthen its strategic position.

EAC milestones and national policies
EAC partner states' decision to harmonise their national policies in developing community rules and regulations is behind its recognition by the AU as the most advanced of the existing RECs. The Treaty emphasizes harmonisation of policies while it allows fast tracking some programmes for willing partner states without jeopardising integration and economic cooperation. Meetings involving Uganda, Kenya, Rwanda and South Sudan were convened to discuss oil discoveries in Uganda and Kenya, but, in addition, discussed infrastructure issues including export hurdles facing South Sudan due to its unpredictable relations with Sudan since the breakup. Top on the agenda were oil pipeline infrastructure linking South Sudan, Uganda, and Kenya, improvements to the NCTS from Mombasa through Uganda to Rwanda to reduce transit time.

Inter-Governmental Authority on Development
IGAD has been discussed extensively in Chapters 9 and 10 with emphasis on regional security challenges, peace and conflict resolution, respectively. Kenya's most successful Foreign Policy on peace has been undertaken

through IGAD namely: the Sudan Peace Process and the Somalia Reconciliation Conference discussed in Chapter 10.

IGAD is a small organisation which has made a significant contribution to peace, security and stability in the Horn of Africa. IGAD's mandate was enhanced in 1984, to include political issues such as peace, security, refugees and proliferation of SALW in the Horn of Africa, when it replaced the Inter-Governmental Authority on Drought and Desertification (IGADD) that dealt with environmental issues only. Kenya chaired the two peace processes.

Common Market for Eastern and Southern Africa
The Common Market for Eastern and Southern Africa (COMESA) groups together countries from eastern and southern Africa. The membership cuts across three RECs, namely, IGAD, EAC and SADC.

COMESA includes Egypt which joined when it recognised COMESA's value as an economic and trade bloc. COMESA was established to promote free trade by addressing tariff and non-tariff trade barriers among its members. The focus on trade has made COMESA dwell less on political issues than the other RECs it cuts across. Kenya's membership serves its economic interests in form of markets for its goods and services, as well as its policy on the integration of African economies.

The EAC, COMESA and SADC countries agreed to negotiate a tripartite arrangement as part of the efforts to create a continent-wide African Economic Community based on the 1980, OAU Lagos Plan of Action. The objective is to improve and harmonise the trade regime for member countries through elimination of overlapping trade regimes of respective RECs. The tripartite free trade area is expected to enable member countries to access a market of over 600 million people in about half of all AU member states with a combined GDP of US$ 1.2 trillion. This is roughly about 58 per cent of Africa's total GDP. Significantly, it will offer excellent opportunities for businesses and will act as a magnet for attracting Direct Foreign Investment (DFI) because of the huge market.

African countries fall into four broad categories, namely: English speaking, French speaking, Portuguese speaking and Arabic speaking. Each language group has tended to align itself in some form of political-cum-economic arrangement with countries outside Africa. The English-speaking countries belong to the Commonwealth, the French speaking to the Francophone group and the Arab speaking to the Arab League. The Portuguese speaking countries are probably the least tied to an outside Africa arrangement. Cultural issues play a significant role in defining the interests of each country. A more daunting challenge is the terrain and the generally underdeveloped infrastructure on the continent. The interconnections by road, rail and air are poor, inefficient and expensive. A great deal of work needs to be done to facilitate trade.

The free trade area may be a game changer in the economic fortunes of member countries, and a step towards the realisation of a continental free market, which would include the ECOWAS member countries and the North African Maghreb countries, into one trading bloc. This is a key project of the AU and a first step towards the creation of an African Economic Community using RECs. A continental free trade area will facilitate the development of infrastructure and harmonise rules on the movement of goods, people, services and capital.

African Union

The African Union (AU) is a platform for Kenya to project its image and interests, particularly, to promote economic integration. Its mandate is to seek, not just unity, solidarity and cooperation among African peoples; but to build necessary institutions for deepening political, economic and social integration of Africa. The promotion of the cultural dialogue and the development of new partnerships falls within Kenya's Foreign Policy framework.

Kenya has participated in developing the organisation's policies on peace and security and international cooperation to strengthen multilateral diplomacy. Kenya's objective has been to promote these ideals in a manner which is beneficial to its Foreign Policy objectives namely; the sanctity of its sovereignty and territorial integrity, peaceful co-existence with neighbours and other nations and respect for international law. Kenya participates in collective positions taken by the AU on political, economic and social issues affecting individual countries or the whole continent, which include decolonisation and abolition of apartheid, the recognition of Western Sahara Democratic Republic (SAHRAWI) as an independent state, the Middle East conflict, and the ICC, among many others.

Kenya considers the AU as a springboard for articulation of its Foreign Policy in the region. This requires close bilateral relations with other African countries in key areas such as trade, health, science and technology, education and culture. Kenya should actively participate in AU's policy organs in order to influence decisions to favour its interests. Membership to critical organs of the AU such as the Peace and Security Council is critical for Kenya to acknowledge and consolidate its position as a peace maker. However, Kenya must be prepared to face competition from other countries in the sub-region for such positions.

Kenya's engagement in collective dialogue and cooperation through the AU is critical to its Foreign Policy in constantly evolving international dynamics. It requires Kenya to adopt innovative ways of international engagement by asserting its position on issues on which it shares common views with other states. Kenya played its card well when it granted temporary rent-free offices for the AU Liaison Office in 2004, in preparation for the International Conference on the Great Lakes. Kenya's role in the peace processes in South Sudan and Somalia are notable examples of what it can do as an active member of the community of nations. Such gestures will enhance its credentials in the organisation and enhance its recognition as an important and dependable player.

Kenya's active participation in the AU's flagship programme, the New Partnership for Africa's Development (NEPAD), has enhanced its role in an integrated framework for sustainable development of the African continent. Through its African Peer Review Mechanism (APRM), NEPAD promotes democracy and good governance. Kenya should take advantage of programmes such as NEPAD to provide leadership on issues such as economic development strategies and workable partnerships in the drive for faster integration. It should contribute to the implementation of the AU's Vision 2063 through participation in the development of infrastructure and industry to enhance intra-African trade. Kenya should take a lead role and strengthen NEPAD as a framework for development in energy, road and rail networks and ICT infrastructure, guided by the AU's ambitious Vision 2063.

The changing dynamics in international relations made the AU re-admit Morocco in January, 2017, thirty-three years since it walked out of the then OAU. Morocco's campaign to re-join the continental body confirmed the AU's potential as a collective forum for bargaining concessions for Africa. The SAHRAWI dispute which forced out Morocco remains unresolved. Kenya needs to take a collective re-examination of the SAHRAWI issue to let the country gain independence. Morocco's re-admission has created new realities in the organisation with regard to the balance of power, particularly, in northern Africa where Egypt has been the dominant power, almost unchallenged.

CHAPTER 12

Multilateral Diplomacy

Kenya's Foreign Policy and diplomacy, guided by internationally accepted principles, has evolved in response to changing dynamics in international relations. The Foreign Policy during the Cold War took into count the realities of super power rivalry between the US and the Soviet Union. Kenya's adoption of a non-aligned Foreign Policy made it possible for Kenya to deal with both sides of the ideological divide. Evolution helped Kenya optimise on its relations with other states in either bloc to pursue its domestic and Foreign Policy agenda. Kenya recognised the economic benefits in maintaining economic partnerships with both the western countries and good cooperation with the East bloc countries during the Cold War.

Kenya's Foreign Policy recognises the link between peace, security and political stability without which there could be no economic development. This link informs its pursuit of economic diplomacy, whose objective is to secure its national interest as projected in the Vision 2030. For this reason, Kenya is fully engaged in the international fight against terrorism, human and drug trafficking, proliferation of SALW, and collaborates in the maintenance of international peace and security. The policy fosters the attraction of trade and investment, capital, affordable and appropriate technology to support its economic development such as exploration of traditional and renewable energy, among others.

Kenya has established diplomatic missions in many countries which it uses in articulating its Foreign Policy. To sustain an effective Foreign Policy, Kenya needs to provide adequate financial and human resources and build the capacity for its representation to make an impact in promoting, projecting and defending its interests and international image. A proper utilisation of the vast diplomatic network will enhance Kenya's international recognition as a dependable player.

Increasingly, the world has become a global village. Developments in one region have dramatic and immediate effect in other regions across the world. Technological developments and advanced modern communication systems have dramatically improved relay of news on major events taking place around the world. Social media has made things even more dramatic through viral dissemination of raw information from one group to another. Furthermore, globalisation has made the world more economically intertwined resulting in flexibility in the movement of goods, labour and capital.

Kenya has to adapt to these changes with a Foreign Policy that is responsive and flexible. The *Kenya Foreign Policy, 2014* acknowledges these developments in its projections. It states:

> "Some of the international challenges Kenya has to respond to require global efforts. They include: threats to international peace and security, fight against international terrorism, drug and human trafficking, and money laundering. Others are non-political threats such as the outbreak of deadly diseases like Acquired Immune Deficiency Syndrome (AIDS), malaria and Ebola, which explode on the scene unexpectedly but require global efforts to combat. This calls for intensive international engagement by all the countries of the world to deal with. Kenya has cooperated and must continue to do so in efforts to combat them."[78]

Kenya must deploy its primary Foreign Policy tool – diplomacy – to negotiate economic and trade partnerships for active engagement and participation in the global economy. It hosted two international trade conferences, the first by the WTO in 2015 and the second by the UNCTAD in July, 2016 – which gave it a diplomatic boost. This was a departure from the gloom it suffered from the fall out over the ICC cases against Uhuru Kenyatta and William Ruto and the damage they had on its international image.

Hosting the two conferences improved the environment for the tourist industry and made the citizens enjoy a feel-good factor and national prestige in a long time. The meetings were important to correct the imbalance in the international economic order, after the traditional considerations for economic partnerships between the developed and developing countries shifted from ideological issues, to democracy and good governance.

Kenya faces unprecedented challenges in its economic and diplomatic engagement with its traditional development partners over issues of democracy, good governance and corruption. International concern about these issues will not fade away.

Kenya must remain active and make a constructive contribution to international efforts in trade negotiations through WTO for fairer terms of trade and how to advance its cooperation with the EU, through the EPA under the auspices of the EAC, in order to continue benefiting from

---

78   *The Kenya Foreign Policy, 2014.*

preferential trade arrangements. Kenya should further explore how its membership to Afro-Asia Economic Cooperation (AAEC), Indian Ocean Rim-Association for Regional Cooperation (IOR-ARC) and African Growth and Opportunity Act (AGOA), can advance its national interest.

The Non-Aligned Movement

A non-alignment Foreign Policy enabled Kenya to pursue its Foreign Policy objectives without suspicion from its partners on either side of the ideological divide. It helped rationalise its Foreign Policy strategies and objectives during the Cold War. Western countries developed close relations with Kenya through official development assistance, investment and trade. The liberal economic model which Kenya adopted at independence attracted foreign capital and accelerated Kenya's economic development. The economic model vindicated the founding fathers' bold steps to keep away from the socialist system practised in many countries in Africa in the immediate post-independence period.

Non-alignment helped Kenya to attract and maintain investment, trade and bilateral assistance from both the West and the East. Kenya had to guard against being held hostage by the interests of one or the other side. Furthermore, the non-aligned Foreign Policy helped Kenya win the right to host UNEP and UN-HABITAT, as it was able to count on both western and eastern support, and the developing countries, organised under the G77 plus China.

The Middle East conflict

The Middle East conflict, also known as "The question of Palestine" has been raging since 1948, when the State of Israel was established by the UN. The conflict remains the most protracted agenda for the UN General Assembly and the UN Security Council to date. Kenya's position on the conflict has been informed by its interest to maintain good relations with the USA, the principal backer of Israel, and Israel itself on the one hand, and Arab countries on the other.

As a former colony itself, Kenya sympathises with the plight of the people of Palestine. Kenya's position takes into account the USA policy towards Israel which the USA considers to be a strategic partner in the Middle East, and has vowed to defend it in the UN Security Council, and militarily if necessary. Both the USA and Israel are Kenya's important development partners. Both countries cooperate not only in many fields of development but are also partners in sharing key security intelligence on issues of global concern such as international terrorism, drug and human trafficking, and illicit trade in endangered species.

Kenya pursues its Foreign Policy on the Middle East conflict, conscious of the right of the Palestinian people to self-determination. It fully subscribes to all UN Security Council resolutions on the matter. It has established diplomatic relations with the Palestinian Authority by which the Palestinian diplomatic mission in Addis Ababa is concurrently accredited to Kenya.

In principle, Kenya subscribes to the AU position on the Middle East conflict and supports the position taken by Arab countries and other developing countries. At the UN, Kenya abstains in votes on the Middle East conflict. Kenya's position is guided by its interest and recognises the need to balance between the right of Israel to exist, and the right of the Palestinian people to self-determination. Kenya, therefore, supports any peace process and the two-state solution to the conflict.

Before 1948 when the UN established the State of Israel, Palestine was administered by the British as a UN Trustee territory. Palestinian anger on the alienation of their land for the Jewish State was to be expected. Jews and the Palestinians, have age old claims to this land rooted in religion and race. Arabs call it Palestine and Jews refer to it as Israel, Samaria and Judea. To Israel, all of West Bank is Samaria and Judea, which it considers as God given land exclusively for Jews. Palestinians are unlikely to give up the fight for their land in a conflict that has sharply divided international opinion and divided the UN Security Council.

Palestinian grievances and the Middle East stalemate
Radical Islamic groups have sprung in defence of Palestinian rights as an expression of resentment to Israeli occupation and discrimination. Groups like Hezbollah, Hamas and the Palestinian Liberation Front (PLF), which fight for Palestinian rights, have been labelled as terrorists, a factor that makes it difficult to find a solution to the problem. The international community should be alert to complications which have side-lined Palestinian and Arab opinion and interests.

The world should be alive to their perception as a marginalised group estranged from their own homeland. The treatment meted to Israeli-Arabs supports this perception. Susan Nathan, an Israeli Jew who migrated from London to Israel but decided to live among Israeli-Arabs, makes interesting and poignant observations of how Israeli-Arabs are treated in their own country. Her account gives graphic details of their status in Israel. She observes that:

> "There cannot be an Arab-Israeli who has travelled around and does not have his or her own personal horror story of dealing with the security procedures at Israel's main Ben Gurion airport just outside Tel Aviv. An Arab's status as a citizen inside the Jewish State is immediately made clear the moment he enters the airport and produces his passport for inspection by one of the young Jewish officials who are charged with assessing the security threat posed by each passenger. The main criterion used by the security personnel is not whether the traveller is Israeli or not, but a Jew or non-Jew, Jewish passengers will almost always be allowed to pass without further checks. Foreigners will be asked questions about their activities, including whether they have had any dealings with Arabs, including Arab citizens and their bags will be X-rayed and possibly inspected. Arab citizens are assumed by definition to pose a security danger and are treated accordingly. They will be subjected to lengthy questioning about their activities and their acquaintances, and their reasons for travelling. If they pass these checks they will have their bags X-rayed, then intimately searched, and finally they may be body searched."[79]

USA and other western countries' support for Israel shields it from international censure on its handling of the peace process, expansion of Jewish settlements in East Jerusalem and the West Bank, which are considered to be illegal under international law. The USA's use of its veto in the UN Security Council against any censure of Israel has virtually assured Israel of inconsequential international repercussions on its actions in the Middle East conflict. Israel routinely ignores UN Security Council resolutions on the issue. A two-state solution is unlikely to be achieved under the prevailing circumstances through direct negotiations between Israel and the Palestinian Authority. Susan Nathan's account describes well the Arab claim that they have been marginalised.

The 1967 and 1973 Arab-Israeli wars entrenched further Western view that Israel must be supported by any means to survive in a hostile Arab region. It fails to take into account the views and interests of Palestinian people, which were major causes of the two wars. Instead, it has led to the birth of groups such as the Hezbollah in Lebanon and Syria, Hamas in Gaza

---

79   Susan Nathan, *The Other Side of Israel.*

in support of the Palestinian right to self-determination. The establishment of Israel incensed Arab opinion to an extent that Arab countries rejected a proposed Palestinian state in the remainder of Palestinian territory after the creation of Israel. In their anger, through the Arab League, Arab countries helped establish the Palestinian Liberation Organisation (PLO), to fight for the total liberation of Palestine from the settlement of Jews, who survived the holocaust, on alienated Palestinian territory. Arabs viewed the settlement as a grave injustice by the international community against the Palestinian people. The narrative continues because of several factors including: the perception of Palestinians that western countries are biased towards Israel and the USA's strategic and economic interests in the region.

US support has made Israel accelerate expansion of settlements in East Jerusalem and the West Bank and the blockade of Gaza and control of all points of entry into Palestinian territory. This amounts to a policy of absolute control of all Palestinian activities in their own land. The policy has effectively condemned Palestinians to the biggest open-air prison in the world.

International terrorism

Terrorism has become a major issue in international relations. It is one of the emerging issues which has attracted the attention of all nations, big or small. Terrorists target interests of certain countries to make a political point. The 1998 bombing of US embassies in Nairobi, Kenya and Dar es Salaam, Tanzania, the World Trade Centre (WTC), New York, USA in 2001, the underground tube system in London in 2007, and the attacks in Paris and Brussels in 2015, by radical groups linked to Al Qaeda, targeted western interests. Terrorists have no regard for even the most powerful countries. Advanced technology in modern communication systems makes it possible to plan more easily and discretely. Kenya has been a frequent victim. In addition to the attack on the US embassy in Nairobi, the Al-Shabaab, a group based in Somalia, has attacked targets in Kenya such as the Westgate shopping mall in 2013, and the Garissa University College in 2015. It has attacked other countries in East Africa including a daring attack on a Kenyan garrison in Somalia itself.

The international community sometimes finds itself in a dilemma on how to deal with the menace. It is more difficult to pin down the real causes for terrorist attacks. It is more confusing when some liberation movements are labelled and characterised as terrorist groups as it happened during the struggle for independence, and others because of religious affiliations. Such simplistic characterisation is not helpful in the fight against international terrorism.

Kenya has been a victim of terrorist attacks on many occasions. Its Foreign Policy is therefore alive to the threat posed by terrorism. A terrorist attack on the Norfolk hotel in 1980 was later blamed on the refuelling stop Israeli jets made in 1976, en route to a rescue mission to Entebbe, Uganda, to free Israeli citizens who had been hijacked by a Palestinian group. The second major attack took place on 7th August, 1998, when Al-Qaeda carried out twin attacks on USA embassies in Nairobi, Kenya and Dar es Salaam, Tanzania. The Nairobi attack caused the death of more than two hundred people, majority of them Kenyans. The third attack was on the Paradise Hotel, Mombasa in December 2002. The attacks, linked to radical groups, took place long before the Al-Shabaab, an affiliate of Al-Qaeda took centre stage in East Africa.

Kenya is alert to the threat of international terrorism to international peace and security. Perpetrators of international terrorism are invisible individuals or groups whose activities are difficult to monitor or predict. It is a global problem which manifests itself in different forms with devastating effects. International terrorism is hard to detect, track and contain. Known terrorist groups such as Al-Qaeda, based in Afghanistan, Hezbollah (Party of God) in Lebanon, Al-Shabaab and Boko Haram (western education is prohibited), Hamas and Islamic State of Iraq and al-Sham (ISIS) carry out their activities in a most lethal way. The terrorist attacks which Kenya has suffered constitute the most serious security challenge to the country and require concerted international efforts to combat.

Rise of militant Islamic groups in the Middle East

The rise of Islamic fundamentalism is not new but gained momentum with the emergence of Al-Qaeda and the Taliban in Afghanistan and Pakistan. Al-Qaeda was an off-shoot of the Mujahidin who fought against Soviet invasion of Afghanistan in the late 1970s with the support of the USA. Al-Qaeda, under the leadership of Osama Bin Laden, developed into a world phenomenon vowing to attack western interests, especially those of the USA. The bombing of the US embassies in Kenya and Tanzania began a wave of such attacks on western interests including the Israel owned Paradise Hotel in Kikambala, near Mombasa in December, 2002. The Al-Shabaab group, based in Somalia is the most active in Kenya.

Al-Qaeda carried out attacks in the UK in 2007, in Kenya (Westgate Mall) in September, 2013, in France (Charlie Hebdo) in January, 2014, Garissa University College in April, 2015, in France in November, 2015 and Belgium (Airport and train station) in March, 2016. The rise of ISIS may be attributed to the US-led war in Iraq to remove President Saddam Hussein from power. Their spread into Syria complicated the situation further in the wake of the so called "Arab Spring" uprising which began in Tunisia and through Libya, Egypt and Syria.

The uprising in Tunisia, Libya, Egypt in 2010, overthrew leaders who had been in power for long periods. President Ahmed Ben Ali of Tunisia fled to Saudi Arabia, Colonel Muammar Gaddafi of Libya was killed in the rebellion which overthrew him while President Hosni Mubarak was tried and convicted; later his conviction was quashed. President Mubarak's democratically elected successor President Mohamed Morsi was later overthrown and jailed for being a member of the Muslim Brotherhood. In Syria, the insurgence did not manage to overthrow President Bishar Al-Assad, thanks to Russia, with the support of Iran and Hezbollah. Opposition groups teamed up with some radical groups such as the ISIS and Al-Qaeda to get rid of President Assad. Ironically, the US has supported some opposition group calling itself the Free Syrian Army (FSR), but the group has not been a match to Russian support for the regime. The overthrow, and subsequent killing of Muammar Gaddafi in Libya, accelerated its degeneration into a failed state. Some of which have inflicted damage to the country directly or through their affiliates such as Al-Shabaab. CDR Youssef H. Aboul-Enein, defines an Islamic militant as:

> "Militant Islamist: a group or individual advocating Islamic ideological goals principally by violent means. Militant Islamists call for the strictest possible interpretation of both the Qur'an (Muslim book of divine revelation) and the Hadith (the Prophet Muhammad's actions and deeds). This narrow interpretation opposes the beliefs of Muslims and non-Muslims alike; Militant Islamists stand against Western democracies, Middle Eastern institutions of government and Islamic political parties that participate non-violently in elections. Although Militant Islamists call for the establishment of an Islamic state, they are characterised by a lack of any socio-economic agenda and impose their narrow views by force upon other Muslims as well as non-Muslims."[80]

---

80   CDR Youssef H. Aboul-Enein, *Militant Islamic Ideology.*

Apart from dealing with the Middle East crisis and radical groups, Kenya's Foreign Policy in the Middle East should actively promote economic diplomacy. As economic relations blossom between Kenya and Middle East countries, its Foreign Policy has to be directed towards enhancing bilateral relations in the region. Linked to economic ties, another phenomenon has emerged which requires consideration. Kenya should deal with the plight of its citizens who get into trouble in some countries in the region such as Saudi Arabia and Lebanon because of unexplained circumstances of their employment. Many such Kenyans take up employment opportunities without an understanding of the terms and conditions applicable to them. It is an issue to be taken up through diplomatic channels with the destination countries to protect Kenyans from exploitation and abuse.

Islamic State of Iraq and al-Sham

The Islamic State of Iraq and al-Sham (ISIS), also known as Daesh, is an off shoot of Al-Qaeda. It operates mainly in the Middle East from where it declared a Caliphate or Islamic government in parts of Iraq and Syria. ISIS presents the most complex threat to international peace and security. US intelligence and counter-terrorism analysts and diplomats believe that ISIS is the latest front in a bloody culmination of a long-running dispute within the ranks of international jihadism on how the holy war should be waged and on whom.

In their book titled, *Inside the Army of Terror*, Michael Weiss and Hassan-Hassan observe that the backbone of ISIS is Sunni Arabs who lost power in Iraq when President Saddam Hussein's military and security forces were disbanded by Paul Bremer, the US appointed administrator of Iraq after the invasion. They describe ISIS as:

> "ISIS is a terrorist organisation, but it isn't only a terrorist organisation. It is also a mafia adept at exploiting decades-old transnational grey markets for oil and arms trafficking. It is a conventional military that mobilises and deploys foot soldiers with a professional acumen that has impressed members of the US military. It is a sophisticated intelligence-gathering apparatus that infiltrates rival organisations and silently recruits within their ranks before taking them over, routing them in combat, or seizing their land. It is a sleek propaganda machine effective at disseminating its message and calling in new recruits via social media. ISIS is also a spectral holdover of an even earlier foe than Al-Qaeda. Most of its decision-makers served either in Saddam Hussein's military or security forces.[81]

---

81   Michael Weiss and Hassan-Hassan: *Inside the Army of Terror.*

The debate on Islamic government dates back to Prophet Mohammed, the founder of Islam. ISIS has become too radical and has no sympathy for religious minorities in Iraq and Syria such as the Yazidis and Christians or what they consider as moderate Islamic groups in Egypt and other parts of the world.

The stalemate in the Middle East conflict, particularly, the US recognition of Jerusalem as the capital of Israel, invasion of Iraq, and the Arab uneasiness with the USA's Foreign Policy strategies and objectives in the Middle East, could be influencing the spread of radical groups in the region. Donald Trump's election as president of the USA in 2016, exacerbated the problem. It emboldened Israel to act more decisively against Palestinian self-determination and hardened Arab countries' attitude towards Iran and Syria. It led to conservative countries such as Saudi Arabia and the United Arab Emirates (UAE) to break ties with Qatar in 2017, which they accuse of supporting terrorism and Iran. The conflict in Yemen reflects these differences where by Saudi Arabia leads Arab countries against the Heuthi rebels believed to be supported by Iran. The USA has classified Iran as a state sponsor of terrorism.

Democratisation has opened up political systems around the world but use of "Tomahawk Diplomacy" is not the answer to dictatorships and will not force the rest of the world to embrace western value systems whole-heartedly. Writing in the *Daily Nation*, Kenya, columnist Rasna Warah observes:

"Thousands of people have died and millions have been displaced since 2003. Meanwhile the terrorists are wreaking havoc on the world's oldest civilisations. Ancient cities and monuments of immeasurable historic value are being destroyed in Iraq and Syria by zealots who appear to be using a Nazi manual to carry out their heinous deeds.

In their bid to bring about regime change in Iraq and Libya, the USA and NATO powers unleashed turmoil, anarchy, bloodshed and displacement in the Middle East and Libya. Nearly four million Syrians have fled their country in the past few years. These refugees are risking their lives and those of their families to reach Europe.

American and European leaders are acting as if this crisis is not of their making. Except for German Chancellor, Angel Merkel, who has an open-door policy towards Syrian refugees, Western leaders are viewing the refugee crisis as an unfortunate intrusion into their ordered lives,

the refugees are being depicted as barbarians at the gate, even though
it was the destabilisation policies and actions of Western leaders that
created conditions that led to the refugee crisis in the first place."[82]

Western Powers' drive to eliminate dictatorships and establish democratic
systems should be well thought out to avoid creating political vacuums
which lead to collapse of states like it happened in Libya. Proliferation of
radical groups has emerged in response to the Arab perception that they
are being marginalised over the question of Palestine.

Foreign Policy dilemma over the International Criminal Court

The ICC is an organ of the UN established under the Rome Statute, as
an international instrument to tackle impunity and punish perpetrators
of crimes against humanity and genocide. Kenya played an active role in
its establishment and became a founding member of the Rome Statute. It
ratified it in 2005.

At the time of ratification, Kenya resisted the USA's request to adopt
Article 98 of the Statute which provides for nationals of a country accused
of genocide and crimes against humanity to be tried in their own countries,
the move would have committed Kenya to this provision to allow the
repatriation of USA citizens who commit crimes against humanity or
genocide back to the USA for trial instead of facing the law in countries
where the crimes were committed. The USA declined to accede to the
Rome Statute when it failed to win support on Article 98.

Background to ICC's involvement with Kenya

The background to the ICC dilemma lies in the 2007 disputed presidential
results. After holding successful elections in 2002, which brought to an end
the twenty-four-year reign of President Moi as well as the dominance of the
independence party, KANU, Kenyans expected a trouble-free election in
2007. Like in December 2002, Kenyans voted in the December 2007 elections
with enthusiasm, hope and full of expectations. The main competitors were
President Mwai Kibaki of PNU and Raila Odinga, running on the ODM
party ticket.

It took most people by surprise when President Kibaki was announced
the winner against the trend and results in the parliamentary and local
government elections across the country which had put ODM in the lead.
The announcement was greeted with shock, anger and disbelief among

---

82   Rasna Warah, *West engineered Middle East crisis and must allow in Syrian Refugees,*
      Daily Nation, 14th September, 2015.

ODM supporters. Violence exploded in ODM strongholds especially in Nairobi, Rift Valley, Nyanza and Western regions because supporters believed their choice for president had been stolen.

The AU quickly despatched its Chairman, then President John Kufuor of Ghana, to intervene. Soon after, high profile eminent persons were identified to seek a solution to the problem, among them the former UN Secretary General, Kofi Annan, former President of the United Republic of Tanzania, Benjamin Mkapa, and Graca Machel, widow of Samora Machel and wife of Nelson Mandela.

Kofi Annan led the team which negotiated a settlement by which the opposition acknowledged the re-election of Mwai Kibaki as president. Raila Odinga became Prime Minister in a power-sharing Grand Coalition Government.

The 2007/2008 post-election violence presented Kenya with a major dilemma. It needed to address two publics – domestic and international. The domestic public comprised the victims of the violence and the opposition leadership which felt cheated. First, the plight of victims of post-election violence demanded a just and fair trial of perpetrators of the violence and compensation for losses incurred. Second, appeasing the political leaders' entrenched interests, often interpreted as synonymous with state interests.

Kenya did not fairly address the plight of the victims. Kenya's failure to observe the rule of law exposed it to accusations of non-compliance with international treaties and conventions it was party to. Many such treaties and instruments relate to upholding human rights, democracy, good governance and corruption.

Kenya's dilemma over the ICC began when six Kenyans, among them Uhuru Kenyatta and William Ruto, were indicted for crimes against humanity because of their perceived role in the 2007/2008 post-election violence. The situation was aggravated by their election as President and Deputy President, respectively, in 2013. Uhuru Kenyatta and William Ruto's indictment made the coalition parties in power, TNA party and URP, consider withdrawing Kenya from the Rome Statute.

More ominous was the removal of immunity from prosecution of a sitting president on charges for crimes against humanity. Any move in this direction would cause further division.

Assembly of State Parties' Conference at The Hague
The Assembly of State Parties is the highest decision-making organ of the Rome Statute. It determines the mandate and procedures of the ICC. Kenya set out to convince the Assembly to consider amendments to the rules of

procedure for the ICC ahead of President Kenyatta's appearance for the status conference at the ICC in October, 2013.

Shuttle diplomacy by President Kibaki and later Uhuru Kenyatta administrations were constrained by Kenya's reluctance to establish a local judicial mechanism to try the perpetrators of the 2007/2008 violence. Kenya further failed to acknowledge the international public opinion against impunity and lack of sufficient safeguards for the victims of the post-election violence. The Constitution of Kenya, 2010, has clarified safeguards in Chapter 1 and Chapter 9, Article 143 on how to treat international treaties and conventions to which Kenya is party and the legal position of a sitting president facing crimes against humanity and genocide.

Kenya must continue to cooperate with the ICC. Calls by some leaders to withdraw from the Rome Statute are misleading and could be counter-productive to Kenya's Foreign Policy and image. Kenya should uphold the rule of law, exercise good governance, combat corruption, and, respect human rights and fundamental freedoms as provided in Chapter 4 of the Constitution to remain a credible and dependable actor of international law.

United Nations Organisation

Victorious powers in World War II – the USA, Great Britain, France, the Soviet Union and China (then represented by Taiwan) – negotiated a framework for the maintenance of international peace and security after the war which led to the formation of the United Nations Organisation (UNO) in 1945. The UN has two principal organs for this purpose, namely, the UN Security Council and the UN General Assembly.

The UN Security Council is the decision-making organ. It comprises of five permanent members (P5) – the USA, the UK, France, Russia and China. These permanent members all have the veto power. Its resolutions are binding to member states. The UN Security Council has the mandate for the maintenance of international peace and security.

In 1971, the People's Republic of China took over the permanent seat from Taiwan after a titanic stand-off between the USA which resisted the change and the USSR, which put its diplomacy on the line in support of the People's Republic of China.

Kenya joined the UN after independence and committed itself to its ideals. Kenya has actively participated in UN peace-keeping missions around the world, including Lebanon, former Yugoslavia, Liberia, Sierra Leone, Sudan, the DRC, and East Timor.

Kenya fully supports international cooperation in tackling issues which may threaten international peace and security. Similarly, it is committed to international efforts in dealing with emerging issues such as international terrorism, human and drug trafficking, environment, and climate change.

UN Security Council reforms

The UN was established at a time when majority of its current members, especially African countries, were colonies of the United Kingdom, France, Portugal or Spain. Other members were parts of independent states which broke up into new independent states. Examples include the Soviet Union (1989), Yugoslavia (1992), and Ethiopia (1991).

The composition of the UN Security Council is biased towards developed countries because of the balance of power at the time the UN was formed. Africa was represented by two former colonial masters, Britain and France, and now wants a permanent seat on the Council. The imbalance created by colonial interests needs addressing to reflect regional representation. The UN Charter needs review to respond to challenges of an evolving world.

Kenya must continue to support on-going calls for UN reforms to revitalise it to become a more democratic and representative organisation. Besides, it should reflect the new demographic and economic realities in the world. The focus on the UN Security Council reforms is informed by the growing concern on the indiscriminate use of the veto power exercised by the five permanent members of the Council.

Developing countries do not have representation on the UN Security Council except for the rotational non-permanent seats allocated to specific regions of the world. Africa has fifty-four (54) members at the UN, which constitutes one third of the entire membership. Yet the continent does not have permanent representation on the Council. New economic realities show that executive authority lies with the UN Security Council whose composition is made up of three western powers, Russia and China. African countries seek its reconstitution to reflect the changed political and economic realities in the world. The geographical spread is not a new argument in the reform debate. Australia raised the debate at the end of World War II, right at the time of establishing the UN security Council, but only agreed to sign the Charter after the USA agreed to defend it in the event of war. The USA's commitment resulted in the security arrangement between Australia, New Zealand and the USA – the ANZUS Treaty.

India and Brazil have economies which are larger than some of the P5 members, with far bigger populations. Africa deserves a permanent seat for its size and complex political and security situation obtaining in some of the countries on the continent. Kenya is a strategically pivotal country in Africa alongside South Africa, Nigeria and Egypt. It should continue to support UN reforms and work within the framework of the AU to negotiate a seat for Africa under the AU on rotational basis.

The creation of the UNON has consolidated the status of UNEP and UN-HABITAT as the fourth UN headquarters in the world. Its location makes it the only one among developing countries hosting UN headquarters. That puts Nairobi at par with New York, Geneva and Vienna. The presence of the UN bodies in Nairobi is a huge boost to Kenya's image and prestige. Kenya must continue to be vigilant and cooperate with other UN members to strengthen its mandate. Developing countries continue to support Kenya as host of the UNON.

Over all, Kenya has established useful diplomatic contacts which it should put to use to strengthen its diplomacy in pursuit of its national interest. Kenya has served as a temporary member of the UN Security Council twice since independence. The last time was in 1997/1998. Kenya should use the experience gained to pursue international partnerships which will promote its interests globally.

CHAPTER 13

Environmental Diplomacy

Environment and climate change have emerged as major Foreign Policy concerns. Immediate issues of concern to the international community are the effects on climate change by chlorofluorocarbon emissions (CFCs) in the atmosphere, discharge of industrial waste, use of fossil energy (oil, coal), deforestation, destruction of flora and fauna and trade in endangered species. Many diplomatic conferences held over the years under the auspices of the UN have tried to reach a consensus on a framework on these issues to mitigate on environmental degradation. The lack of political will, an enforcement mechanism, and diverse interests remain major obstacles to implementation of the agreements reached at the conferences. Barston observes that:

> "The first major post-war high-level global conference to discuss environmental questions was held in Stockholm in 1972. An important and continuing influence on the environment diplomacy, apart from the Stockholm conference, was the convening of the third UNCLOS in 1973. International attention began to be increasingly focussed on environmental regulation again at a global level from the mid-1980s... A fourth development, the United Nations Conference on Environment and Development (Rio Summit, 1992) has, despite limitations, brought high-level attention to environmental issues."[83]

The Paris conference on climate change in 2015, acknowledged that high levels of emissions are by industrialised countries, notably the USA, China, European countries, Japan, Australia, Canada and, newly industrialised countries like India, Brazil and South Korea. The Paris agreement raised international expectations on concerted efforts to address climate change. US President Trump dashed the expectations when he withdrew the US from the Paris agreement soon after taking office. The USA withdrawal from the agreement is a major drawback in global efforts to tackle environmental issues. Industrialised countries constitute the core pockets of resistance to change so as to reduce emission levels because of their economic interests. China, Russia, India, and Brazil argue that their economies cannot afford

---

83   R. P Barston, *Modern Diplomacy.*

to take drastic action to limit use of certain fuels like coal as this is bound to stunt their economic development.

Kenya's role in international diplomatic efforts on environment and climate change encourages collective international action to deal with the problem. Kenya must work together with other developing countries to put pressure on developed countries to take responsibility for the damage their industries have on environment. Developing countries are forced to balance their development needs with climate change initiatives of the UN such as the Kyoto Protocol and the Green Energy Processes. As host to UNEP and the UN-HABITAT, Kenya should continue to play an active role in the negotiations.

Fourth UN Headquarters

Kenya successfully lobbied to host the UNEP and UN-HABITAT headquarters in the early 1970s on account of support from the western countries, East bloc countries and the developing countries. Jomo Kenyatta, a Pan-Africanist, galvanised African support and with the help of leaders like Josip Broz Tito of Yugoslavia and Jawaharlal Nehru of India for his commitment to the Non-Aligned Movement (NAM). The Ministry of Foreign Affairs and other government agencies successfully lobbied against stiff competition from the USA, Mexico, Japan and Congo-Kinshasa, to win the right to host the UNEP headquarters during the United Nations Environment Conference in Stockholm, Sweden in 1972. Kenya achieved a similar result to host UN-HABITAT during the 1976 first UN-HABITAT Conference in Vancouver, Canada.

Kenya's standing among the G77 plus China and its contacts within the Non-Aligned Movement (NAM) was invaluable. Its pragmatic approach in its economic and foreign policies placed it in good standing with both western and East bloc countries. Developing countries, as a block, fought hard to have the two agencies established in a developing country so as to secure a geographical representation against the other three agencies established in the developed countries, namely: New York, USA, Geneva, Switzerland, and Vienna, Austria.

UNEP and UN-HABITAT have placed Kenya at the centre of environmental diplomacy, not just in Africa and the developing world, but across the whole world. It makes it imperative for Kenya to pursue an environmental policy which will draw international confidence and support. It should ensure that a conducive environment exists for the operations of UNEP and UN-HABITAT in Nairobi. Kenya must assure the international community of security, good infrastructure and fast action on administrative issues including administration of the diplomatic privileges such as VAT refunds agreed to under the Headquarters Agreement. It should intensify its pursuit of a pro-active environmental policy which will ensure Kenya remains at the forefront of environmental diplomacy.

Security, cleanliness and amenities convinced the international community to locate UNEP and UN-HABITAT in Nairobi. Security was good and the city clean; easily available social and economic services should be maintained and where possible, improved to keep Nairobi attractive. The diplomatic community need to be assured of security, good infrastructure and cleanliness in Nairobi. Deterioration in security especially robberies with violence and killings caused the UN system to downgrade Nairobi's security rating to category C. The developments heightened calls by some countries to seek relocation of the two bodies to Germany or France. Germany promised to provide free office accommodation in Bonn where its former offices as seat of government were available.

The upgrade of UNEP into a fully-fledged UN organisation for all its member states instead of the 54 or which had been members as an agency is welcome. That, together with the establishment of the UNON has affirmed Nairobi as the Fourth UN Headquarters.

In 2005, the then Director General of UNEP intervened on a string of concerns such as insecurity, deterioration of physical facilities (roads and street lighting) and tax exemptions. The concerns were discussed at the highest level of government where the Director General issued veiled threats that failure to improve would jeopardise the future of the two agencies in Kenya. The intervention led to the establishment of the Diplomatic Police Unit at Gigiri, construction of the road linking United Nations Avenue to Ruaka road, improvement of security, lighting and re-carpeting of the city's main streets.

Further improvements included the creation of a contact desk at the Ministry of Foreign Affairs Headquarters. The contact desk deals with all enquiries from the diplomatic community and directs those which need quick attention to appropriate authorities for action. Moreover, Kenya established a Host Country Liaison Committee for regular consultations between the government and the UN office. These extraordinary measures were taken to address the concerns of the diplomatic community and forestall any talk of moving the UN bodies from Nairobi. Kenya enjoys immense economic benefits accruing from capital inflows from a large number of international civil servants working for the UN agencies and other international organisations as well as diplomatic missions based in Nairobi.

Deforestation

Deforestation has a major impact on climate change. It adversely affects rain patterns, amount of rainfall and vegetation growth, and could lead to desertification. President Moi underlined the problem of deforestation in a speech delivered during the inauguration of the UN in Nairobi in 1984. He observed that:

> "It is underdevelopment and poverty that are forcing citizens in the third world to overgraze the land, cut down the trees, plough thin and unproductive soils, pollute and misuse water supplies. The consequences are the destruction of the priceless renewable resources. It is not enough to pass resolutions without implementing them. We should provide financial support to implement the resolutions we pass at international fora...The developed countries should support and encourage young bodies such as UNEP and UN-HABITAT. I believe that the day the developed countries will cease to politicize contributions; the United Nations will be able to succeed in fulfilling its objectives for the benefit of mankind. Let us show more concern for our environment beyond political divisions and ideologies."[84]

Moi's statement sent a powerful message to both domestic and foreign audiences about Kenya's commitment to environmental conservation. This was encouraging, yet he allowed excision of forests to settle landless Kenyans as well as reward political supporters. The latter were allocated huge tracks of land when squatters were given small unviable pieces of land to camouflage the illegal land acquisition. The allocations depleted the forest cover from the 10% recommended by the UN to 1.7% of Kenya's land mass by 2002.

Mau Forest saga

The Mau forest covers parts of Nakuru, Kericho, Narok, and Trans Mara counties. It serves the largest water tower of Kenya and is the source of the Mara and Sondu rivers which flow into Lake Victoria through Tanzania and Kenya, respectively. Its eco-system includes the rich agricultural land in these counties as well as the world famous Maasai Mara National

---

84 President Daniel arap Moi in a speech during the inauguration of the United Nations at Gigiri, Nairobi on 21st May, 1984.

Reserve in Kenya, and, Serengeti National Park in Tanzania. Extensive excision of the forest, most actively pursued during Moi's presidency, led to severe depletion of the water tower and the controversy around it damaged Kenya's international image on environmental conservation.

The debate on the Mau forest evokes emotions, controversy and has effectively overshadowed any restoration efforts to save the largest tropical forest in Kenya. The Mau forest is home to the Ogiek community, who have lived there for centuries. The community's lifestyle, by itself, does not threaten the forest. The policy debate should be in public interest and should not be allowed to serve regional, ethnic, political or personal interests. The Mau forest's importance to Kenya as a national treasure must be preserved and protected at all costs. Sustainable forest cover should be maintained to support agricultural farming, electricity generation and other rain-dependant economic activities.

The damage to the eco-system can be seen as one flies over the Mau forest, and the Kericho tea zone in Kericho and Bomet counties which twenty years ago were wet with rain most of the day. Kericho, full of tea estates, has less rain today than only a few years ago. The Constitution of Kenya, 2010 has provided for checks and balances in the governance structure to protect public interest and has outlawed situations where a single individual possesses the power to dish out national resources for political expedience. The degradation of the Mau forest has taken the country many years back. Development has a cost. Extraordinary measures should be taken, whatever the circumstances, to save the forest and support Kenya's role in international diplomacy on global warming, conservation of forests and population growth.

Convention on prohibition of international trade in endangered species
Kenya is endowed with rich natural flora and fauna, favourable climate all year round and a warm and welcoming people. The flora and fauna, especially its world-famous wildlife and national parks, should be preserved for posterity. Kenya should build on the measures it has taken to conserve its natural heritage. President Moi's decision to burn twelve tonnes of ivory worth Kshs 60 million on 8th July, 1989, seized from poachers and traffickers, signified Kenya's commitment to wildlife conservation. During the occasion, he said:

> "If the elephant is to be saved from extinction, poaching must be stopped. To stop the poachers, the traders must also be stopped, and to stop the trader, the final buyer must be convinced not to buy ivory.

I appeal to people all over the world to stop buying ivory. Do not be tempted to buy jewellery, ornaments or other objects carved out of ivory, for to do so will be to support the needless illegal killing of elephants."[85]

President Moi's decision was a wakeup call to save the elephant population which had dropped from 65,000 to 17,000, in Kenya alone and 1.7 million, in Africa in less than thirty years. It placed Kenya at the centre of conservation efforts which was capped by hosting the summit on the Convention on the Prohibition of International Trade in Endangered Species (CITES) in 1999, in Nairobi. The convention imposed a moratorium on the illicit trade for ten years, against opposition from southern African countries, some of who had chided Kenya for burning the elephant tusks instead of selling them to invest in conservation. The war against poaching will be difficult to win without the end market, appreciating the destruction it causes on the natural heritage of mankind.

Developments thereafter
The global ban which the conference imposed in 1999, on trade in ivory enabled Kenya's elephant population growth for nearly 17 years. Kenya was still complicit in the ivory trade as a conduit for illegal ivory from southern African countries. Elephants and rhino poaching, which resumed from 2008, culminated in a rebuke for the country at the Conference of Parties (CoP) in 2013, in Bangkok, Thailand. Kenya and seven other countries were given an ultimatum to come up with a tight formula on how to rein in illegal trade and trafficking in ivory, and rhino horns before the next CoP in South Africa in 2016. The relapse in conservation efforts hurt Kenya's image, especially the moral authority it attained when Moi burnt illegally poached ivory. Kenya must quickly reverse the adverse report on its conservation efforts to regain respect in conservation, Kenya's record in destroying elephant tusks – 12 tons in 1989, five tons in 2011, 15 tons in 2013, and, 105 tons and 1.35 tons of rhino tusks in 2016 – improved its international image on conservation efforts. The extension of the ban on the illicit trade in endangered species was re-affirmed by the CITES conference in South Africa in September, 2016, after successful lobbying by Kenya and other like-minded states.

Kenya should strengthen its governance structures to tackle corruption in the wildlife conservation sector which is the main driver of the raging poaching of elephants and the illegal trafficking of ivory tusks through the country. It should engage the CoP to prevail upon countries like China

---

85   President Moi on the occasion of burning twelve tonnes of ivory on 9th July, 1989.

and Cambodia to take action to minimize interest in the trade and make it unattractive to poachers and traffickers. Further, Kenya should take urgent action on the wanton degradation of its wildlife habitats through uncontrolled massive illegal grazing by domestic animals to sustain the tourism industry. It requires a delicate balance between human settlements and wildlife habitats to avoid conflicts like those which took place in Laikipia County in 2016 in order to maintain its conservation efforts and tourism for posterity.

Kenya's track record and commitment to saving the elephant and the rhino should be maintained as an inspiration for international action. Burning of the tusks alone is not enough and may come to naught if bold steps are not taken to deal with poaching and illegal trafficking to save the elephant and the rhino and preserve the flora and fauna for future generations. Illicit trade in endangered species is not restricted to elephants and rhinos alone. Trade in chimpanzees, a rare species, has been unravelled in West Africa where whole adult populations are eliminated to retrieve baby chimpanzees sought as pets in developed countries.

PART V

LOOK EAST POLICY, EVALUATION, CONCLUSION

This part discusses orientation of Kenya's Foreign Policy and diplomacy towards the East in response to dynamics in its relations with its traditional western development partners after the end of the Cold War in 1989. It focuses on Kenya's Foreign Policy on China, its major financier of road and rail infrastructure. It shows how Africa is the theatre for big power rivalry between China and the USA.

The Part further examines the achievements of Kenya's Foreign Policy and diplomacy since independence. The analysis and conclusions define the extent to which Kenya has successfully articulated its Foreign Policy and diplomacy to secure its national interest.

It also examines the impact of emerging issues in international relations such as democracy, good governance, international terrorism, human and drug trafficking, and the proliferation of SALW and how they have influenced the country's Foreign Policy and diplomacy.

It concludes with a way forward on the future of Kenya's Foreign Policy and diplomacy in the constantly changing dynamics in international relations.

CHAPTER 14

Look East Policy

Kenya articulated a non-aligned Foreign Policy from independence to maintain economically beneficial partnerships from either side of the political divide during the Cold War rivalry. In practice though, it preferred the western free market economic system over the socialist/communist economic system as practised by East bloc countries. Jomo Kenyatta's ideological and policy differences with Oginga Odinga played a role in settling for a non-aligned Foreign Policy. The differences, similarly, led to the proscription of Mao Zedong's red book and denunciation of Chou en Lai, Chinese Premier's visit in 1964, to some countries Africa.

However, the "Look East" Policy started under President Moi when he visited China in 1984 after US/China established a working relationship. One of the benefits of President Moi's visit was the construction of Moi International Sports Complex, Kasarani, by China. The Look East Policy was accelerated during the Kibaki presidency. The Look East Policy was Kenya's response to the new dynamics in international relations towards the end of the Cold War. The policy re-orientation was necessary for the country to find new sources of foreign capital and assistance in the changed new circumstances.

In taking cognisance of the dynamic developments in international relations since the end of the Cold War, Kenya's Foreign Policy was under scrutiny after the collapse of the Soviet Union, which left the USA unchallenged as the only superpower. Hitherto, Kenya enjoyed good relations with western countries. The dramatic end of the Cold War suddenly changed fortunes for Kenya. At first, Kenya seemed reluctant to accept the new realities. Its failure to immediately acknowledge the realities of the New World Order isolated it from its traditional development partners. This cost the country dearly in terms of development. Therefore, the "Look East Policy" was designed to find a balance in Kenya's international economic partnerships.

The end of the Cold War in 1989, left Kenya in a precarious position. The strategic position it held as a bastion against communist expansion in Africa suddenly evaporated. Its western development partners introduced tough political and economic conditions to be met to maintain uninterrupted economic partnership. It then turned to the East, in particular, China, which had emerged from Mao Zedong's doctrinaire, socialism, to market economy. The Look East Foreign Policy was a response to the realities of the post-Cold War era.

Kenya's relations with its western development partners began to deteriorate in the 1980s before the end of the Cold War when the country was forced to implement tough Structural Adjustment Programmes (SAPs) on the recommendation of the International Monetary Fund (IMF). As the world moved closer to the end of the Cold War, China began its modernisation programme after the death of Mao Zedong. Mao's successor, Deng Zhao Ping introduced market economy to make China competitive. USA President Richard Nixon's visit to China in 1981 opened up international interest in China. President Moi was one of the early leaders to visit China in 1984. That was the beginning of the détente with China which began the Look East orientation in Kenya's Foreign Policy.

New thinking

In 2002, the opposition won a landslide victory in the first truly democratic elections since the country's independence. Mwai Kibaki assumed the reins of power from President Moi after a twenty-four-year stint as President of Kenya. Kenya's economic performance had substantially deteriorated during Moi's tenure due to reduced international support and in response to his strong-arm tactics, resistance to political change and high levels of corruption in government. Western countries, hitherto the main source of development funds and investment capital, became reluctant to deal with Kenya. Oginga Odinga's fears of over reliance on one side of the ideological divide had returned to haunt Kenya more than twenty years later.

President Kibaki's focus on resuscitating the economy introduced the challenge of injecting new capital to spur development. The experience Kenya had undergone with its western development partners did not inspire confidence on how quickly such capital could be raised at short notice. He turned to the East, notably China.

President Kibaki made his first State visit to China in the autumn of 2005, which was followed by a return visit by Hu Jintao, then President of China, in April, 2006. These two visits laid down the foundation of a very strong bilateral engagement, which built on previous Chinese engagement with Kenya such as the construction of Kasarani stadium. China has been and continues to finance the construction of roads and other infrastructure projects including the SGR in the country. President Kibaki's flagship project, the Thika Super Highway was constructed by China.

President Kibaki's state visit attracted the interest of envoys of western countries based in Nairobi who were keen to know the outcome of the visit. USA Ambassador Andrew Bellamy and British High Commissioner Adam Wood made a joint demarche to the Ministry of Foreign Affairs to inquire about aspects of the visit of interest to them. First, they wanted to know why the president chose to visit China. Second, whether this interest signified a shift in the country's Foreign Policy towards the East.

On face value, the visit would not have raised any eyebrows, yet it was unusual for an US Ambassador and British High Commissioner to jointly and personally seek to find out about an issue which did not directly affect their countries. The joint intervention demonstrated their anxiety about the direction Kenya was taking in its international relations. Kenya's geo-strategic importance as a long-standing collaborator and anchor for their, respective, as well as collective, economic and security interest in East Africa, seemed to have been their main concern.

A few weeks after President Kibaki's visit, the then British Prime Minister, Tony Blair, made an official visit to China accompanied by a large trade delegation. The British High Commissioner to Kenya was at pains to explain the visit. He observed that China was a very important country with huge business potential to become a major economic power with whom Britain was consciously working hard to engage. That was obviously double speak for an envoy who appeared frantic about a visit to the same country by the president of Kenya.

Big powers unashamedly display undisguised national interest by determining what small countries must do or how they should behave. Invariably, the message appears to be that the interests of the USA and the UK, respectively, must be taken seriously than those of Kenya in relation to engagement with China. Between 2005 and 2014, many official visits have been exchanged between the USA and China, and between individual European countries and China, respectively. This is in addition to a structured annual engagement between, the EU as a block, and China, with a standing agenda on economic partnership and trade.

Kenya, a preferred country by the West during the Cold War, found itself in this position – between a rock and a hard place. It was clear that its leaders did not seem ready to embrace the fundamental changes which took place in the world after the end of the Cold War. The move towards the East was intriguing, recalling the rebuke Oginga Odinga received when he showed preference for a socialist mode of development for Kenya. He was forced to quit KANU and the government due to ideological differences with Jomo Kenyatta. Kenya's Look East Foreign Policy was, therefore, not accidental.

China's emergence from a peasant society to a global power

China's transformation from a peasant society to a global power was not accidental. The establishment of the People's Republic of China under Mao Zedong in 1949 was the first step in the evolution of the country. Mao focussed on creating an identity for China and its people. He was well aware of the huddles China needed to overcome. Mao may have gone overboard in some areas like the Cultural Revolution, but he managed to inculcate nationalism in the minds of the Chinese people. Deng Zhao Ping reforms took China to a higher level.

China's phenomenal economic growth took the world by surprise. China developed into the second largest economy in the world overtaking Japan in three decades of economic reforms. Deng's approach avoided the pitfalls of *glasnost* (openness) and *perestroika* (restructuring) which were the hallmarks of Gorbachev's attempt to reform the Soviet Union. China has since pursued an economic liberalisation programme which embraces market economics (capitalism), while ignoring constant criticism over human rights violations to this day, yet China remains a socialist state.

Once western countries acknowledged China's potential, they calibrated human rights criticisms in such terms as not to directly confront China. Instead, western leaders trooped to China accompanied by large trade delegations to conclude economic partnership agreements. Many large western companies including car manufacturers, computer, ICT, aviation industry, electronics and transport infrastructure, moved to invest in China.

All countries in the world want to benefit from China's breathtaking transformation into a developed economy seemingly against all odds and expectations. China is the largest foreign creditor to the USA through the holding of USA Treasury Bonds as well as its largest trading partner. China's importance as an economic power in the world cannot be underestimated. It has emerged as a major global player and in the process, presenting a big challenge to the USA's hitherto unchallenged global economic leadership.

New economic realities

Western countries hold economic sway in the world through advanced technology, favourable terms of trade, and influence in important international economic institutions including the International Bank for Reconstruction and Development (World Bank), and the International Monetary Fund (IMF). The US and its allies in the EU, the OECD, the G7 (Group of 7) and NATO, pursue their foreign policies through influencing the decisions of these institutions. Apart from the UN Security Council where Russia and China exercise the veto power, the influence by the West on the World Bank and IMF is enormous.

New centres of economic power have emerged since the end of the Cold War, which are beginning to compete for global influence. China and India, for example, have GDPs which are larger than some of the G7 countries, yet they do not have as much influence in international institutions compared to the G7 countries collectively or individually. Russia, jilted from the G8 (Group of 8), has joined hands in forming an economic group known as Brazil, Russia, India, China and South Africa (BRICS). As the name suggests, the group comprises of Brazil, Russia, India, China and South Africa, and could be critical in the balance of power in the future.

Chinese interests in Africa

China's economic transformation and rapid economic development has taken the world by storm. Unlike Mikhail Gorbachev who attempted a complete package of restructuring the Soviet society transparently through the policy of *glasnost* and *perestroika*, Deng Zhao Ping opted for economic transformation, observing that China needed economic development to deal with poverty and backwardness, before addressing political issues. The approach has witnessed China develop fast into the second biggest economy in the world with the potential of overtaking the USA by 2050. The speed and magnitude of China's development depends on availability of raw materials to fire its industries for sustainable economic development.

China sees Africa as a major source of raw materials. The continent possesses some of the largest mineral deposits known to man. Minerals such as gold, platinum, diamonds and virgin oil fields abound. China is already heavily involved in oil exploitation in Sudan, South Sudan, Libya, Angola, among other countries. Second, Africa has the potential of a huge market for Chinese goods. The visits by Chinese President Xi Jinping to Tanzania, DRC and South Africa, and that by Prime Minister Li Keqiang to Kenya, Ethiopia, Nigeria, and Angola, within a year of assuming office, should not surprise anyone. Elles Morgan, Ben Lambert, May Tan-Mullins and Daphne Chang support this observation. They state that:

"The dominant explanation for the Chinese presence in Africa is to access the continent's vast resources and emerging markets. In such accounts, aid is used as a form of 'soft power' to smooth entry into these markets that have hitherto been the preserve of western multinational companies. This materialistic and realist explanation has much traction and tends to be tied to state actors (although in China the distinction between state and non-state is complex) in the shape of large state-owned enterprises (SOEs) (e.g. Sino hydro) and banks (e.g. Exim). In terms of geopolitical discourse, this has been a shift from ideological solidarity in the Cold War period, where African regimes were courted as part of an 'anti-imperialist movement', to a more clear-cut and agreeable business footing in the recent past."[86]

The projection by the World Bank and IMF that China will soon become the largest economy in the world ahead of the USA adds to the urgency of securing the sources of raw materials as well as markets for its industrial production. China is, therefore, doing what a sensible country would do – seek markets for its manufactured products to advance its economic agenda.

Assertive China

China's engagement with Africa has attracted unprecedented interest by western countries who seem to worry about China's surge towards becoming a global economic and military power. Western countries' concern with China's engagement with Africa presents challenges on three fronts. First, as an economic giant, China wields immense influence among developing countries in which it has heavily invested in infrastructure development. Second, politically, China's policy of non-interference in the internal affairs of other states is less intrusive, compared to the conditionalities imposed by western countries.

Third, an assertive China threatens to neutralise Western countries' influence in the world. A combination of economic and political power has, therefore, made China project an unprecedented image of a powerful nation. China can challenge any world power in pursuit of its national interest. The realities of the post-Cold War period influenced developing countries to shift to China, out of their frustration on the manner in which the West ruthlessly dictated terms and conditions of engagement. China took the opposite view, and as a result, now attracts many developing countries seeking economic assistance.

---

86   Elles Morgan, Ben Lambert, May Tan-Mullins and Daphne Chang, *Chinese Migrants and Africa's Development.*

President Kibaki's ascend to power in 2002 helped attract interest from South East Asia, beginning with the visit to Kenya by Thaksin Sinawatra, then Prime Minister of Thailand and a State visit to China in 2005 already alluded to. It is worth noting, as discussed earlier, that the West showed interest in the direction Kenya was taking in its international relations. The real concern was the possible loss of their dominant position in Kenya and East Africa, and their long-term fear of China encroaching on what they perceived to be their traditional sphere of influence.

Strategic decision

Kenya took a bold step to pursue a Foreign Policy to support a liberal economic policy for fast growth. It was neither ground-breaking nor the last to shift in its Foreign Policy. Many countries have taken similar steps with regard to China. Western countries themselves troop to China for trade and investment, yet they disapprove when developing countries do the same.

However, Kenya's Look East policy in the wake of difficult relations with traditional development partners should not overlook the Chinese practice of sending manual workers, disguised as engineers of sorts, to undertake jobs which do not require any technical expertise, and can easily be done by Kenyans. Chinese assistance in the development of infrastructure is welcome, not just in Kenya, but across Africa. Mutually beneficial and constructive engagement regimes must be agreed upon to carry along the public for inclusive participation and ownership.

No development partner gives free money. Kenya's development agenda requires funding from within and without. It should seek assistance from wherever it can get it, including the East, without abandoning integrity requirements in governance, by merely seeking development partnership from the East. The country must continue to be held accountable for the proper use of development loans wherever they are obtained. Turning East should not mean cutting ties with western development partners.

CHAPTER 15

Kenya's Diplomacy on the World Stage

This chapter evaluates the effectiveness of Kenya's Foreign Policy and diplomacy over the years to address claims that Kenya pursues a "wait and see" Foreign Policy, or has no Foreign Policy at all. It discusses ways in which Kenya has used its diplomacy as an instrument in the implementation of its Foreign Policy. We have seen how Kenya took certain Foreign Policy positions on specific fronts to serve its national interest. Its Foreign Policy's focus on peace and stability was to secure a favourable environment for investment and trade in the region.

Earlier, the non-aligned Foreign Policy moderated Kenya's relations with western countries and the East bloc countries during the Cold War. Kenya adopted a mixed economy at independence to attract economic partnerships which could enable it to grow its economy to serve a thriving and competitive market in Eastern Africa.

Track record
Kenya has been pre-occupied with conflict resolution and mediation to promote peace and tranquillity in neighbouring countries which form the Horn of Africa and the Great Lakes Region. Its role in peace processes especially Sudan, Somalia and Mozambique attest to this fact. In addition to its remarkable participation in UN peacekeeping operations, this approach has helped it to advance the cause of peace and consolidate its role as an important player in the maintenance of world peace and security.

Quality of Kenya's diplomacy
Kenya attained independence without a suitable Foreign Policy infrastructure to manage and administer its foreign service. Its first task was to create institutions of the state to manage its affairs. It did not have trained diplomats to conduct its diplomacy and had to negotiate with friendly Commonwealth countries such as Canada, Australia, New Zealand and the UK, to help it build its own diplomatic capacity through training opportunities. However, the technical assistance provided had its limits with respect to Kenya's interests. Kenya's view of the world was specific to its interests with a road map of how it expected to secure them.

Makumi Mwagiru summarises the limitations and points out the variance in the interpretation of those countries' view of the world versus Kenya's view, as follows:

> "One of the challenges Kenya faced at independence was the lack of trained personnel to man its public institutions. This challenge was experienced in the field of diplomacy.... There were, however, training programmes that were established in agreement with friendly countries. These training programmes were essentially a sandwich type and their bulk consisted of doing internships at the ministries of foreign affairs of these friendly counties....The original programme was the Commonwealth Assistance Programme (CAP) in which Kenyan diplomats (and Commonwealth) were seconded to headquarters or diplomatic missions of the United Kingdom, Australia, New Zealand and Canada... Since it offered this in foreign countries, its emphasis was patterns, procedures and formats that were developed in cultural settings outside the African setting."[87]

Kenya did not have the capacity to run an effective Foreign Policy due to inadequate trained personnel, financial capacity and a sound infrastructure. An effective diplomatic service depends on the quality of its staff. Their selection and deployment should be determined on merit and professional qualifications. They should be able to understand the intricacies of diplomacy. Kenya needs a dedicated Foreign Service, whose members of staff understand the depth of their work. They must be sophisticated, dignified and tactful in carrying out their diplomatic assignments.

Apart from the above attributes, diplomats effectively deal with situations which they come to understand over time. They require reasonable tours of duty to enable them establish relations with their counterparts and, in the process, increase chances of forging long-term contacts to make a mark.

Internal political dynamics in Kenya's Foreign Service

Kenya continuously dilutes the quality of its diplomacy through heavy deployment of non-career diplomats to manage its diplomacy. Good quality diplomacy is grounded on knowledge, experience, patience and professionalism. Kenya's Foreign Service has never been developed to become truly professional. It has been administered as part of the general civil service, making it lose focus and professionalism. The influx of officers from both within and without the mainstream civil service at all levels, has diluted the quality of its diplomacy and effective articulation of the country's Foreign Policy.

---

87   Makumi Mwagiru, *Diplomacy and Its Relations*, p. 25.

Internal political, ethnic and personal interests have increasingly blurred the country's Foreign Policy vision and objectives. Inability or unwillingness to distinguish between the national interest, which its Foreign Policy articulates, and personal and ethnic interests of state actors, make it difficult to articulate a coherent Foreign Policy. The confusion translates into inability to play an influential role on the world stage. Critics have argued that Kenya appears at a loss on when to voice its opinion on issues of concern and interest, or when to take advantage of opportunities open at the sub-regional, regional and international levels.

Kenyan leaders talk and boast too much about themselves, and about what they can do to improve the lives of ordinary Kenyans, with little to show for it. Such loud talk is neither constructive nor is it likely to be productive in articulation of the country's Foreign Policy. Kenya needs leaders who talk less and act more decisively to enable the country achieve its Foreign Policy objectives.

International relations require singularly focused projection of national power. Political discourse in advanced democracies distinguishes between party political agenda and the national interest. Failure to distinguish the two sends wrong signals to friend and foe alike. In Foreign Policy, friendly countries rally together as allies for common causes, while foes generally remain adversarial and almost always act antagonistically against each other. A properly constituted government, which has appointed a shrewd Foreign Minister, should be able to articulate a coherent Foreign Policy to serve the country's national interest.

Richard Woollcott writes:

> As a nation we need less talk, less debate and more decision. [88]

Woollcott's observation supports the view advanced above and should be regarded as sound advice to policy makers in the management of public affairs. Unregulated appointment of non-career officers to plum diplomatic posts has a negative effect on the quality of the country's diplomacy. Kenya should be alert to constant dynamic changes in international relations and adapt its diplomacy to deal with these dynamics.

Promotion, protection and defence of Kenya's interests abroad

Kenya's standing in the world depends on several factors, some domestic and others external. The issues discussed in Chapter 4 on Kenya's Foreign Policy framework, are complemented by the quality of its diplomacy, and the effectiveness of institutions which undertake its diplomacy. If there is no confidence in state institutions by the citizens and the international

---

[88] Richard Woollcott, a onetime Permanent Secretary for Foreign Affairs and International Trade of Australia, "*The Hot Seat*".

community, it becomes much more difficult to successfully engage other states.

Kenya must support its institutions with human and financial capital to enable its diplomats do their work. Its diplomats should undergo intensive training to be knowledgeable on Foreign Policy, diplomatic traditions and sensitivities of receiving states, as required by the Vienna Convention on Diplomatic and Consular Relations.

In situations where Kenya has to reward persons who have made financial contributions to parties by appointing them to plum ambassadorial positions, efforts must be made to pick men and women who can adapt to the challenges of diplomatic work abroad. Kenya must strike a balance between political expedience and professionalism in considering such appointments. Overwhelming bias in favour of political operatives in the Foreign Service is desperate and counter-productive. It creates disillusionment for career officers who feel dejected and often lose enthusiasm and drive in the performance of their work. Experience has shown that political appointees themselves quickly become disillusioned during their postings, as soon as they find out what diplomatic service actually is about, that is, it is not the lucrative gamble they had imagined it to be, but a sacrifice for the nation.

Political appointees serve a short-term convenience and do not advance the national interest. Advanced countries like the USA, which appoint political operatives to selected plum posts, do so for strategic reasons. It may be because of their links to those countries in fields where the USA is seeking cooperation or because of certain historical reasons which augment its national interest.

The transformation from a politician to a diplomat is not easy for the majority of such appointees. The free-wheeling nature of domestic politics to which they may be accustomed to is totally different from the discipline of diplomacy. Factors such as lack of enthusiasm in the job, lack of knowledge of the job, lack of training or false expectations about the job quickly destroy any enthusiasm they may have shown in the assignment. However, not all political appointees have been failures in diplomacy.

Tours of duty for envoys

Diplomatic service is one field in which Kenya has maintained reasonable tours of duty for its envoys, partly because of costs involved in transfers of staff, and partly due to protocols involved in accrediting Ambassadors and High Commissioners. Short stints for diplomatic postings for career and non-career diplomats do not add value to the service. Such appointments only address local political equations and end up as a major burden to the tax payer who ultimately meets the cost of running the Foreign Service.

Diplomacy is a dynamic instrument of Foreign Policy. Kenya needs to engage its diplomatic capacity to exploit opportunities available to it to secure its national interest. It has to manage its relations with other states in such a way as to influence situations in its favour. It must not lose the international goodwill and confidence it enjoys to sustain cooperation on issues such as the war against terrorism, environment, climate change and economic partnerships, as it could affect its role, respect and mileage in respect to collaborative international efforts.

Kenya's diplomacy has suffered irreparable damage due to frequent changes at the Ministry Headquarters, especially of foreign ministers and permanent secretaries. The frequent changes which occurred, specially during both Moi and Kibaki's presidencies, introduced uncertainty in Kenya's Foreign Policy management. The ministers for Foreign Affairs have been shuffled at a frightening pace. For example, under the Kibaki Administration (2002-2013) there were five successive Foreign Ministers as follows: Kalonzo Musyoka, 2003-2004, Chirau Ali Mwakwere, 2004-2005, Raphael Tuju, 2006-2007, Moses Masika Wetangula, 2008-2010, George Saitoti (acting), 2010-2011 and again Moses Masika Wetangula, 2011-2013.

Similarly, there were four successive permanent secretaries in the Ministry of Foreign Affairs between 2003 and 2006. Therefore, these changes affected the chances of Kenya articulating its Foreign Policy effectively.

Diplomacy is most effective through contacts established and maintained over a long period. Such frequent reshuffle of top officials at the Ministry is not healthy in establishing channels for diplomatic engagement to consolidate the country's international standing and respect. The impression created is that Kenya does not place great value to its foreign relations and only grudgingly pursues its interests abroad through lip service. It may be one of the reasons why Kenya's voice, role and influence do not match its regional economic power.

Kenya's diplomacy will be better served if it maintains stability in the top echelons of the country's diplomatic hierarchy. Frequent changes of staff at top levels create instability and inconsistency, which in turn dilutes the effectiveness of diplomacy as a tool for its Foreign Policy. A foreign Minister, for example, who remains in the post for, at least, five years (the expected life of a constitutional term for a government), will be in a position to establish good contacts among his/her colleagues, and is likely to develop a good network for a sound diplomatic discourse than one who stays briefly in the post.

***

In 2004, the EAC Council of Ministers endorsed a Ugandan for the appointive post of Director General of the United Nations Industrial Development Organisation (UNIDO). Rather than support the position, Kenya fronted Ambassador Dr. Kipkorir Rana, for the same post. It played out badly and nearly brought an unnecessary misunderstanding between Kenya and Uganda at the AU summit in Abuja, Nigeria in February, 2005. Kenya was forced to withdraw its candidate when Uganda threatened to intervene at the highest level with Kenya.

Similarly, in 2003, Kenya fronted a candidate, during the first election of members of the Peace and Security Council of the AU in Addis Ababa, Ethiopia. The three-year rotational seat was intended to ensure continuity in sub-regional representation when the two-year tenures expired. North Africa settled for Egypt, West Africa chose Nigeria and Southern Africa selected South Africa. Therefore, Kenya and Ethiopia sought to be the first to be elected for the three-year tenure from Eastern Africa and presented candidates. Kenya lost to Ethiopia.

With hindsight, Kenya should have negotiated with Ethiopia on the rotation of the three-year seat for Eastern Africa, than take the matter to open competition on the floor, where it lost. Whereas West African countries reached an agreement quickly, Eastern Africa countries are unlikely to agree on an arrangement. The move portrayed Kenya as inadequately prepared for sub-regional competition for influence. It assumed that it would be the automatic choice of Eastern Africa on account of the size of its economy. Such plunders must be avoided at all costs in the future.

Setting SMART Objectives

Kenya should continuously set SMART objectives in its Foreign Policy. SMART objectives define clearly the direction of the Foreign Policy and how to achieve the objectives.

Kenya seems reluctant to front candidates for positions at the regional and international levels, or with international UN agencies. Apart from the EAC where the post of Secretary General is rotational, individual Kenyans seek international positions and revert to the government for support.

Countries whose citizens occupy senior positions in international organisations, similarly, influence situations in those organisations to the advantage of their countries. Internal political infighting in support of candidates ends up in factional endorsement, based on ethnicity or narrow political interests.

In 1998, Dr. Henry Chasia contested the post of Secretary General of the International Telecommunications Union (ITU), a plum international position, which should have had the full weight of the government. Instead, he was supported by the then Kenya Posts and Telecommunications Corporation (now Posta). In spite of a spirited campaign, Dr. Chasia narrowly lost to a Japanese candidate.

In 2007, Kenya put forward three candidates, Mr. Erastus Mwencha, for Deputy AU Commissioner, Ambassador Amina Mohamed for Commissioner for Trade, and Dr. Monica Juma for Commissioner for Peace and Security. Each candidate was fronted by different interests in the political system.

Kenya needs to improve its strategy to ensure support of its candidates for important international jobs. It should use its economic leverage to influence events in its favour. For example, in 2017, the EAC's last-minute announcement endorsing Ambassador Amina Mohamed, Kenya's candidate for AU Commission Chairperson, days before the election, underlines this point. Bilateral contracts should be used early enough to build consensus on regional interests.

As a respected member of the international community, Kenya should be prepared to deal with awkward circumstances diplomatically. Diplomacy is transitory; its conduct varies from one situation to another. It responds to prevailing international dynamics of the time. For example, Kenya's public criticism of Uganda for not supporting its candidate to the end, to secure an AU Commission Chairperson's seat, exposed a major weakness in the quality of its diplomacy. Uganda is Kenya's immediate neighbour and the largest trading partner. Its relations with Uganda are bound to expand as both countries develop. Uganda's support alone could not have altered the result of the election.

The re-admission of Morocco tipped the scale in favour of the eventual winner. Kenya should have foreseen this development and adopted a flexible strategy, including its position on the issue of Sarawi. The 40 or so countries which supported Morocco's re-admission voted for Chad's candidate for the AU Commission Chairperson. Support for candidates in AU elections is strategically tactical. Member-states singularly or through RECs progressively shift alliances on candidates, as some are eliminated from the ballot. Uganda was bound to drop one candidate or the other. The AU Commissioner Chairperson's seat cannot be compared with the economic benefits Kenya derives from its relations with Uganda.

Leadership in the region

Kenyans expect the country to take a lead on many issues in relation to its commanding economic position in East Africa. It partly explains why Kenya exerts less influence, is not visible in a region where it commands substantial economic leverage, and why it seems to shy away from taking a leadership role commensurate with its economic strength on issues it can articulate with authority and conviction. The country is bound, as expected, to face competition from its neighbours; it should not shy away from articulating positions at the regional and international levels when situations demand it.

Kenya should work to bring on board partner states in the EAC or IGAD, COMESA and the AU. A common agenda when collectively pursued is likely to succeed because of the weight of joint action. In the process, Kenya is likely to influence events to suit its Foreign Policy objectives and thus secure its national interest without confrontation.

As the lead institution, the Ministry of Foreign Affairs should coordinate Kenya's leadership on issues in the international community relevant to its interests. The Ministry has acted decisively on occasions when the minister enjoyed some degree of latitude in decision making. Dr. Munyua Waiyaki's tenure as Foreign Minister saw Kenya demonstrate strong leadership in supporting the liberation struggle against apartheid in South Africa, in the NAM, and the UN General Assembly. But that was because President Jomo Kenyatta delegated Foreign Policy to the minister largely due to his advanced age and his focus on domestic policies soon after independence. Other ministers like Dr. Robert Ouko and Dr. Bonaya Godana, though articulate, did not enjoy similar latitude under Moi when they held the post.

Pro-action

In general, responses to international developments have been slow, sometimes uncoordinated and ineffective. The name tag "wait and see" has tended to place Kenya in the group of countries known as "fence sitters". The Ministry of Foreign Affairs has been at pains to explain this ambivalent position even when Kenya takes neutral positions (abstention) on controversial issues at the UN or other international fora. The option enables both sides to claim support when in reality, Kenya avoids offending either party. It is a useful tool employed by many countries in tricky circumstances.

On the question of Palestine, for example, Kenya generally abstains on any vote in the UN General Assembly in order to maintain good relations with both Israel and Arab countries, and has adopted a similar position on country-specific resolutions on human rights issues, for pragmatic reasons.

Kenya has, in the past, considered it prudent to pursue a policy of recognising states instead of governments. This move has enabled it to avoid pronouncing itself on the legitimacy of change of government by unconstitutional means. In the past, Kenya adopted this approach when it suited its interests to do so, such as was the case in Uganda when Idi Amin Dada overthrew Milton Obote in 1971.

It is no longer possible to continue with such an ambivalent position. As party to the Constitutive Act of the AU, Kenya is bound by collective action taken by the AU on military coups d'etat where unconstitutional change of governments has occurred. The AU now imposes sanctions on such countries until constitutional governments have been restored.

Clear policy position

Kenya's Foreign Policy framework discussed in chapter 4 sets out the principles which guide the policy. It looks at issues in its Foreign Policy such as good governance, democracy and respect for human rights. The provisions of The Constitution of Kenya, 2010, have anchored the policy in its provisions, which oblige the country to respect internationally accepted norms and behaviour. It is no longer possible to hide under non-interference in the internal affairs of other states or, indeed, of its own in articulating its Foreign Policy. The three consecutive elections; 2007, 2013 and 2017, underline how domestic issues influence Kenya's relations within Africa and with the rest of the international community. The manner in which Kenya manages its own internal affairs is, itself, subject to international interest.

The Constitution of Kenya, 2010 obliges Kenya to uphold the rule of law and respect the country's international obligations. It sets out the conditions of establishing a government in Kenya and extends its application to international law as provided in Chapter 1, Article 3, Section 2 which states that: "Any attempt to establish a government otherwise than in compliance with this Constitution is unlawful," while Article 2, Section 5 states that: "The general rules of international law shall form part of the law of Kenya", and Section 6 which states that: "Any treaty or convention ratified by Kenya shall form part of law of Kenya under this Constitution."[89]

---

89   The Constitution of Kenya, 2010.

Kenya must always pronounce itself on the question of constitution of a government in a foreign country, and in so doing, take into account governance issues, including the legal status of such a government.

Kenya's diplomatic infrastructure

The Ministry of Foreign Affairs is the lead institution in the formulation and implementation of Kenya's Foreign Policy, in consultation with other stakeholders. It is a strategic arm of the government which is ranked immediately after the office of the chief executive of the country. Its pivotal role means that its coordination mandate is critical to developing country positions on international issues. The Ministry must be adequately funded for it to develop the pre-requisite capacity to enable it to formulate, articulate and implement a credible Foreign Policy. The Foreign Policy must be innovative, flexible and sensitive to developments in the world, which requires adequately trained staff, able to cope with technological advancements in information and communication technology.

The ability of the Foreign Policy to be flexible without digressing from the Foreign Policy framework enables Kenya to maintain friendly relations with different actors in its national interest. At the multilateral level, Kenya has adopted the policy of abstention on country specific resolutions principally to avoid antagonising itself with friendly countries that are at loggerheads or in conflict. This approach has been deviated from only when there is consensus by the AU or sub-regional groups, to which it is a member. The policy recognises the enormous influence of countries like the US, China and Russia, and institutions such as the EU, the World Bank, the IMF and the UN itself.

In 2005, Kenya found itself in an awkward position during the UN conference on Human Rights in Geneva. The conference evaluates, on an annual basis, human rights situations globally, and censures countries which are deemed to have violated them. The then Minister for Justice and Constitutional Affairs who was leading the Kenyan delegation announced publicly that Kenya would support Cuba on a resolution sponsored by the USA, designed to condemn Cuba for its violation of human rights against its people.

The announcement enraged the USA, the EU and their allies who sharply rebuked Kenya and threatened economic consequences if it went ahead to support Cuba. The threat by the US and the EU presented a serious challenge to Kenya in the light of their influence in the international system, unlike Cuba, of which the minister had publicly pledged Kenya's support.

After weighing the situation, it was decided that Kenya's interests were paramount. The Ministry of Foreign Affairs directed the mission in Geneva to abstain on the vote as was the tradition or support the AU position if there was one. That, in effect, would maintain relations with both Cuba and the US. That experience revealed the dangers of uncoordinated action by an arm of government not familiar with intricacies of Foreign Policy. It re-affirmed the ministry's role as the principal organ responsible for Kenya's Foreign Policy.

The implementation of Foreign Policy is a complex process which demands intensive consultations and coordination in its articulation. If the Minister for Foreign Affairs falls short of expectations, Kenya stands to lose out on important contacts, consultations and negotiations with other international actors. It makes it harder for the country to engage its diplomacy successfully. The Ministry usually has, under its direction, qualified and trained career Foreign Service officers, and specialised staff from other ministries and departments, who provide expert advice on foreign, trade, consular, security and other policy issues.

The Minister for Foreign Affairs should ensure that policy direction and the deployment of staff at all levels is based on merit as far as possible, qualifications and suitability to undertake assignments efficiently. It is critical to carry out a sound capacity evaluation before deployment is done, in order to avoid any compromises in the stated objective of Foreign Policy.

The ministry will be best served by staff with adequate skills to ensure professional execution of Foreign Policy. The establishment of the Foreign Service Academy is well placed to provide practical training to its staff, as well as provide similar diplomatic skills to Foreign Service officers from friendly countries in the sub-region, especially those emerging from conflict, as part of Kenya's post-conflict engagement and contribution to peace.

The usefulness of the Academy depends on how the Ministry intends to use it as a tool of diplomacy. The Academy should become the backbone of the Ministry in the development of capacity, in liaison with the Institute of Diplomacy and International Studies at the University of Nairobi, or similar institutes in other public universities, as well as the National Defence College (NDC). The Academy needs to develop tailor-made courses for junior, middle level and senior officers, including refresher courses.

Suitable deployment

Suitable staff deployment enhances stability of staff and the Ministry's ability to shoulder the responsibility of diplomatic expectations for the nation. The Minister represents the face of the country at international fora where the Chief Executive is not present, and through him/her the Foreign Policy of the country. He/she should be someone who is prepared to spend more time travelling on diplomatic assignments. It works better when the Minister is a professional who does not have other domestic challenges like being an MP at the same time.

Countries which maintain foreign ministers for at least the parliamentary term, enjoy good diplomatic stability because the Minister is able to maintain contacts made during his/her tenure. Other foreign Ministers are able to understand and relate to him/her professionally. The rapport, thus created, translates into benefits. Stability at the top political management levels improves chances of successful engagement with other foreign ministers through telecommunication or at a personal level. Diplomacy is a game of brinkmanship and is best conducted when the interlocutors know one another and have developed confidence to discuss issues freely.

Kenyans in the diaspora

Kenya has a large number of its citizens living abroad as students, businesspersons or working as professionals. Many gave up their Kenyan and took up foreign citizenship before the Kenya Constitution, 2010, which allows dual citizenship was promulgated. The Constitution recognises the economic contribution made by the Kenyan diaspora community largely via repatriation of their money to support families or for investment. It has granted dual citizenship to Kenyan nationals in the diaspora as an incentive to invest in their country. Chapter 3, Article 16 of the Constitution, grants Kenyans who live abroad dual citizenship. It states that:

> "A citizen by birth does not lose citizenship by acquiring the citizenship of another country."[90]

Before the current Constitution, Kenyans in the diaspora relentlessly campaigned for dual citizenship to enable them maintain strong ancestral connections in their country of birth as well as benefit from rights as citizens of their adopted countries.

In 2012, Kenyans in the diaspora estimated at over 3 million, repatriated Kshs. 170 billion.[91] This is a major contribution to Kenya's GDP. The diaspora, therefore, constitutes an important means of transfer

---

90   The Constitution of Kenya, 2010.
91   See Migration and remittances data – World Bank Group.

of technology to Kenya. Both remittances and transfer of technology are critical in consolidating on-going, long-term Vision 2030.

Kenyans in the diaspora are keen to exercise their right to participate in the elections as citizens of Kenya. The *Kenya Foreign Policy, 2014,* has identified the diaspora as one of the pillars of the Foreign Policy of the country. It states on p. 23 that:

> "The Diaspora pillar aims to harness the diverse skills, knowledge, expertise and resources of Kenyans living abroad and facilitating their integration into the national development agenda."[92]

This position has probably not been given due consideration as Kenyans in diaspora do not remit money or participate in the transfer of technology as part of government policy. They do so for personal reasons, commitment and priorities. Many of them are not sure of what to do or how to relate to a government which has little to do with their daily lives. It is also not clear whether the actual number of Kenyans in the diaspora is known. A programme should be put in place to map out and establish the number of Kenyans in the diaspora, with a view to determining how to deal with them.

The *Diaspora Policy* should determine how Kenyans abroad may be influenced as many of them hold dual nationalities and cannot be wholly relied upon for loyalty to the country of birth. It would be more sensible to consider them as an important target group which the country should continuously court for interest and investment. To do so, Kenya must develop a simple, transparent and flexible investment policy to attract them to invest in the country and to make them feel that their investments will be protected. One of the areas to be thought through regards the taxation policy which, at present, is prohibitive and appears to be punitive to investors.

It is far-fetched to imagine that all Kenyans in the diaspora are people of good conduct. Some could very well be involved in suspicious under-hand dealings.

The *Diaspora Policy* should also have a robust implementation mechanism which will deal with concerns of those in the diaspora willing to invest in the country. It should, for example, pay closer attention to the perennial problems facing Kenyan domestic workers in the Middle East countries to ensure their safety and meaningful contribution to the national economy.

---

92 *Kenya Foreign Policy, 2014*

Goodwill ambassadors

Kenya has an array of talent among its nationals which can be utilised to market the country. Some Kenyans have outstanding credentials in fields such as athletics, education, environment and diplomacy. They could be appointed as goodwill ambassadors and role models to influence Kenyans in the diaspora to cultivate, promote and project a positive image of the country in their adopted countries. Use of goodwill ambassadors is not new. Professor Wangari Maathai was bestowed with the honour shortly after her award of the Nobel in 2005, for her work on environment conservation.

CHAPTER 16

Conclusion

This book has established that Kenya's Foreign Policy is determined by its national interest. Based on the national interest, which is permanent and eternal, articulation of the Foreign Policy for the future is straightforward. Kenya's national interest is not only an expression of its national power, it is critical to its survival as a state. It drives all state activities and defines what Kenya stands for both at home and abroad. Kenya's Foreign Policy objectives have been designed to secure its national interest as a priority. As conclusions are made from the narrative, pointed questions will continue to be asked about its relevance, value and effectiveness. It will not be in vain to pose the questions about the direction Kenya's Foreign Policy might take in the future. The dynamics of international relations will continue to shape the Foreign Policy as Kenya strategizes to respond to them. The basic tenets will remain as long as the core elements of its national interest remain its determinants.

Conduct of Kenya's Foreign Policy
Kenya conducts its Foreign Policy guided by internationally accepted principles on Foreign Policy discussed in Chapter 4. Furthermore, it respects the principles, meets its international commitments and obligations. It also practises good governance, democracy, respects human rights, fundamental freedoms enshrined in its Constitution, and upholds the rule of law. These attributes make Kenya articulate a pragmatic Foreign Policy of peace, regional and international cooperation. As a result, Kenya plays a role in the search for peaceful settlement of disputes in the sub-region, which has earned it a reputation as a respected member of the international community. It has played a role in the search for solutions to conflicts in the Sudan, Somalia, Ethiopia and Uganda in the Horn of Africa, and DRC in the Great Lakes Region. Kenya will continue to pursue this policy as long as insecurity, conflict, and instability persist in some of its neighbours. The objective of pursuing the policy continues to be the search for markets in the region, attraction of foreign investment and trade.

Kenya's Foreign Policy from independence was designed to secure much needed financial aid and investment from development partners.

Most of the economic support came from the West, which saw Kenya as a beacon of peace in a turbulent Horn of Africa and Great Lakes Region. Its non-aligned policy made it possible for Kenya to develop a working relationship with the East bloc and western countries. It helped Kenya adopt a non-confrontational Foreign Policy and made it possible to secure the right to host UNEP and UN-HABITAT in the 1970s.

Throughout the Cold War period, Kenya maintained a strong non-aligned position, although it preferred to engage more with western countries for its economic development needs and on security issues. The UK maintained military training facilities in northern Kenya while the USA carried out its Africa operations from Nairobi. Kenya became a strategic partner for the West against the Soviet Union in their competition for global dominance until 1989 when the Cold War ended. The realities of the New World Order presented Kenya with difficult choices when it ceased to be a proxy in the post-Cold War era.

Mwai Kibaki propelled Kenya's Foreign Policy towards the East, particularly, China. The orientation attracted instant attention by western countries, notably the USA and the UK, whose ambassadors in Nairobi made a joint demarche to the Ministry of Foreign Affairs to inquire on what had transpired during Kibaki's visit to China in the autumn of 2005.

Uhuru Kenyatta intensified the new Foreign Policy orientation through exchange of visits and partnership in infrastructure development. Apart from road infrastructure, Kenya signed a cooperation agreement with China to finance the construction of the SGR from Mombasa to Malaba, as well as other infrastructural projects around the country.

The Constitution of Kenya, 2010

Kenya's early realisation that its national interest would be best served with a flexible and prudent Foreign Policy influenced its Foreign Policy on regional and international cooperation as pillars of its economic development to secure its national interest. This meant that Kenya adjusts its Foreign Policy from time to time to attain its Foreign Policy objectives. World issues which were previously regarded as internal affairs of states such as governance, democracy, human rights, accountability and corruption became critical in international relations.

The Constitution of Kenya, 2010, gave fresh impetus to articulation of a pragmatic Foreign Policy after years of confusion and reluctance to accept political change. Its provisions on new governance structures, a comprehensive Bill of Rights, democracy and good governance have provided the country with a fresh start and the flexibility to respond to changing international dynamics from time to time. Kenya's adoption of international treaties and conventions it has signed or acceded to commits it to uphold international law. Kenya's Foreign Policy must articulate its values, beliefs and aspirations to secure support and secure a role and place on the world stage.

Kenya Foreign Policy, 2014

Kenya Foreign Policy 2014, defines the strategic objectives of Kenya's Foreign Policy. It states:

> "Kenya's long struggle for national liberation from colonialism set a strong foundation for its Foreign Policy orientation. The architects of our Republic underscored the inextricable link between national independence and humanity's larger freedom, equity and the inalienable right to a shared Heritage... In order to strategically place the country in the international arena, the architects of Kenya's Foreign Policy charted a pragmatic approach, informed by several principles, which have stood the test of time. This approach has ensured that Kenya successfully forges mutually beneficial alliances with the West while constructively engaging the East through its policy of positive economic and political non-alignment."[93]

Kenya Foreign Policy, 2014, underscores pragmatism and continuity. It underlines flexibility and adaptation in pursuit of its objectives. Kenya's geographical location, resource endowment, strategic interests and its capacity to act to promote, protect and defend them are critical factors. Kenya's Foreign Policy should remain flexible to enable it respond to the challenges of the dynamics of international relations.

Kenya's diplomatic engagement must remain consistently pro-active, allowing it to argue each case backed by facts to secure its national interest. Kenya's diplomatic style should be explained to its citizens. Sometimes silence could be a positive stand to take. On some occasions, Kenya should be ready to take a stand on issues it views strongly, even if it is at odds with its partners. It must decide what position suits it best on any issue under different circumstances. Kenya's Foreign Policy should be about prudent judgement of situations with a view to converting them into opportunities for its benefit.

Kenya's regional Foreign Policy began at independence when it joined Tanganyika and Uganda to establish the EAC. Although the Community collapsed in 1977, the EAC is particularly critical to this policy approach. The EAC established in 2000, provides mechanisms to facilitate agreement

---

93   *Kenya Foreign Policy, 2014, pp. 14-15.*

on common positions as a Community. It has set four milestones intended to be achieved towards a political federation. In principle, this arrangement should eliminate unnecessary competition in other areas of common interest such as seeking opportunities for international jobs for the citizens of East Africa. Kenya's Foreign Policy acknowledges the importance of collective action in circumstances which demand such an approach.

Internal dynamics in Kenya's Foreign Policy

Issues such as good governance, democracy and accountability define Kenya's Foreign Policy. They include the values, beliefs and aspirations which its Foreign Policy articulates. Calls for national dialogue and cohesion should take into account the need to address people's perception on inclusiveness and demonstrate action to address historical injustices which affect the feel-good factor for the citizens. Kenya's readiness to uphold the Constitution and the rule of law will help it transform itself from a backward to a modern state to unleash the potential of its citizens.

Other issues such as HIV and AIDS, malaria, gender equity and gender-based violence, and poverty must be addressed urgently to allow Kenya's economy to grow at a reasonable percentage to create employment opportunities for citizens so as to improve their standards of living. Specific efforts and steps must be taken to revive its agriculture, manufacturing, and the tourism sectors and, to attract foreign investment and accelerate the economic recovery strategy in order to achieve Vision 2030.

Kenya's Foreign Policy on environment should be matched with specific programmes to exploit its potential for rapid economic development. Its participation in international conferences on environment and climate change means very little, if the destruction of its water towers, through deforestation and illegal acquisition of forest land hurts, its conservation efforts. Forest degradation leads to less rainfall and consequently, poor agricultural production. It negatively impacts on power generation, which makes it difficult to produce sufficient energy for domestic and industrial use. Kenya stands a better chance of achieving Sustainable Development Goals (SDGs) and Vision 2030, if it strikes a balance between its environmental policy and population growth.

Kenya needs to diversify its development partners to avoid over-reliance on just a few countries, and to strengthen its relations with emerging and fast industrialising countries in Asia, the Middle East and Latin America, to attain the balance. Countries from these regions are likely to attach less stringent conditionalities to economic partnerships with Kenya, than the traditional development partners. Diversification should not be used to ignore its commitment to democracy, accountability and good governance. Its Foreign Policy should respond to both domestic and external challenges of the 21st century.

ICT in diplomacy

Information and communication technology (ICT) has overtaken the traditional diplomatic communications in many respects. The traditional methods of envoys physically conveying diplomatic messages by land, sea or even air have been overtaken by electronic systems such as telephones, live news coverage and other forms of social media.

ICT has become the central means of communication in modern diplomacy. Events happening in one corner of the world are instantaneously transmitted live to the rest of the world. Internet has revolutionised communication and the way of doing business all over the world. The optic fibre undersea cable that has already been laid from the Red Sea to Mombasa to improve internet connectivity in Eastern Africa, is a major development. Kenya should develop an effective communication network to link its diplomatic missions across the world to the ministry headquarters.

Kenya should likewise remain alert to global cyber threats to its interests. Other threats it should be conscious of in the support of efforts to secure international peace and security include terrorism, piracy, and human and drug trafficking. Its Foreign Policy should, therefore, include programmes which integrate politics, trade, infrastructure development, investment, tourism, and technology, as envisioned in the AU's Vision 2063 as an incentive to accelerate its economic development.

Kenyans in the diaspora are a significant constituency. They are, however, an elusive group who prefer to invest in the country of birth by choice. Many of them hold dual citizenship which makes it difficult to meaningfully engage them. Dual nationality may help Kenyans in the diaspora to engage meaningfully in nation-building by investing some of their savings in their country of birth. Such investment will augment the repatriation of funds as a source of foreign exchange earnings.

Furthermore, as a major sporting nation, Kenya should underscore the importance of sports as a diplomatic tool. Already, Kenyan athletes are powerful goodwill ambassadors in their own right, promoting the good image of the country, by their outstanding performances, without due acknowledgement by the state.

A good sports policy and efficient administration of various sports organisations should harness benefits from mass sports like football, and help develop emerging ones such as golf, for sports tourism. Golf, on its own, is a major tourist attraction. Kenya could harness it for its economic potential, by encouraging major tourist facilities to develop golf courses like in South Africa and Middle East countries of Abu Dhabi, Bahrain and Qatar. These countries have turned hostile climactic conditions into great investment opportunities. The existence of good facilities will encourage high end tourists who pay for their stay in Kenya, and contribute in the creation of employment opportunities for the people. This requires an assurance of adequate security, as the long-term future of tourism and other industries depends on peace and security in the country.

The Foreign Policy should be dynamic, to position Kenya, to adapt to new situations to sustain its role and place at the regional and international levels. It will increase Kenya's comparative advantage over its competitors. Kenya must maintain a high standard of professionalism in the Foreign Service. Diplomacy is a cherished profession which deserves only the best brains Kenya can produce, noting that it is expensive and tedious to fully train a Foreign Service officer.

The future

A robust Foreign Policy must be subjected to review from time to time. Such a review should take into account domestic circumstances and the external environment, and seek to balance economic partnerships the country seeks, from friendly countries and international organisations. A sound Foreign Policy will enable Kenya to maintain good relations with its traditional partners from the West, even as it seeks new ones in the East. This balance is critical to ensuring that Kenya does not compromise its potential through blackmail following the wishes or interests of one group or the other.

The executive, which by law is responsible for the formulation and implementation of Kenya's Foreign Policy, should seek the views of all stakeholders on its management and administration. The legislature should play its part as an important stakeholder in the articulation of the Foreign Policy as a strategy to pursue its objectives in line with Vision 2030.

Kenya should jealously guard the right to host the Fourth UN Headquarters comprising UNEP and UN-HABITAT, whose umbrella office, UNON, is at par with other UN offices in New York, Geneva and Vienna in the UN system. It must guarantee security, good infrastructure and other amenities to ensure the environment is conducive to their operations.

Kenya must continue with its policy of interacting with all actors to complete its ambitious programme of infrastructure development so as to achieve Vision 2030. Kenya's Foreign Policy should anchor the country firmly in the international system as a credible and active player for all seasons.

Bibliography

Aboul-Enein, CDR Youssef, *Militant Islamic Ideology*, p. 192.

Acemoglu, Daron & Robinson, James, *Why Nations Fail,* p. 125.

African Socialism and its Application to Planning in Kenya, Sessional Paper No. 10, 1965, p. 70.

Ahtisaari, Martti, *Conversations with Ahtisaari*, p. 127.

Aller, Aber, Southern Sudan; *Too many Agreements Dishonoured*, p. 133.

Barston, R. P., *Modern Diplomacy*, pp. 31, 32, 200.

Carson, Johnnie, former US Ambassador to Kenya, p. 100.

Foreign Service Institute, *Reminisces of Kenya's early Diplomacy 1963-1993.*

Francis, David J., *Peace and Conflict in Africa*, p. 123.

Gujral, Inder Kumar, *A Foreign Policy for India*, p. 5.

Karimi, Joseph & Ochieng, Philip, *The Kenyatta Succession*, p. 76.

Kenya Foreign Policy, 2014, pp. xxv, 104, 234, 239.

Kissinger, Henry A., *Diplomacy, Third Edition*, p. 11.

Leys, Colin, *Underdevelopment in Kenya*, p. 59.

Mohiuddin, Ahmed, *African Socialism in Two Countries*, p. xix.

Morgan, Elles, Lambart, Ben, Tan-Mullins, May & Chang, Douglas, *Chinese Migrants and Africa's Development*, p. 216.

Morgenthau, Hans J., *Politics Among Nations*, Fourth Edition.

Mutiso, Gideon-Cyrus & Rohio, S.W., *Readings in African Political Thought,* p. 62.

Mwagiru, Makumi, *Diplomacy and Its Relations*, p. 220.

Nathan, Susan, *The Other Side of Israel*, p. 188.

Ndegwa, Duncan, *Walking in Jomo Kenyatta's Struggles*, My Story, pp. 65, 67.

Nicholson, Harod, *Diplomacy, Third Edition*, pp. 17, 25.

Nyerere, Julius, *Freedom and Unity*, p. 167.

Odinga, Jaramogi Oginga, *Not Yet Uhuru*, pp. 67, 68.

Oxford English Dictionary, p. 24.

Satow's *Guide to Diplomatic Practice*, p. 24.

Sen, B., *A Diplomat's Handbook of International Law and Practice*, p. 4.

Sumbeiywo, Lazarus, *To be A Negotiator*, p. 136.

The Constitution of Kenya, 2010, pp. 101, 230, 234.

Walcott, Richard, *The Hot Sear*, p. 222.

Warah, Rasna, *Middle East Crisis and the Refugee Problem*, Daily Nation, 14th September, 2015.

Woodward, Peter, *Crisis in the Horn of Africa*, p. 131.

Index

A

Abbottabad, 32

Abdullah, Abdullah, 80

Abdullah, King, 90

Aboul-Enein, CDR Youssef H., 155

Abyei, 114, 116

Acemoglu, Daron, 103-104

Adan, Sharif Hassan Sheik, 125

Afghanistan, 34, 80, 109, 154

African Growth and Opportunity
Act (AGOA), 9-10, 32, 150

African Peer Review Mechanism
(APRM), 147

African Union (AU), 12, 16, 24-25,
40, 72, 77, 84-85, 95, 103, 123,
127, 134, 136, 139, 141,
144-147, 151, 158, 161, 183-188;
Commission Chairperson, 184;
Constitutive Act, 40,186;
liaison office, 147;
Peace and Security Council,
24, 146, 183;
summit in Abuja, 183;
Vision 2063, 147, 196;
Mission to Somalia (AMISOM),
16, 94-95

Afro-Asian Economic Cooperation
(AAEC), 150

Afwerki, Isaias, 69, 121

Ahmed, President Abdullahi Yusuf,
16, 126

Ahtisaari, Martti, 105

Akol, Dr. Lam, 115

al-Assad, President Bishar, 156

al-Bashir, President Omar, 113, 115

Algeria, xxix

Ali, Major General Hussein
Mohamed, xxxii, 80

Ali, Mohamed, 109

Ali, President Ahmed Ben, 155

Alier, Abel, 109

Al-Qaeda, 32, 34, 50, 93-94,
153-156

Al-Shabaab, 16, 34, 50, 93-95, 99,
126, 153-155

Ambassadors, Appointment of,
35-36

Amin, Idi, xxxiv, 5, 17, 62, 96,
117-118, 120, 141, 186

Angola, 61, 105, 128, 135, 175

Anyanya I, 110

Anyanya II, 110

Arab, 109, 151-153, 157;
Arab countries, 150-152, 157,
186; Arab League, 145,
152; Arab North (Sudan), 110,
116; Arab Spring, 155;
Arabic language, 134, 145;
Arab-Israeli wars, 151-152;
opinion, 151, 153; region, 152;
population in Kenya, 50;
Sunni Arabs, 156

Arusha Declaration (1967), xx, 58,
138

Asia, 195; South East, xxxiii, 177

Assange, Julian, 27, 29

Assembly of State Parties (ASP), 85

Athens, 21-22

Australia, New Zealand, United States (ANZUS), 161

Austria, 46, 87, 164

B

Bagisu, 99

Banda, Dr. Kamuzu, 130

Barre, President Siad, 71, 93, 103, 124, 126

Barrow, President Adama, 25

Barston, R. P., 27-28, 163

Beira, 128-129, 133

Belgium, 33, 90, 154

Birigwa, Wasswa, 141

Blair, Tony, 109, 173

Borana, 99

Bosnia-Herzegovina, 3

Botswana, 69

Brazil, 38, 134, 161, 163, 175

Brazil, Russia, India, China and South Africa (BRICS), 175

British, 7, 12, 14, 51, 53, 55-56, 94, 96, 103, 109, 115, 117, 122, 137-138, 151, 173; colonial heritage, 122, 138; East Africa, 96, 117, 137; interests, 109; trustee territory, 137, 151

Bukusu, 99

Burundi, xxxiii, 80, 92, 96-97, 102-103, 118-119, 134-135, 139, 143-144

Bush, President George W., 82, 128

C

Cambodia, 6, 168

Central African Republic (CAR), 135

Chagga, 99

Chang, Daphne, 175-176

Chasia, Dr. Henry, 184

China, xxxi, 6, 8-9, 13, 22, 24-25, 32, 56, 81, 83, 86, 90, 96, 136, 150, 160-161, 163-164, 168, 170-177, 187, 193; as global power, 8, 174, 176; interests in Africa, 175-176; south sea, 9

Chissano, Joaquim President, 72, 128-130, 132

Chlorofluorocarbon emissions (CFCs), 163

Clinton, Hillary Rodham, 7, 31

Clinton, President Bill, 9, 69-70

Cold War, xv, xxviii, xxxi, xxxiv, 1, 9, 29, 37, 39-40, 64, 67-68, 73, 83, 128, 135-136, 148, 150, 170-173, 175-176, 178, 193; end of, 170, 172, 175-176, 178; post-Cold War, xxxi, 1, 29, 37, 64, 68, 73, 83, 128, 136, 171-173, 176, 193; rivalries, xxx

Collective action, xvii, 16-20, 33, 91, 186, 195

Columbia University, 54

Commission of Inquiry into Post-Election Violence (Kenya), xxxii, 78, 80

Common Man's Charter, xx, 52, 58, 138

Common Market for Eastern and Southern African (COMESA), 120, 134, 136, 139, 143, 145, 185

Commonwealth (of Independent States), 12, 24, 38, 54, 136, 145, 178-179

Comprehensive Peace Agreement (CPA), 3, 71, 98, 103, 107, 110, 112-114, 116

Congo-Brazzaville, 135

Congo-Kinshasa, xxxiv, 58-60, 135, 164. *see also* DRC and Zaire

Constitution of Kenya, 2010, xxx, xxxii, 40-41, 43-44, 46-47, 78-79, 84-86, 88, 140, 160, 167, 186, 189, 193; amendments, 38, 86, 159

Constitutional monarchy, 5

Constitutional Review Commission of Kenya (CRCK), 71, 74

Corinth, 21-22

Cote d'Ivoire, 24

Crimea, 8, 23

Croatia, 3

Cuba, 6, 13, 33, 56, 187-188

D

Dadaab refugee camp, 94, 102

Darod clan, 125

Declaration of Principles (DoP), 112

Deforestation, xxxi, 163, 166, 195

Democracy and good governance, 43, 46, 69, 82, 147, 149, 193

Democratic Republic of Congo (DRC), xxxiii, 71-72, 80, 92, 96-97, 99, 102-103, 108-109, 117-119, 121, 129, 134-135, 139, 160, 175, 192; Eastern DRC, xxxii, 80, 92, 96-97, 118-119, 134-135; Inga, 134; River Congo, 134. *see also* Zaire *and* Congo-Kinshasa

Desertification, 145, 166

Dhlakama, Afonso, 130-131, 134

Diaspora Policy (Kenya), 89, 189-191, 196

Diouf, President Abdu, 121, 128

Diplomatic missions, 12, 15, 20, 22, 26, 29-30, 33-34, 76, 148, 166, 179, 196

Diplomatic Notes, 19, 50

Djibouti, 103, 121-123, 126

Domingos, Raul, 133

Drug trafficking, 7, 33, 39, 48,136, 148, 161, 170, 196

E

East Africa, xxix, xxxiii, 34, 43, 47, 52, 59, 70, 79, 88, 92, 96-97, 105, 116-117, 127, 137-139, 141-144, 153-154, 173, 177, 185, 195; court, 143

East African Airways (EAA), 138

East African Community (EAC), xxix, 58, 61, 62, 74, 98, 114, 116-118, 120, 127, 134, 136-137, 139-145, 149, 185, 194

Legislative Assembly, 143;
milestones, 144;
mission, 142;
New EAC, 142, 143; vision, 142
East African Development Bank
(EADB), 138
East African Posts and
Telecommunications (EAP&T),
138
East African Railways (EAR), 138
East Timor, xxx, 160
Eastern Africa, xxxiii, 62, 103, 135,
178, 183, 196
Ebola, xxxiv, 17, 149
Economic Community of West
African States (ECOWAS),
24-25, 146
Economic Partnership Agreements
(EPAs), 32, 143, 150, 174
Egypt, 24, 109-111, 114, 145, 147,
155, 157, 162, 183
Elemi Triangle, 114, 115
Emerging issues, xxxiii-xxxiv, 29,
33, 153, 161, 170
Endangered species, xxxiv, 33, 48,
136, 151, 163, 167-169;
Convention on International Trade
in (CITES), 168
Environmental diplomacy, xvii,
xxxiv, 89, 163-169
Equatorial Guinea, 25
Eritrea, 3, 69, 103, 121, 122;
independence, 121; People's
Liberation Front (EPLF), 121
Establishment and recognition
of a state, 2-3; recognition of a
government, 5-6
Ethiopia, xxxiii, 3, 16, 25, 42-43, 48,
68-69, 71, 94, 97, 99-103,
107-109, 111, 112, 114, 116, 117,
121-123, 139, 161,
175, 183, 192; border with
Kenya, 99, 101-102; defence pact
with Kenya, 100-101; peace
process, 120-121, 139
Europe, xxxiii, 6, 24, 37, 48, 52,
67-68, 135, 157, 163,
173; Central, 68; Eastern, 6,
67; Western, 6, 135
European Union (EU), 9, 22, 28, 30,
32, 68, 86, 90, 96, 143-144, 149,
173, 175, 187

F

Foreign policy, articulation, xvii,
14-15; coordination and
strategy, 27-29; framework, xvii,
12, 14, 37-39, 139, 146, 180,
186-187; instruments,
sanctions, 21-26, mediation,
106-108; military, 17;
diplomacy, 21, 178; other tools,
33; strategy, 33-34
Fort Hare University, 61
France, xxxi, 8, 12, 22, 30, 33, 38,
155, 160-161, 165

Francis, David J., 101-102
Free Syrian Army (FSR), 155
French, troops, 25; tourists, 94
Front for the Liberation of
    Mozambique (FRELIMO), 72,
    128-130, 134

G
Gaddafi, Colonel Muammar, 72,
    155
Gambia, 13, 25
Garissa University College, 95,
    153, 155
Gaza, 152-153
Gender Based Violence, 195
Geneva, 162, 164, 187-188, 197
Germany, 6, 8, 13, 25, 30, 98, 137,
    165
Gethi, Ben, 63
Ghai, Prof. Yash Pal, 71, 74
Ghana, xxix, 58, 69, 77, 159
Ghani, Ashraf, 80
Ghedi, Prof. Mohamed, 125
Global Fund for Africa, 128
Godana, Dr. Bonaya, 75, 103, 185
Gonzales, Archbishop, 129
Goodwill Ambassadors, 191
Gorbachev, Mikhail, 175
Gorongosa, 130, 132
Grand Coalition Government
    (Kenya), 26, 43, 47, 77, 78,
    80-81, 159
Great Lakes Region, xxx, xxxiii, 6,

42, 70-72, 80, 91-92, 98-99, 103,
    106-107, 109, 116, 134-135, 139,
    178, 192-193
Greek, 3, 21-22
Gross Domestic Product (GDP), 67,
    73-74, 140, 144-145, 189
Group of 20 (G20), 12
Group of 7 (G7), 175
Group of 77 (G77), 136, 150, 164
Group of 8 (G8), 175
Guinea, xxix, 17, 58
Gujiral, Inder Kumar, 4

H
Habyarimana, President Juvenile,
    135
Hamas, 151-152, 154
Hawiye clan, 125
Hebdo, Charlie, 155
Hezbollah, 151-152, 154-155
Hong Kong, 71
Horn of Africa, xxx, xxxiii, 5-6, 42,
    70-71, 80, 91-94, 96, 98-99, 103,
    106-109, 116-117, 122-123, 145,
    178, 192-193
Human Immuno-Deficiency Virus/
    Acquired Immune Deficiency
    Syndrome (HIV and AIDS),
    xxxiv, 149, 195
Human trafficking, xxxiv, 31, 33,
    149, 151
Hussein, President Saddam, 16, 155,
    156

I

Independent Review Commission
(Kenya), 78

India, xxxi, 4, 13, 86, 90, 161, 163-164, 175

Indian Ocean Rim-Association for Regional Cooperation (IOR-ARC), 150

Indian Ocean, 94-95, 150

Information, Communication and Technology (ICT), 140, 147, 174; in Diplomacy, 196-197

Institute of Diplomacy and International Studies *see* University of Nairobi

Intelligence Gathering, 30-33, 156

Interahamwe, 135

Inter-Governmental Authority on Development (IGAD), 65, 72, 91, 94, 107, 109, 110-111, 116-117, 120-121, 123-124, 134, 136, 144-145, 185

Inter-Governmental Authority on Drought and Development (IGADD), 145

International Criminal Court (ICC), xxxi, xxxii, 25, 43, 81, 84-86, 90, 128, 135, 146, 149, 158-160; Conference of Parties (CoP), 168; status conference, 85, 160

International Monetary Fund (IMF), 4, 30, 59, 73, 172, 175-176, 187

Inter-Parliamentary Parties Group (IPPG), 71

Iran, 5, 8, 13, 33, 155, 157

Islamabad, 32

Islamic Courts Union (ICU), 16, 94

Islamic militant groups, 50, 155; faith 123; fundamentalism, 154; government 156; radicals 151;

Islamic State of Iraq and al-Sham (ISIS), 154-157

Islamic State of Iraq and the Levant (ISIL), 34

Israel, 9, 90, 150-154, 157, 186; Jerusalem recognition, 9, 152-153, 157

Italy, 123, 129, 133; Italian system, 103, 122

J

Jammeh, President Yahya, 25

Japan, xxxi, 25, 32, 163-164, 174

Jinping, President Xi, 86, 90, 175

Joint Comprehensive Plan of Action (JCPOA), 8

Jong-Un, Kim, 25

Jordan, 90

Jubilee Alliance Party (JAP), 87, 90

Juma, Dr. Monica, 184

K

Kagame, President Paul, 68

Kaggia, Bildad, 57

Karamojong, 99-100

Karimi, Joseph, 63

Kaunda, President Kenneth, 121, 128

Kazakhstan, 13

Keita, Modibo, 58

Kenya African Democratic Union (KADU), 54, 57, 65

Kenya African National Union (KANU), 42, 51, 54, 57, 65, 73-74, 77, 87, 158, 174; Manifesto, 51

Kenya Defence Forces (KDF), 16, 95

Kenya Foreign Policy, 2014, xxxii-xxxiii, 40, 59, 75-77, 83, 89, 149, 190, 194

Kenya National Accord and Reconciliation Act, 2008, xxxi, 77-78, 127

Kenya National Anthem, xvii, 41-42

Kenya People's Union (KPU), 55, 65

Kenya School of Government (KSG), 59

Kenya's diplomatic infrastructure, 15, 88, 187-188

Kenya's foreign policy, evolution, xxxii, 37, 75, 89, 42-43; formulating, 13-14, 40, 111; framework, xvii, 12, 14-15, 37-39, 145, 146, 180, 186-187; international dynamics at independence, 39

Kenya's Foreign Service, xv, xxviii, 35-36, 178-179, 181-182, 188, 197; Institute, xxviii, 59

Kenya-Ethiopia Memorandum of Understanding (MoU), 100-101

Kenyatta Home Again (KHA), 51

Kenyatta, President Mzee Jomo, xv, xvii, xxix, 5, 26, 37, 40-42, 50-65, 82, 96, 100, 105-106, 118-119, 121, 137-139, 164, 171, 174, 185; differences with Odinga, 54-57; foreign policy legacy, 60-62

Kenyatta, Uhuru Muigai, xvii, xxxii, 37, 40, 42, 43, 46, 48, 53, 55-57, 74, 79-80, 83-90, 101, 128, 149, 159-160, 193; first term, 43, 86-87; foreign policy legacy, 90

Kibaki, Mwai, xvii, xx, xxx, 37, 40, 42, 57, 73-83, 113, 120, 126, 158-160, 171-173, 177, 182, 193; foreign policy legacy, 83

Kikwete, President Jakaya Mrisho, 127

Kiplagat, Ambassador Bethwel A., 112, 131

Kivuitu, Mr. Samuel, 77

Koinange, Mbiyu, 60, 63

Kosgey, Henry, xxxii, 81

Kosovo, 3

Kriegler Commission *see* Independent Review Commission

Kriegler, Justice Johann, 78

Kuria, 99

L

Laden, Osama bin, 32, 154

Lai, Chou en, 171

Laikipia County, 169

Lambert, Ben, 175-176

Lamu Port, South Sudan, Ethiopia (LAPSSET), xxxiii, 43, 97, 116-117

Latin America (countries), 38, 195

Law of the sea, 136

Lebanon, xxx, 152, 154, 156, 160

Legislative Council (LEGCO), 65

Lenaola, Justice Isaac, 45

Letters of Credence, 82

Leys, Colin, 49

Liberia, xxx, 17, 160

Libya, 17, 72, 111, 119, 155, 157-158, 175

London Rhodesia (Lonrho), 129

Look west policy, 52, 59

Lumumba, Patrice, 58, 60, 135

Luo groups, 99

M

Maasai Mara National Reserve, 166

Maasai, 99-100, 127

Maathai, Prof. Wangari, 191

Mabior, Dr. John Garang de, 110-116

Machar, Dr. Riek, 114-117

Machel, Graca, 77, 127, 159

Machel, Samora Moisés, 129, 159

Magufuli, John Pombe, 90

Majaritan clan, 5

Making America Great Again (MAGA), 7

Malaria, xxxiv, 149, 195

Malawi, 130-131, 133

Maldives Islands, 46, 87

Mali, xxix, 24, 58

Mandela, Nelson, 68-69, 77, 159

Mangachi, Ambassador, 141

Manicaland Province, 131

Maraga, Justice David, 45, 87

Mariam, Mengistu Haile, 3, 69, 71, 100, 121

Marshall Plan, 6

Marxist model, 13, 130

Massawa port, 121-122

Mau Forest Saga, 166-167

Mayadit, Salva Kiir, 113-114, 116-117

Mboya, Tom, 56-57, 60

Megara, 21-22

Middle East, xxxiii, 9, 34, 146, 150-152, 154, 156-158, 190, 195, 197

Migingo Islands, xxxiv, 92, 96, 120, 140

Ministry of Foreign Affairs (Kenya), xviii, xxi, xxviii, 13, 26-29, 75-76, 89, 131, 164-165, 173, 182, 185, 187-188, 193

Mkapa, Benjamin William, 77, 127, 141, 159

Mochache, Rev., 129

Modi, Prime Minister Narendra, 86, 90

Mohamed, Ambassador Amina, 84, 184

Mohamed, General Mahmoud, 124

Mohiuddin, Ahmed, xxix, 57

Moi International Sports Complex, Kasarani, 171

Moi, President Daniel arap, xvii, xxxi, 37, 41-42, 46, 61, 63-72, 74-75, 77, 106, 112-113, 119, 121, 124, 129, 131-132, 134, 141, 158, 166, 168, 171-172, 182, 185;

politics of, 65; foreign policy legacy, 71-72

Mombasa port, xxxiii, 5, 43, 83, 92, 96, 117, 120, 139, 143

Mombasa Republican Council (MRC), 50

Montenegro, 3

Montevideo Convention, xxvii, 1-2, 4

Morgan, Elles, 175-176

Morgenthau, Hans J., 6-7, 20-21, 47-48

Morsi, President Mohamed, 155

Movement for Democratic Change (MDC), 80

Mozambique National Resistance Movement (RENAMO), 72, 128-134

Mozambique, xxx, 42, 61, 72, 77, 128-134, 178

Mubarak, President Hosni, 155

Mugabe, President Robert, 61, 80, 128-129

Mujahidin, 154

Mungai, Njoroge, 60, 63

Murumbi, Joseph Zuzarte, 60, 63, 65

Museveni, President Yoweri Kaguta, 68-69, 111, 118-119, 141

Muslim Brotherhood, 155

Musyoka, Stephen Kalonzo, 77, 87, 112, 182

Muteesa II, King Fredrick, 118, 139

Muthaura, Francis, xxxii, 80

Mutiso, Gideon-Cyrus, 52

Mwagiru, Makumi, 179

Mwakwere, Chirau Ali, 182

Mwencha, Mr. Erastus, 184

N

Nadapal, 92, 98, 114, 115

Nakodok, xxxiv, 92, 98, 115

Napotpot River, 114

National Alliance of Kenya (NAK), 74

National Alliance Rainbow Coalition (NARC), 74, 76-77: manifesto, 76; MoU, 74

National interest, xiv, xvii, xxi, xxviii-xxix, 1, 3-9, 14, 16, 20, 22-24, 28, 33, 38, 41, 43-44, 46, 48, 60, 73, 75-76, 83, 89, 95, 102, 108, 110, 129, 139-140, 148, 150, 162, 170, 172, 173, 176, 178, 180-182, 185-187, 192-194; as a driver of State activities, 6-7; in foreign policy, 2-10

Ndegwa, Duncan, 51, 53, 55-56,

Ndegwa, Philip, 57

Netanyahu, Prime Minister Benjamin, 90

Neto, Agostino, 60

New Partnership for Africa's Development (NEPAD), 147

New World Order, 67-69, 171, 193

New York, 72, 113, 153, 162, 164, 197

Ngumba, Andrew Kimani, 61

Nicholson, Harold, 14, 21-22

Nigeria, 33-34, 69, 86, 93, 111, 141, 162, 175, 183
Nile Treaty, 114
Nile waters, 110, 114
Njonjo, Charles Mugane, 60-61, 63
Nkomo, Joshua, 61
Nkrumah, President Kwame, 58
Non-Aligned Movement (NAM), 61, 150-151, 164, 185
Non-refoulement principle, 45
Norfolk Hotel, 154
North American Free Trade Agreement (NAFTA), 8
North Atlantic Treaty Organisation (NATO), 4, 9, 16, 30, 68, 157, 175
North Kordofan, 116
North Korea, 13, 16, 23, 25-26
Northern Corridor Transport System (NCTS), xxxiii, 5, 80, 92, 97, 101, 117, 119, 143-144
Northern Frontier District (NFD), 93, 101, 123
Northern Rhodesia, 23-24, 61, 129. *see also* Zimbabwe
Ntanyirira, Cyprian, 135
Nyerere, Julius Kambarage President, 17, 58, 118-119, 126, 137-139, 141

O
Governance, public participation in, 43-44 Kenya, 2007/2008 post-election violence in, xxx-xxxiii, 25, 77-81, 87-88, 97, 84, 86, 143, 158-160; impact, 79

Kenya, interests abroad, promotion, protection and defence of, 28, 180-182
Marine piracy, 31, 39, 94-96, 99, 104, 196
Obama Snr., Barack, 57, 82
Obama, Dr. Auma, 90
Obama, President Barack, 30-31, 57, 82-83, 86, 90, 127-128
Obote, President Milton, 7, 17, 71, 117-119, 137-139, 141, 186
Ochieng, Philip, 63
Odinga, Jaramogi Oginga, 26, 52-53, 171-173; differences with Kenyatta, 54-57
Odinga, Raila Amolo, 53, 66, 74-75, 77-78, 82, 87, 90, 158-159
Ogaden, 122; Ogaden war (Ethiopia), 100-101, 122-123
Ogiek community, 167
Okello, Gen. Tito, 68, 119
Oneko, Achieng, 57
Operation Lifeline Sudan (OLS), 98
Orange Democratic Movement (ODM), xxxii, 75, 77-79, 81, 158
Orange Democratic Movement-Kenya (ODM-K), 77
Organisation for Economic Cooperation and Development (OECD), 30, 175
Organisation of African Unity (OAU), xxx, 3, 24, 59, 61, 72, 93, 97, 105-107, 120, 134, 139-140, 145, 147. see also African Union
Oromo, 99
Ouattara, Alassane, 24-25

Ouko, Dr. Robert, 185
Oxfam-UK, 31

P
Pakistan, 32, 34, 154
Palestine, 9, 150-151, 153, 158; and Israel, 151; Authority, 151-152; grievances, 151-153; Palestinian Liberation Front (PLF), 151; Palestinian Liberation Organisation (PLO), 153; question, 150, 186; self-determination, 153, 157; State, 153; territory, 153
Palmerstone, Lord, 14
Paradise Hotel, Kikambala, Mombasa, 154
Paris Accord on environment, 8
Paris conference on climate change (2015), 163
Party of National Unity (PNU), xxxii, 77-78, 80, 158
Pentagon, USA, 32, 108
Pokot, 99
Portugal, 38, 61, 134, 145-146, 161, 213; rule 61
Projection of power, xiv, xvii, 15-17, 141, 180
Puntland, 123, 125

R
Progressive leadership in Africa, rise to power of, 68-69
Rana, Ambassador Dr. Kipkorir, 183
Red Sea, 95, 196

Refugee problem, 76, 92, 94, 98, 101-104, 106, 108, 145, 157; influx in Kenya, xxx, 39, 42-43,
Renison, Governor Sir Patrick, 53
Roberto, Holden, 60
Rohio, S. W., 52
Rowland, Tiny, 129
Russia, 3, 6-9, 17, 22, 24-25, 29-31; 90, 155, 160-161, 163, 175, 187; hospital 56. *see also* USSR and Soviet Union
Ruto, William, xxxii, 81, 84-85, 87, 90, 149, 159
Rwanda, xxxiii, 68, 70, 80, 92, 96-97, 99, 102-103, 118-120, 134-135, 139, 143-144; Rwanda genocide, 70, 135

S
Sabaoti, 99
Saitoti, Prof. George, 182
Samia, 99
Sang, Joshua arap, xxxii, 81
Santos, Cardinal Dos, 129, 131
Satow, 21
Saudi Arabia, 13, 17, 119, 155-157
Sauti Kuu (NGO), 90
Savimbi, Jonas, 60
Security Laws (Amendment) Act (Kenya), 45
Security of Diplomats, 34
Sen, B., 2-3
Senegal, 58, 121, 128
Senghor, Léopold Sédar, 58-59
Sengulane, Anglican Archbishop, 129, 131

Serbia, 3

Sese Seko, President Mobutu, 121, 128, 134-135

Sessional Paper No. 10 of 1965 (Kenya), 40, 50, 52, 55, 57-58, 101, 138

Shifta insurrection, xxxiv, 93, 100-101, 122-123

Sierra Leone, xxx, 17, 160

Sinawatra, Thaksin, 177

Slovenia, 3

Small Arms and Light Weapons, xxx, 31, 39, 42, 92-93, 103, 104, 106, 108, 145, 148, 170

SMART objectives (in foreign policy), 44, 89, 183-184

Smith, Ian, 24, 129

Somali: ethnic group, 99, 123; Kenyan-, 62, 93, 122; language, 93, 122-123; nation, 93; rebellion, 99, 22-123; youths, 123

Somalia Reconstruction and Reconciliation (SRRC), 125

Somalia Youth League (SYL), 123

Somalia, xxx, xxxiv, 16, 33-34, 42, 48, 65, 71-72, 92-96, 99-104, 107-109, 122-126, 129, 139, 145, 147, 153-154, 178, 192: peace process, 94

Somaliland, 103, 122-123, 125

South Africa, 12, 23-24, 48, 61, 68-69, 78, 86, 90, 95, 119, 128-131, 139, 161, 168, 175, 183, 185, 197

South Kordofan, 116

South Sudan, xxx, xxxiii, xxxiv, 3, 43, 71, 92, 96-100, 108-110, 113-117, 135, 144, 147, 175; impact of violence on regional economies, 115-117; instability, 98; power struggle, 114; Sudan People's Liberation Movement/ Army (SPLM/A), 71, 92, 98, 107, 110-11

Southern Africa, xxxiii, 12, 60-61, 69, 139, 145, 168, 183

Southern African Development Community (SADC), 134, 143, 145

Soviet Union, xxviii, xxix, 6, 16-17, 22-25, 40, 56, 59, 67, 113, 128, 135, 148, 160-161, 171, 174, 193. see also Russia and USSR

Spain, 5, 38, 161

Sparta, 21-22

St Egidio Catholic, Rome, 129, 133

Standard Gauge Railway (SGR), 43, 80-81, 83, 97, 120, 173, 193

Structural Adjustment Programmes (SAPs), 172

Sudan, xxx, 3, 42, 65, 71-72, 92-94, 98, 102-103, 108-111, 113-117, 119, 128, 144, 160, 175, 178: Arab North, 109-110; Christian South, 93, 110, 112-113, 115; peace process, 107, 112, 139, 145; SPLM/A–Nasr, 115; Sudanese, 109-110

Sultan of Zanzibar, 50, 109

Sumbeiywo, Lt. Gen Lazarus, 112

Sung, Kim Il, 25

Supreme Court (Kenya), 46, 79, 87-88, 140

Sustainable Development Goals (SDGs), 195

Swaziland, 13

Swynnerton plan, 49

Syria, 8, 13, 34, 152, 155-157

T

Taita, 99

Taiwan, 22, 25, 160

Taliban, 34, 154

Tan-Mullins, May, 175-176

Tanzania, xxix, 10, 17, 52, 58, 61, 76-77, 80, 90, 97, 99-100, 103, 118-120, 126-128, 130, 134-135, 138-139, 141, 143-144, 153-154, 159, 166, 175; border with Kenya, 99

Tanzanian People's Defence Forces (TPDF), 17

Terrorism, international, xxxii, xxxiv, 7, 31-33, 39, 43, 92, 94, 102, 104, 108, 136, 148-149, 151, 153-154, 156-157, 161, 170, 182, 196; attacks, 32, 94, 157

Teso, 99

Thailand, 168, 177

The National Alliance (TNA), 90, 159

Thucydides, 21-22

Tigrinya People's Liberation Front (TPLF), 121

Tokyo International Conference on Africa's (TICAD), 32, 86

Touré, Ahmed Sekou, 58

Tours of duty for envoys, 179, 181-182

Trans-boundary security, 39, 92, 99-100, 127

Transitional Federal Government, Somalia (TFG), 16, 94-95, 125-126; institutions, 94, 125; parliament, 125; Charter, 125

Trans-Pacific Partnership (TPP), 8

Trump, President Donald J., 7-10, 31, 157, 163

Tsvangirai, Morgan, 80

Tuju, Raphael, 182

Tunisia, 155

Turco-Egyptian administration, 109-110

Turkana, 97-100; county, 92

U

Uganda, xxx, xxxiii, 5, 10, 17, 33, 42, 52, 58, 62, 68-71, 76, 80, 92, 94, 96-100, 102-103, 107-109, 111, 114-115, 117-120, 127, 129, 134-135, 137-141, 143-144, 154, 183-184, 186, 192, 194; border with Kenya, 5, 99; peace process, 117; threats to Kenya, 95

Ujamaa (socialism), 52

Ukraine, 6, 8, 17, 23, 46, 87

Unilateral Declaration of independence (UDI), 23-24

Union of Soviet Socialist Republics (USSR), 39, 160. see also Russia and Soviet Union
United Arab Emirates (UAE), 90, 157
United Kingdom (UK), xxix, 5, 8, 10, 12, 17, 22, 24-25, 31, 33, 35, 38, 83, 114, 119, 155, 160-161, 173, 178-179, 193. *see also* Britain
United Nations (UN), xxxiv, 3, 4, 8-9, 13, 15, 30, 33, 61, 64, 80, 103, 122-123, 160, 185, 187; UN Agencies, 183; UN Charter, 18, 40, 59, 93, 161; UN Conference on human rights, 187; UN Conference on the Law of the Sea (UNCLOS), 163; UN Conference on Trade and (UNCTAD), xv, 86, 149; UN Convention on the Status of Refugees, 45; UN Educational Scientific and Cultural (UNESCO), 8; UN Environment Conference in Stockholm, Sweden, 164; UN Environmental Programme (UNEP), xxix, 39, 60, 72, 150, 162, 164-166, 193, 197; UN Framework Convention on Climate Change (UNFCC), 8; UN General Assembly, 103, 150, 160, 185-186; UN Headquarters in Kenya, 164; UN High Commissioner for Refugees (UNHCR), 102; UN Human

Settlements (UN-HABITAT), xxix, 39, 60, 72, 150, 162, 164-166, 193, 197; UN Industrial Development Organisation (UNIDO), 183; UN International Children's Educational Fund (UNICEF), 98; UN Legal instruments, 97; UN Office at Nairobi (UNON), 60, 162, 165, 197; UN Peace keeping missions, xxx, 72, 117, 134, 178; UN Reforms, 161-162; UN Resolutions, 140; UN Sanctions, North Korea, 23, 25-26; South Africa, 23; UN Secretary General, 77, 117, 159; UN Security Council, 3, 16, 18, 22-25, 85, 122, 134, 150-152, 160-162, 175; permanent members, 22, 160-161; UN System, 22, 165; UN Tribunal, 121; UN Trustee territory, 138, 151
United Republican Party (URP), 90, 159
United States of America (USA),xxviii-xxxiv, 4, 6-10, 13, 16-17, 22-23-25, 29, 31-32, 38-40, 48, 53-54, 57, 60, 67, 69-70, 82-84, 86, 90, 96, 108-109, 127-128, 150-154, 156-158, 160-161, 163-134, 170-176, 181, 187-188, 193; Congress, 13, 24; embassy, Kenya, 153-154; foreign policy under Trump, 7-10

University of Nairobi, 82, 188
  Institute of Diplomacy and
  International Studies, 188

V

Venezuela, 13
Vienna Convention on Consular
Relations (VCCR), 36
Vienna Convention on Diplomatic
Relations (VCDR), 1, 30, 36, 81, 100
Vienna, 162, 164, 181, 197
Vision 2030, Kenya, 40, 48, 73, 83,
148, 190, 195, 197

W

Waiyaki, Dr. Munyua, 61, 185
Waki Commission *see* Commission
  of Inquiry into Post-Election
Violence (Kenya)
Waki, Phillip, 78
Warah, Rasna, 157
West Africa, xxxiii, 24, 69, 169, 183
Western Sahara Democratic
  Republic (SAHRAWI), 146-147
Westgate Mall (Kenya), 95, 153, 155

Wetangula, Moses Masika, 182
White Nile, 109
Wiki Leaks, 27, 29
Woodward, Peter, 108-109, 123
World Trade Centre (WTC), 32,
  108, 153
World Trade Organisation (WTO),
  9, 24, 149
World War I, 6, 137
World War II, 6, 8-9, 15, 23, 123,
  160-161

Y

Yugoslavia, xxx, 3, 16, 160-161, 164,

Z

Zaire, 121, 128-129, 134. *see also*
  DRC
Zambia, 61, 119, 121, 128, 135
Zedong, Mao, 13, 56, 171-172, 174
Zenawi, Meles, 68-69, 121
Zimbabwe, 23-24, 61, 80, 121,
  128-131, 133
Zuma, President Jacob, 61, 86, 90

About the Author

Ambassador Boaz Kidiga Mbaya was born on 14th March, 1951, to Joram Kidiga and Dorika Kaluhi at Gaigedi Sub-Location, Vihiga County. He attended Gaigedi Primary School, 1960-68, Chavakali High School (O-Levels), 1969-72 and Chesamisi High School (A-Levels), 1973-74. He joined the University of Nairobi in 1975 from where he graduated with a BA (Hons) in Political Science and Literature in 1978, and a Post-Graduate Diploma in International Relations in 1982.

He joined the Civil Service at the level of District Officer (DO) and was seconded to the Ministry of Home Affairs as Registrar of Persons for one year. He transferred to the Ministry of Foreign Affairs in 1980 where he rose through the ranks to become Director of Political Affairs in 1987, before he was appointed Ambassador to France, with multiple accreditation to Portugal, Spain, Yugoslavia and the Holy See, as well as Permanent Delegate to UNESCO (2000-2003), and as Ambassador to Ethiopia with multiple accreditation to Djibouti, and Permanent Representative to the African Union in Addis Ababa, from 2004 to February, 2005.

Ambassador Mbaya was appointed Permanent Secretary, Ministry of Foreign Affairs in February, 2005, and retired in April 2006. After this, he was recalled to serve as High Commissioner to the United Republic of Tanzania from 2006-2009, when he finally left the Foreign Service, he founded the Centre for Policy Analysis, a think tank and consultancy firm in public policy, training, management and research, where he is the Executive Director/Chief Executive Officer.

www.ingramcontent.com/pod-product-compliance
Lightning Source LLC
Chambersburg PA
CBHW060034030426

42334CB00019B/2320